HERBAL SIMPLES

Approved for Modern Uses of Cure

"Jamque aderat Phœbo ante alios dilectus Iapis
Iasides : acri quondam cui captus amore
Ipse suas artes, sua munera, lætus Apollo
Augurium, citharamque dabat, celeresque sagittas:
Ille ut *depositi* proferret fata *clientis*,
Scire potestates herbarum, usumque medendi
Maluit, et mutas agitare inglorius artes."

Virgil, *Æneid:* Libr. xii. v. 391-8

HERBAL SIMPLES

Approved for Modern Uses of Cure

VOLUME TWO

M – Z

BY

W.T. FERNIE, M.D.

Author of "Botanical Outlines," etc., etc.

> "Medicine is mine; what herbs and *Simples* grow
> In fields and forests, all their powers I know."
>
> ***Dryden***

LOGOS PRESS

New Delhi-110 002

"And now Iapis had appeared,
Blest leech! to Phœbus-self endeared
Beyond all men below;
On whom the fond, indulgent God
His augury had fain bestowed,
His lyre—his sounding bow!
But he, the further to prolong
A fellow creature's span,
The humbler art of Medicine chose,
The knowledge of each plant that grows,
Plying a craft not known to song,
An unambitious man!"

ISBN-13: 978-81-7268-184-5 (Set)
ISBN-10: 81-7268-184-4 (Set)

ISBN-13: 978-81-7268-185-2 (Vol. I)
ISBN-13: 978-81-7268-186-9 (Vol. II)
ISBN-10: 81-7268-185-2 (Vol. I)
ISBN-10: 81-7268-186-0 (Vol. II)

Reprinted 2008

Printed and Published by

LOGOS PRESS

Building No. 4788-90, Street No. 23, Ansari Road, Darya Ganj
New Delhi-110 002 (India)
Phone : 23272187

PREFACE TO THE FIRST EDITION

It may happen that one or another enquirer taking up this book will ask, to begin with, "What is a Herbal Simple?" The English word "Simple," composed of two Latin words, *Singula plica* (a single fold), means "Singleness," whether of material or purpose.

From primitive times the term "Herbal Simple" has been applied to any homely curative remedy consisting of one ingredient only, and that of a vegetable nature. Many such a native medicine found favour and success with our single-minded forefathers, this being the "reverent simplicity of ancienter times."

In our own nursery days, as we now fondly remember, it was: "Simple Simon met a pieman going to the fair; said Simple Simon to the pieman, 'Let me taste your ware.' " That ingenuous youth had but one idea, connected simply with his stomach; and his sole thought was how to devour the contents of the pieman's tin. We venture to hope our readers may be equally eager to stock their minds with the sound knowledge of Herbal Simples which this modest Manual seeks to provide for their use.

Healing by herbs has always been popular both with the classic nations of old, and with the British islanders of more recent times. Two hundred and sixty years before the date of Hippocrates (460 B.C.) the prophet Isaiah bade King Hezekiah, when sick unto death, "take a lump of Figs, and lay it on the boil; and straightway the King recovered."

Iapis, the favourite pupil of Apollo, was offered endowments of skill in augury, music, or archery. But he preferred to acquire a knowledge of herbs for service of cure in sickness; and, armed with this knowledge, he saved the life of Æneas when grievously wounded by an arrow. He averted the hero's death by applying the plant "Dittany," smooth of leaf, and purple of blossom, as plucked on the mountain Ida.

It is told in *Malvern Chase* that Mary of Eldersfield (1454), "whom some called a witch," famous for her knowledge of herbs and medicaments, "descending the hill from her hut, with a small phial of oil, and a bunch of the 'Danewort,' speedily enabled Lord Edward of March, who had just then heavily sprained his knee, to avoid danger by mounting 'Roan Roland' freed from pain, as it were by magic, through the plant-rubbing which Mary administered."

In Shakespeare's time there was a London street, named Bucklersbury (near the present Mansion House), noted for its number of druggists who sold Simples and sweet-smelling herbs. We read, in *The Merry Wives of Windsor*, that Sir John Falstaff flouted the effeminate fops of his day as "Lisping hawthorn buds that smell like Bucklersbury in simple time."

Various British herbalists have produced works, more or less learned and voluminous, about our native medicinal plants; but no author has hitherto radically explained the why and wherefore of their ultimate curative action. In common with their early predecessors, these several writers have recognised the healing virtues of the herbs, but have failed to explore the chemical principles on which such virtues depend. Some have attributed the herbal properties to the planets which rule their growth. Others have associated the remedial herbs with certain cognate colours, ordaining red flowers for disorders of the blood, and yellow for those of the liver. "The exorcised demon of jaundice," says Conway, "was consigned to yellow parrots; that of inflammatory disease to scarlet, or red weeds." Again, other herbalists have selected their healing plants on the doctrine of allied signatures, choosing, for instance, the Viper's Bugloss as effectual against venomous bites, because of its resembling a snake; and the sweet little English Eyebright, which shows a dark pupil in the centre of its white ocular corolla, as of signal benefit for sore and inflamed eyes.

Thus it has continued to happen that until the last half-century Herbal Physic has remained only speculative and experimental, instead of gaining a solid foothold in the field of medical science. Its claims have been merely empirical, and its curative methods those of a blind art :–

"Si vis curari, de morbo nescio quali,
Accipias herbam; sed quale nescio; nec quâ
Ponas; nescio quo; curabere, nescio quando."

"Your sore, I know not what, be not foreslow
To cure with herbs, which, where, I do not know;
Place them, well pounc't, I know not how, and then
You shall be perfect whole, I know not when."

Happliy now-a-days, as our French neighbours would say, *Nous avons changé tout cela,* "Old things are passed away; behold all things are become new!" Herbal Simples stand today safely determined on sure ground by the help of the accurate chemist. They hold their own with the best, and rank high for homely cures, because of their proved constituents. Their manifest healing virtues are shown to depend on medicinal elements plainly disclosed by analysis. Henceforward the curtain of oblivion must fall on cordial waters distilled mechanically from sweet herbs, and on electuaries artlessly compounded of seeds and roots by a Lady Monmouth, or a Countess of Arundel, as in the Stuart and Tudor times. Our Herbal Simples are fairly entitled at last to independent promotion from the shelves of the amateur still-room, from the rustic ventures of the village grandam, and from the shallow practices of self-styled botanical doctors in the back streets of our cities.

"I do remember an apothecary,—
And hereabouts he dwells,—whom late I noted
In tatter'd weeds, with overwhelming brows,
Culling of Simples; meagre were his looks;
And in his needy shop a tortoise hung,
An alligator stuff'd, and other skins
Of ill-shap'd fishes; and about his shelves
A beggarly account of empty boxes,
Green earthen pots, bladders, and musty seeds,
Remnants of packthread, and old cakes of roses
Were thinly scattered to make up a show."
Romeo and Juliet, Act V. Sc. 1.

Chemically assured, therefore, of the sterling curative powers which our Herbal Simples possess, and anxious to expound them with a competent pen, the present author approaches his task with a zealous purpose, taking as his pattern, from the *Comus* of Milton:–

"A certain shepherd lad
Of small regard to see to, yet well skilled
In every virtuous plant, and healing herb;
He would beg me sing;
Which, when I did, he on the tender grass
Would sit, and hearken even to constancy;
And in requital ope his leathern scrip,
And show me *Simples*, of a thousand names,
Telling their strange, and vigorous faculties."

Shakespeare said, three centuries ago, "throw physic to the dogs." But prior to him, one Doctor Key, self-styled Caius, had written in the Latin tongue (*tempore* Henry VIII), a Medical History of the British Canine Race. His book became popular, though abounding in false concords; insomuch that from then until now medical classics have been held by scholars in poor repute for grammar, and sound construction. Natwithstanding which risk, many a passage is quoted here of ancient Herbal lore in the past tongues of Greece, Rome, and the Gauls. It is fondly hoped that the apt lines thus borrowed from old faultless sources will escape reproach for a defective modern rendering in Dog Latin, Mongrel Greek, or the "French of Stratford atte bowe."

Lastly, quaint old Fuller shall lend an appropriate Epilogue. "I stand ready," said he (1672), "with a pencil in one hand, and a spunge in the other, to add, alter, insert, efface, enlarge, and delete, according to better information. And if these my pains shall be found worthy to passe a second Impression, my faults I will confess with shame, and amend with thankfulnesse, to such as will contribute clearer intelligence unto me."

1895.

PREFACE TO THE SECOND EDITION

On its First Reading, a Bill drafted in Parliament meets with acquiescence from the House on both sides mainly because its merits and demerits are to be more deliberately questioned when it comes up again in the future for a second closer Reading. Meanwhile its faults can be amended, and its omissions supplied; fresh clauses can be introduced; and the whole scheme of the Bill can be better adapted to the spirit of the House inferred from its first reception.

In somewhat similar fashion the Second Edition of "Herbal Simples" is now submitted to a Parliament of readers with the belief that its ultimate success, or failure of purpose, is to depend on its present revised contents, and the amplified scope of its chapters.

The criticisms which public journalists, not a few, thought proper to pass on its First Edition have been attentively considered herein. It is true their comments were in some cases so conflicting as to be difficult of practical appliance. The fabled old man and his ass stand always in traditional warning against futile attempts to satisfy inconsistent objectors, or to carry into effect suggestions made by irreconcilable censors. "*Quot homines, tot sententiæ*," is an adage signally verified when a fresh venture is made on the waters of chartered opinion. How shall the perplexed navigator steer his course when monitors in office accuse him on the one hand of lax precision throughout, and belaud him on the other for careful observance of detail? Or how shall he trim his sails when a contemptuous Standard-bearer, strangely uninformed on the point, ignores, as a leader of any repute, "one Gerard," a former famous Captain of the Herbal fleet? With the would-be Spectator's lament that Gerard's graphic drawings are regrettedly wanting here, the author is fain to concur. He feels that the absence of appropriate cuts to depict the various herbs is quite a deficiency; but the hope is inspired that a still future

Edition may serve to supply this need. Certain botanical mistakes pointed out with authority by the *Pharmaceutical Journal* have here been duly corrected; and as many as fifty additional Simples will be found described in the present Enlarged Edition. At the same time a higher claim than hitherto made for the paramount importance of the whole subject is now courageously advanced.

To all who accept as literal truth the Scriptural account of the Garden of Eden it must be evident how intimately man's welfare from the first was made to depend on his uses of trees and herbs. The labour of earning his bread in the sweat of his brow by tilling the ground; and the penalty of thorns and thistles produced thereupon, were alike incurred by Eve's disobedience in plucking the forbidden fruit; and a signified possibility of man's eventful share in the tree of life, to "put forth his hand, and eat, and live for ever," has been more than vaguely revealed. So that with almost a sacred mission, and with an exalted motive of supreme usefulness, this *Manual of Healing Herbs* is published anew, to reach, it is hoped, and to rescue many an ailing mortal.

Against its main principle an objection has been speciously raised, which at first sight appears of subversive weight; though, when further examined, it is found to be clearly fallacious. By and able but carping critic it was alleged that the mere chemical analysis of old-fashioned Herbal Simples makes their medicinal actions no less empirical than before; and that a pedantic knowledge of their constituent parts, invested with fine technical names, gives them no more scientific a position than that which our fathers understood.

But, taking, for instance, the herb Rue, which was formerly brought into Court to protect a Judge and the Bench from gaol fever, and other infectious disease; no one knew at the time by what particular virtue the Rue could exercise this salutary power. But more recent research has taught, that the essential oil contained in this, and other allied aromatic herbs, such as Elecampane, Rosemary, and Cinnamon, serves by its germicidal principles (stearoptens, methyl-ethers, and camphors), to extinguish bacterial life which underlies all contagion. In a parallel way the antiseptic diffusible oils of Pine, Peppermint, and Thyme, are likewise employed with marked success for inhalation into the lungs by consumptive patients. Their volatile vapours reach remote parts of the diseased air-passages, and heal by destroying the morbid germs which perpetuate mischief therein. It need scarcely be said the very existence of these causative microbes, much less any mode of cure by their abolishment, was quite unknown to former Herbal Simplers.

Again, in past times a large number of our native plants acquired a well-deserved, but purely empirical celebrity, for curing scrofula and scurvy. But later discovery has shown that each of these several herbs contains lime, and earthy salts, in a subtle form of high natural sub-division; whilst, at the same time, the law of cure by medicinal similars has established the cognate fact that to those who inherit a strumous taint, infinitesimal doses of these earth salts are incontestably curative. The parents had first undergone a gradual impairment of health because of calcareous matters to excess in their general conditions of sustenance; and the lime proves potent to cure in the offspring what, through the parental surfeit, was entailed as a heritage of disease. Just in the same way the mineral waters of Missisquoi, and Bethesda, in America, through containing siliceous qualities so sublimated as almost to defy the analyst, are effective to cure cancer, albuminuria, and other organic complaints.

Nor is this by any means a new policy of cure. Its barbaric practice has long since obtained, even in African wilds, where the native snake doctor inoculates with his prepared snake poison to save the life of a victim otherwise fatally bitten by another snake of the same deadly virus. To Ovid, of Roman fame (20 B.C.), the same sanative axiom was also indisputably known as we learn from his lines:—

"Tunc observatas augur descendit in herbas;
Usus et auxilio est anguis ab angue dato."

"Then searched the Augur low mid grass close scanned
For snake to heal a snake-envenomed hand."

And with equal cogency other arguments, which are manifold, might be readily adduced, as of congruous force, to vindicate our claim in favour of analytical knowledge over blind experience in the methods of Herbal cure, especially if this be pursued on the broad lines of enlightened practice by similars.

So now, to be brief, and to change our allegory, "on the banks of the Nile," as Mrs. Malaprop would have pervertingly put it, with "a nice derangement of epitaphs," we invite our many guests to a simple "dinner of herbs." Such was man's primitive food in Paradise: "every green herb bearing seed, and every tree in which is the fruit of a tree yielding seed;" "the green herb for meat for every beast of the earth, and every fowl of the air." What better Preface can we indite than a grace to be said before sitting down to the meal? "Sallets," it is hoped, will be found "in the lines to make the matter savoury." Far be it from our object to preach a prelude of texts, or to weary those at our board with a meaningless long benediction. " 'Tis not so plain as the old Hill of Howth," said tender-hearted witty Tom Hood, with serio-comic truth, "a man has got his belly full of meat, because he talks with victuals in his mouth." Rather would we choose the "russet Yeas and honest kersey Noes" of sturdy yeoman speech; and cheerfully taking the head of our well-stocked table, ask in homely terms that "God will bless these the good creatures of His Herbal Simples to our saving uses, and us to His grateful service."

1897.

CONTENTS

Volume One

Volume Two

DETAILED CONTENTS

VOLUME TWO
M – Z

MALLOWS.

ALL the Mallows (*Malvacēæ*) to the number of a thousand, agree in containing mucilage freely, and in possessing no unwholesome properties.

Their family name "Mallow" is derived from the Greek *malassein*, "to soften," as alluding to the demulcent qualities of these mucilaginous plants. The Common Mallow is a well-known roadside plant, with large downy leaves, and streaked trumpet-shaped purple flowers, which later on furnish round button-like seeds, known to the rustics as "pickcheeses" in Norfolk and elsewhere, whilst beloved by schoolboys, because of their nutty flavour, and called by them "Bread and Cheese."

Clare tells playfully of the fairies, borne by mice at a gallop :—

> "In chariots lolling at their ease,
> Made of whate'er their fancies please,
> With wheels at hand of Mallow seeds,
> Which childish sport had strung as beads."

And recalls the time when he sat as a boy :—

> "Picking from Mallows, sport to please,
> The crumpled seed we called a cheese."

Both this plant and its twin sister, the Marsh Mallow (*Althœa hibiscus*, from *altho*, to cure), possess medicinal virtues, which entitle them to take rank as curative Herbal Simples. The Sussex peasant knows the Common Mallow as "Maller," so that "aller and maller" means with him Alehoof (Ground Ivy) and Mallow. Pliny said: "Whosoever shall take a spoonful of the

Mallows shall that day be free from all diseases that may come to him."

This plant is often named "Round Dock," and was formerly called "Hock Herb": our Hollyhock being of the Mallow tribe, and first brought to us from China. Pythagoras held *Malvæ folium sanctissimum;* and we read of Epimenides in *Plato,* "at his Mallows and Asphodels." The Romans esteemed the plant *in deliciis* among their dainties, and placed it of old as the first dish at their tables. The laxative properties of the Mallow, both as regards its emollient leaves, and its *radix altheæ efficacior,* were told of by Cicero and Horace.

The *Marsh Mallow* grows wild abundantly in many parts of England, especially in marshes near the sea coast. It gets its generic name *althæa,* from the Greek *althos,* "a remedy," because exercising so many curative virtues. Its old appellations were *Vismalva, Bismalva, Malvaviscus,* being twice as medicinally efficacious as the ordinary Mallow (*Sylvestris*).

Virgil in one of his eclogues teaches how to coax goats with the Marsh Mallow :—

> "Hædorumque gregem viridi compellere hibisco."

The root is sweet and very mucilaginous when chewed, containing more than half its weight of saccharine viscous mucilage. It is, therefore, emollient, demulcent, pain-soothing, and lubricating; serving to subdue heat and irritation, whilst, if applied externally, diminishing the painful soreness of inflamed parts. It is, for these reasons, much employed in domestic poultices, and in decoction as a medicine for pulmonary catarrhs, hoarseness, and irritative diarrhœa or dysentery. Also the decoction acts well as a bland soothing collyrium for bathing inflamed eyes. Gerard says: "The leaves be with good effect mixed with fomentations and poultices against pains of the sides, of the stone, and of the bladder; also in a bath they serve to take away any manner of pain."

The mucilaginous matter with which the Marsh Mallow abounds is the medicinal part of the plant; the roots of the Common Mallow being useless to yield it for such purposes, whilst those of the Marsh Mallow are of singular efficacy. A decoction of Marsh Mallow is made by adding five pints of water to a quarter-of-a-pound of the dried root, then boiling down to three pints, and straining through calico. Also Marsh Mallow ointment is a popular remedy, especially for mollifying heat, and hence it was thought invaluable by those who had to undergo the ordeal of holding red hot iron in their hands, to rapidly test their moral integrity. The sap of the Marsh Mallow was combined together with seeds of Fleabane, and the white of an hen's egg, to make a paste which was so adhesive that the hands when coated with it were safe from harm through holding for a few moments the glowing iron.

French druggists prepare a famous medicinal sweetmeat, known as *Pate de gimauve* from the root of the Marsh Mallow. In Palestine, the plant is employed by the poor to eke out their food; thus we read in the book of Job (chap. xxx. ver. 4), "Who cut up Mallows by the bushes, and juniper roots for their meat."

In France, the young tops and tender leaves of the Marsh Mallow are added to spring salads, as stimulating the kidneys healthily, for which purpose is likewise prepared a syrup of Marsh Mallows *(Syrupus Althæus)* from the roots with cold water, to which the sugar is afterwards added. The leaves, flowers, and roots, are employed for making ptisans. In Devonshire, this plant is termed by the farmers, "Meshmellish," also "Drunkards," because growing close by the water; and in the West of England, "Bulls-eyes"; whilst being known in Somerset as "Bull Flowers" (pool flowers). The root of the Marsh Mallow contains starch, mucilage, pectin, oil, sugar, asparagin, phosphate of lime, glutinous matter and cellulose. An infusion made with cold water takes up the mucilage, sugar, and asparagin, then the hot water dissolves the starch.

The flowers were used formerly on May-day by country people for strewing before their doors, and weaving into garlands.

The Geranium is said to have been originally a Mallow. Mahomet having washed his shirt while on a journey, hung it on a Mallow to dry, and the plant became therefore promoted to be a Geranium.

Most probably, the modern French *Pate de gimauve* contains actually nothing of the plant or its constituents; but the root is given in France to infants, on which they may try their teeth during dentition, much as Orris root is used elsewhere.

The laxative quality of the common Mallow was mentioned by Martial:—

> "Exoneraturas ventrem mihi villica malvas
> Attulit, et varias quas habet hortus opes."

The Musk Mallow *(Malva moschata)* is another common variety of this plant, which emits from its leaves a faint musky odour, especially in warm weather, or when they are drawn lightly through the hand. Its virtues are similar in kind, but less powerful in degree, to those of the Marsh Mallow.

MARIGOLD.

IN the *Grete Herball* this plant was called Mary Gowles. Three varieties of the Marigold exercise medicinal virtues which constitute them Herbal Simples of a useful nature — the Corn Marigold (*Chrysanthemum segetum*), found in our cornfields ; the cultivated garden Marigold (*Calendula officinalis*) ; and the Marsh Marigold (*Caltha palustris*), growing in moist grass lands, and popularly known as "Mareblobs."

The Corn Marigold, a Composite flower, called also Bigold, and the Yellow Oxeye, grows freely, though locally, in English cornfields, its brilliant yellow flowers contrasting handsomely with adjacent Scarlet-hued Poppies and Bluebottles (*Centaurea cyanus*). It is also named Buddle or Boodle, from *buidel*, a purse, because it bears *gools* or *goldins*, representing gold coins, in the form of the flat, round, brightly yellow blossoms, which were formerly known, too, as *Ruddes* (red flowers). The botanical title of the species, *Chrysanthemum segetum*, signifies "golden flower."

Hill named this Marigold, "the husbandman's dyall." In common with the larger Oxeye Daisy (*Chrysanthemum leucanthemum*) it has proved of late very successful in checking the night sweats of pulmonary consumption. A tincture and an infusion of the herb have been made ; from five to ten drops of the former being given for a dose, and from two to three tablespoonfuls of the latter.

The garden Marigold, often called African Marigold, came originally from Southern France, and has been cultivated in England since 1570. It is a Composite plant, and bears the name *Calendula* from the Latin *calendæ*, the first days of each month, because it flowers all the year round. Whittier styles it "the grateful and obsequious Marigold." The leaves are somewhat thick and sapid ; when chewed, they communicate straightway a viscid sweetness, which is followed by a sharp, penetrating taste, very persistent in the mouth, and not of the warm, aromatic kind, but of an acrid, saline nature. This Marigold has always been grown, chiefly for its flowers, which were esteemed of old as a cordial to cheer the spirits, and when dried were put into broths as a condiment. Charles Lamb (Elia) says, in his *Essay on Christ's Hospital :* "In lieu of our half-pickled Sundays, or quite fresh boiled beef on Tuesdays (strong as *caro equina*), with detestable Marigolds floating in the pail to poison the broth." The strap-like florets of the rays are the parts of the flowers used for such a purpose. They should be gathered on a fine day when the blossoms are fully expanded, which having been divested of their outer green leaves, should be next spread on a cloth in an airy room to become dry. After having been turned frequently for a few days, they may be put by in paper bags or in drawers.

Gerard says : "The yellow leaves of the flowers are dried and kept throughout Dutch-land against winter, to put into broths and physical potions, and for divers other purposes, in such quantity that the stores of some grocers or spice-sellers contain barrels filled with them, and to be retailed by the penny, more or less ; insomuch, that no broths are well made without dried Marigolds" ; and, "The herb drank after the coming forth from the bath of them that hath the yellow jaundice doth in short time make them well coloured." (This is probably conjectured on the doctrine of signatures.)

A decoction of the flowers is employed by country people as a posset drink in measles and small-pox ; and the expressed fresh juice proves a useful remedy against costiveness, as well as for jaundice and suppression of the monthly flow—from one to two tablespoonfuls being taken as a dose.

The plant has been considered also of service for scrofulous children, when given to them as a salad. One of the flowers if rubbed on any part recently stung by a bee or wasp, will quickly relieve it.

Buttercups and Marigolds, when growing close to each other, are called in Devonshire, "publicans and sinners." The active, bitter principle of the Marigold is "calendulin," which is yellow and tasteless, whilst swelling in water into a transparent jelly. Druggists now make a medicinal tincture (H.) of the common Marigold, using four ounces of the dried florets to a pint of proof spirit, the dose being from half a teaspoonful to two teaspoonfuls in water, twice or three times in the day. It is advised as a sudorific stimulant in low fevers, and to relieve spasms. Also, the Marigold has been employed both as a medicine and externally in treating cancer, being thought to "dispose cancerous sores to heal." A saturated tincture of the flowers when mixed with water, promotes the cure of contusions, wounds, and simple sores or ulcers; also the extract will allay chronic vomiting, if given in doses of two grains, several times a day. One drop of the tincture with two grains of powdered borax when sprayed into the ear, is very useful if a discharge has become established therefrom.

The plant, especially its flowers, was used on a large scale by the American surgeons, to treat wounds and injuries sustained during the last civil war; and obtained their warmest commendation. It quite prevented all exhausting suppurative discharges and drainings. *Succus Calendulæ* (the fresh juice) is the best form—say American surgeons—in which the *Calendula* is obtainable for ready practice. Just sufficient alcohol should be added to the juice as will prevent fermentation. For these purposes as a vulnerary, the *Calendula* owes its introduction and first use altogether to homœopathic methods, as signally valuable for healing wounds, ulcers, burns, and other breaches of the skin surface. Dr. Hughes (Brighton) says: "The Marigold is a precious vulnerary. You will find it invaluable in surgical practice."

On exposure to the sun the yellow colour of the garden Marigold becomes bleached. Some writers spell the name "Marygold," as if it, and its synonyms bore reference to the Virgin Mary; but this is a mistake, though there is a fancied resemblance of the disc's florets to rays of glory. It comes into blossom about March 25th (the Annunciation of the Virgin Mary).

> "What flower is this which bears the Virgin's name,
> And richest metal joinëd with the same?"

In the chancel of Burynarbon Church, Devonshire, is an epitaph containing a quaint allusion to this old idea respecting the Marigold:—"To the pretious memory of Mary, ye dear, and only daughter of George Westwood. January 31st, 1648."

> "This Mary Gold, lo! here doth show
> Mari's worth gold lies here below;
> The Marigold in sunshine spread,
> When cloudie closed doth bow the head."

Margaret of Orleans had for her device a Marigold turning towards the sun, with the motto, "*je ne veux suivre que lui seul.*"

Dairy women used to churn the petals of the Marigold with their cream for giving to their butter a yellow colour.

The Marsh Marigold (*Caltha poetarum*) or the Marsh

Horsegowl of old writers, grows commonly in our wet meadows, and resembles a gigantic buttercup, being of the same order of plants (*Ranunculaceæ*). The term, Marsh Marigold, is a pleonasm for Marigold, which means of itself the Marsh Gowl or Marsh Golden Flower, being an abbreviation of the old Saxon *mear-gealla*. So that the term "Marsh" has become prefixed unnecessarily. Presently, the name "Marigold," "Marsh Gowl," was passed on to the *Calendula* of the corn fields of Southern Europe, and to the garden Marigold. Furthermore, the botanical title, *Caltha*, of the Mare Blob, is got from *calathus*, a small round basket of twigs or osiers made two thousand years and more ago, which the concave golden bowl of the Marsh Marigold was thought to resemble. Persephone was collecting wild flowers in a *Calathus* when carried off by the admiring Pluto. The earliest use of the floral name *Caltha* occurs in Virgil's second Pastoral, "*Mollia luteolâ pingit vaccinia Calthâ.*" The title Mare Blob comes from the Anglo-Saxon, "*mere*" (a marsh), and "*bleb*" or "*blob*" (a bladder). These flowers were the *flaventia lumina Calthæ* of Columella, described by Shakespeare in the *Winter's Tale*. They are also known as "Bublicans," "Meadowbrights," "Crazies," "Christ's Eyes," "Bull's Eyes," "May Blobs," "Drunkards," "Water Caltrops," and wild "Batchelor's Buttons." A tincture is made (H.) from the whole plant when in flower, and may be given with success for that form of bloodlessness with great impairment of the whole health, known as pernicious anæmia. In toxic quantities the marsh Marigold has produced in its provers, a pallid, yellow, swollen state of the face, constant headache and giddiness, a thickly-coated tongue, diarrhœa, a small rapid pulse sometimes intermittent, heaviness of the limbs, and an unhealthy, eruptive state of the skin; so that the tincture of the plant in small, well-diluted doses will slowly overcome this totality of symptoms, and serve to establish a sound state of restored health. Five drops of the tincture diluted to the third strength should be given three times a day with water. Dr. Withering tells that on a large quantity of the flowers being put in the bed-room of a girl subject to fits, the attacks ceased; and an infusion of the flowers has been since given with success for similar fits.

The Marsh Marigold has been called *Verrucaria*, because efficacious in curing warts; also *Solsequia*, or *Solsequium*; and *Sponsa Solis*, since the flower opens at the rising, and shuts at the setting of the sun.

MARJORAM.

THE common Marjoram (*Origanum*) grows frequently as a wild labiate plant on dry, bushy places, especially in chalky districts throughout Britain, the whole herb being fragrantly aromatic, and bearing flowers of a deep red colour. When cultivated in our kitchen gardens it becomes a favourite pot herb, as "Sweet Marjoram," with thin compact spikes, and more elliptical leaves than the wild Marjoram. Its generic title, *Origanum*, means in Greek, the joy of the mountains (*oros-ganos*) on which it grows.

This plant and the Pennyroyal are often called "Organ." Its dried leaves are put as a pleasant condiment into soups and stuffings, being also sometimes substituted for tea. Together with the flowering tops they contain an essential volatile fragrant oil, which is carminative, warming, and tonic. An infusion made from the fresh plant will excellently relieve nervous headaches by virtue of the camphoraceous principle contained in the oil; and externally the herb may be applied with benefit in bags as a hot fomentation to painful swellings and rheumatism, as likewise for colic. "Organy," says Gerard, "is very good against the wambling of the stomacke, and stayeth the desire to vomit, especially at sea. It may be used to good purpose for such as cannot brooke their meate."

The sweet Marjoram has also been successfully employed externally for healing scirrhous tumours of the breast. Murray says: "Tumores mammarum dolentes scirrhosos herba recens, viridis, per tempus applicata feliciter dissipavit." The essential oil, when long kept, assumes a solid form, and was at one time much esteemed for being rubbed into stiff joints. The Greeks and Romans crowned young couples with Marjoram, which is in some countries the symbol of honour. Probably the name was originally, "Majoram," in Latin, *Majorana*. Our forefathers scoured their furniture with its odorous juice. In the *Merry Wives of Windsor*, Act v, Scene 5, we read:—

> "The several chairs of order look you scour
> With juice of balm, and every precious flower."

MERCURY—DOG'S (*Euphorbiaceæ*).

THE *Mercuriallis perennis* (Dog's Mercury) grows commonly in our hedges and ditches, occurring in large patches, with egg-shaped pointed leaves, square stems, and light green flowers, developed in spikes. The old herbalists called it Smerewort, and gave it for agues, as well as to cure melancholy humours. It has been eaten in mistake for Good King Henry, which is sometimes called Mercury Goosefoot; but it is decidedly poisonous, even when cooked. Some persons style it "Kentish Balsam."

The name Dog's Mercury or Dog's Cole was given either because of its supposed worthlessness, or to distinguish it from the Mercury Goosefoot aforesaid. A medicinal tincture is made (H.) from the whole plant freshly collected when in flower and fruit, with spirit of wine; and the dose of this in a diluted form is from five to ten drops, of the third decimal strength, two or three times a day, with a spoonful of water. The condition which indicates its medicinal use, is that of a severe catarrh, with chilliness, a heavy head, sneezing, a dry mouth, and general aching, lassitude, with stupor, and heat of face. Its chemical constituents have not been ascertained. In the Isle of Skye it is used for causing salivation as a vegetable mercury; and *per contra* for curing a sore mouth.

Such virtues as the herb possesses were thought to have been taught by the god Mercury. The Greeks called it Mercury's Grass (*Ermou poa*). When boiled and eaten with fried bacon in error for the English spinach, Good King Henry, it has produced sickness, drowsiness, and convulsive twitchings. The root affords both a blue and a crimson colour for dyeing.

MINTS.

(Pennyroyal, Peppermint, and Spearmint).

SEVERAL kinds of the Mints have been used medicinally from the earliest times, such as Balm, Basil, Ground Ivy, Horehound, Marjoram, Pennyroyal, Peppermint, Rosemary, Sage, Savory, Spearmint, and Thyme, some being esteemed rather as pot herbs, than as exercising positive medicinal effects. The most useful as Herbal Simples which have yet to be considered are Pennyroyal, Peppermint, and Spearmint. The Cat Mint (*Nepeta cataria*) and Horse Mint are of minor importance.

All the Mints are severally provided with leaves of a familiar fragrant character, it having been observed that this aromatic vegetation is a feature of deserts, and of other hot, dry places, all over the world. Tyndall showed the power exercised by a spray of perfume when diffused through a room to cool it, or in other words to exclude the passage of the heat rays; and it has been suggested that the presence of essential oils in the leaves of these plants serves to protect them against the intense dry heat of a desert sun as effectively as if they were partly under shelter. Nevertheless Mints, with the exception of "Arvensis," are the inhabitants of wet and marshy wastes.

They have acquired their common name *Mentha* from Minthes (according to Ovid) who was changed into a plant of this sort by Proserpina, the wife of Pluto, in a fit of jealousy. Their flowering tops are all found to contain a certain portion of camphor. Pliny said: "As for the garden Mint, the very smell of it alone recovers and refreshes the spirits, as the taste stirs up the appetite for meat, which is the reason that it is so general in our acid sauces, wherein we are accustomed to dip our meat." The Mints for paying tithes, with respect to which the Pharisees were condemned for their extravagance by our Saviour, included the Horse Mint (*Sylvestris*), the round-leaved Mint, the hairy Mint (*Aquatica*), the Corn Mint (*Arvensis*), the Bergamot Mint, and some others, besides the "Mint, Rue, and Anise," specially mentioned. "Woe unto you Pharisees; for ye tithe Mint and Rue, and all manner of herbs. Ye pay tithe of Mint, and Anise, and Cummin."

The Mint Pennyroyal (*Mentha Pulegiūm*) gets its name from the Latin *puleium regium*, because of its royal efficacy in destroying fleas (*pulices*). The French call this similarly, *Pouliot.* It grows on moist heaths and pastures, and by the margins of brooks, being cultivated further in our herb gardens, for kitchen and market uses. Also, it is produced largely about Mitcham, and is mostly sold in a dry state. The herb was formerly named Pudding Grass, from its being used to make the stuffing for meat, in days when this was termed a pudding. Thus we read in an old play, *The Ordinary* :—

> "Let the corporal
> "Come sweating under a breast of mutton stuffed with
> [pudding."

The Pennyroyal was named by the Greeks *Bleekon* and *Gleekon*, being often used by them as a condiment for seasoning different viands. Formerly it was known in England as "Lurk in ditch," and "Run by the ground," from its creeping nature, and love of a damp soil. Its first titles were "Puliall Royall," and "Hop Marjoram." A chaplet of Pennyroyal was considered admirable for clearing the brain. Treadwell says, the Pennyroyal was especially put into hog's puddings, which were made of flour, currants, and spice, and stuffed into the entrail of a hog.

The oil of Pennyroyal is used commercially in France and Germany. Its distilled water is carminative and anti-spasmodic; whilst the whole plant is essentially stimulating. The fresh herb yields about one per cent. of a volatile oil containing oxygen, but of which the exact composition has not been ascertained. From two to eight drops may be given as a dose in suitable cases, but not where feverish or inflammatory symptoms are present.

If added to an ordinary embrocation the oil of

Pennyroyal increases the reddening and the benumbing (anodyne) effects, acting in the same way as menthol (oil of Peppermint) for promptly dispelling severe neuralgic pain. With respect to the Pennyroyal, folk speak in Devonshire of "Organs," "Organ Tea," and "Organ Broth." An essence is made of the oil, mixed and diluted with spirit of wine. The Pennyroyal has proved useful in whooping cough; but the chief purpose to which it has long been devoted, is that of promoting the monthly flow with women. Haller says he never knew an infusion of the herb in white wine, with steel, to fail of success; *Quod me nunquam fefellit.* It is certain that in some parts of England preparations of Pennyroyal are in considerable demand, and a great number of women ascribe *emmenagogue* properties to it, that is, the power of inducing the periodical monthly flux. Many married women of intelligence and close observation, assert as a positive fact, that Pennyroyal will bring on the periodical flow when suppressed; and yet the eminent jurisprudist, Dr. Taylor, was explicit in declaring that Pennyroyal has no such properties. He stated that it has no more effect on the womb than peppermint or camphor water. So there is difficulty in collecting evidence as regards the real action of Penny royal in such respect. Chemists supply the medicine in the full belief of this eminent opinion just quoted: at the same time they know it is not wanted for "catarrh of the chest," as alleged. The purchaser keeps her secret to herself, and does not communicate her experience to anyone. Dr. Taylor evidently supposed Peppermint water and Camphor water to be almost inert, especially as exercising any toxical effect on the womb. The medicinal basis of the latter is certainly a powerful agent, and its stimulating volatile principles are found to exist in most of the aromatic herbs; in fact, Camphor is a concrete volatile vegetable oil, and camphoraceous properties signalise all the essences derived from carminative Herbal Simples.

The Camphor of commerce is secreted by trees of the laurel sort native to China and Japan, whilst coming also from the West Indies. Everyone knows by sight and smell the white crystalline granular semi-translucent gum, strongly odorous, and having a warm pungent characteristic taste. Branches, leaves, and chips of the trees are soaked in water until it is saturated with the extract, which is then turned out into an earthen basin to coagulate. This is completely soluble in spirit of wine, but scarcely at all in water; nevertheless, if a lump of the Camphor be kept in a bottle of fresh water, to be drawn off from time to time as required, it will constitute Camphor julep. A wineglassful of it serves to relieve nervous headache and hysterical depression.

The domestic uses of Camphor are multiple, and within moderate limits perfectly safe; but a measure of caution should be exercised, as was shown a while ago by the school-boy, whom his mother furnished affectionately after the holidays with a bottle of supersaturated pilules to be taken one or two at a time against any incipient catarrh or cold. The whole bottleful was devoured at once as a sweetmeat, and the lad's life was rescued with difficulty because of intense nervous shock occasioned thereby.

An old Latin adage declares that *Camphora per nares emasculat mares*, "Camphor in excess makes men eunuchs," even when imbibed only through the air as a continuous practice. And, therefore, as a "similar" the odorous gum, in small repeated doses, is an excellent sexual restorative. Likewise, persons who have taken poisonous, or large probative quantities of Camphor found themselves quickly affected by exhausting choleraic diarrhœa; and Hahnemann therefore advised, with much success, to give (in doses of from one to three or four drops on sugar), repeatedly for cholera, a tincture of Camphor (Rubini's) made with spirit of wine above proof. This absorbs as much as is possibly soluble of the drug.

Physiologically Camphor acts by reducing reflex nervous irritability. Externally its spirit makes an admirable warming liniment, either by itself, or when conjoined with other rubefacients. In persons poisoned by the drug, all the superficial blood vessels of the bodily skin have been found immensely dilated; acting on a knowledge of which fact anyone wishing to produce copious general sweating, may do so by sitting over a plate on which Camphor is heated, whilst a blanket envelops the body loosely, and is pinned round the neck so that the fumes do not get down the throat.

In medical books of the last century this substance was called "Camphire." To a certain extent its effluvium is noxious to insects, and it may therefore be employed for preserving specimens, as well as for protecting fabrics against moths. But its volatile odours swiftly evaporate, and become even offensively diffused about the room. In a moderate measure Camphor is antiseptic, and lessens urinary irritation. Recently a dose of ninety-six grains, taken toxically, produced giddiness, then epileptic convulsions, with dilated pupils, and stertor of breathing.

The Peppermint (*Mentha piperita*), or "Brandy Mint," so called because having a pungent smell, and taste of a peppery (*piper*) nature, is a labiate plant, found not uncommonly in moist places throughout Britain, and occurring of several varieties. Both it and the Spearmint probably escaped from cultivation at first, and then became our wild plants. Its leaves and stems exhale a powerful, refreshing, characteristic aroma, and give a taste which, whilst delicate at first, is quickly followed by a sense of numbness and coldness, increased by inspiring strongly. Preparations of Peppermint, when swallowed, diffuse warmth in the stomach and mouth, acting as a stimulating carminative, with some amount of anodyne power to allay the pain of colic, flatulence, spasm, or indigestion. This is through the powerful volatile oil, of which the herb yields one per cent.

Its bruised fresh leaves, if applied, will relieve local pains and headache. A hot infusion, taken as tea, soothes stomach ache, allays sickness, and stays colicky diarrhœa. This will also subdue menstrual colic in the female. The essential oil owes its virtues to the menthol, or mint camphor, which it contains.

The Peppermint is largely grown at Mitcham, and is distilled on the ground at a low temperature, the water which comes away with the oil not being re-distilled, but allowed for the most part to run off.

Chinese oil of Peppermint (*Po Ho Yo*) yields menthol in a solid crystalline form, which, when rubbed over the surface of a painful neuralgic part, will afford speedy and marked relief, as also for neuralgic tooth-ache, tic douloureux, and the like grievous troubles. It is sold in diminutive bottles and cases labelled with Chinese characters. An ethereal tincture of menthol is made officinally with one part of menthol to eight parts of pure ether. If some of this is inhaled by vaporisation from a mouthpiece inhaler, or is sprayed into the nostrils and hindermost throat, it will relieve acute affections thereof, and of the nose, by making the blood vessels contract, and by arresting the flow of mucous discharge, thus diminishing the congestion, and quieting the pain. This camphoraceous oil was formerly applied by the Romans to the temples for the cure of headache. In local rheumatic affections the skin may be painted beneficially with oil of Peppermint. For internal use, from one to three drops of the oil may be given as a dose on sugar, or in a spoonful of milk; but the diluted essence, made from some of the oil admixed with spirit of wine, is to be preferred. Put on cotton wool into the hollow of a carious tooth, a drop or two of the essential oil will often ease the pain speedily. The fresh plant, bruised, and applied against the pit of the stomach over the navel, will allay sickness, and is useful to stay the diarrhœic purging of young children. From half to one teaspoonful of the spirituous essence of Peppermint may be given for a dose with two tablespoonfuls of hot water; or, if Peppermint water be chosen, the dose of this should be from half to one wineglassful. Distilled Peppermint water should be preferred to that prepared by adding the essence to common water. Lozenges made of the oil, or the essence, are admirable for affording ease in colic, flatulence, and nausea. They will also prevent or relieve sea-sickness.

When Tom Hood lay a dying he turned his eyes feebly towards the window on hearing it rattle in the night, whereupon his wife, who was watching him, said softly, "It's only the wind, dear"; to which he replied, with a sense of humour indomitable to the last, "Then put a Peppermint lozenge on the sill."

Two sorts of this herb are cultivated for the market—black and white Peppermint, the first of which furnishes the most, but not the best oil. The former has purple stems, and the latter green. As an antiseptic, and destroyer of disease germs, this oil is signally efficacious, on which important account it is now used for inhalation by consumptive patients as a volatile vapour to reach remote diseased parts of the lung passages, and to heal by destroying the morbid germs which are keeping up mischief therein. Towards proving this preservative power exercised by the oil of Peppermint, pieces of meat, and of fat, wrapped in several layers of gauze medicated with the oil have been kept for seven months sweet, and free from putrescent changes. A simple respirator for inhaling the oil is made from a piece of thin perforated zinc plate adapted to the shape of the mouth and nostrils like a small open funnel, within the narrow end of which is fitted a pledget of cotton wool saturated with twenty drops of the oil, or from twenty to thirty drops of the spirituous essence. This should be renewed each night and morning, whilst the apparatus is to be worn nearly all day. At the same time the oil is agreeable of odour, and is altogether harmless. It may be serviceably admixed with liniments for use to rheumatic parts.

"Peppermint," says Dr. Hughes (Brighton), "should be more largely employed than it is in coughs, especially in a dry cough, however caused, when it seems to act specifically as a cure, just as arnica does for injuries, or aconite for febrile inflammation. It will relieve even the irritative hectic cough of consumptive patients. Eight or ten drops of the essence should be given for this purpose as a dose with a tablespoonful of water. In France continuous inhalations of Peppermint oil combined with creasote and glycerine, have become used most successfully, even when cavities exist in the lungs, with copious bacillary expectoration. The cough, the night sweats, and the heavy phlegm have been arrested, whilst the nutrition and the weight have steadily increased."

A solution of menthol one grain, spirit of wine fifty drops, and oil of cloves ten drops, if painted over the seat of pain, will relieve neuralgia of the face, or sciatica promptly. Unhealthy sores may be cleansed, and their healing promoted, by being dressed with strips of soft rag dipped in sweet oil, to each ounce of which one or two drops of the oil of Peppermint has been added. For diphtheria, Peppermint oil has been of marked use when applied freely twice or three times in the day to the ulcerated parts of the throat. This oil, or the essence, can be used of any strength, in any quantity, without the least harm to the patient. It checks suppuration when applied to a sore or wound, whilst exercising an independent antiseptic influence. "Altogether," says Dr. Braddon, "the oil of Peppermint forms the best, safest, and most agreeable of known antiseptics." Pliny tells that the Greeks and Romans crowned themselves with the Peppermint at their feasts, and adorned their *al fresco* tables with its sprays. The "chefs" introduced this herb into all their sauces, and scented their wines with its essence. The Roman housewives made a paste of the Peppermint with honey, which they esteemed highly, partaking of it to sweeten their breath, and to conceal their passion for wine at a time when the law punished with death every woman convicted of quaffing the ruby seductive liquor. Seneca perished in a bath scented with woolly mint.

The Spearmint (*Mentha viridis*) is found growing apparently wild in England, but is probably not an indigenous herb. It occurs in watery places, and on the banks of rivers, such as the Thames, and the Exe. If used externally, its strong decoction will heal chaps and indolent eruptions.

It possesses a warm, aromatic odour and taste, much

resembling those of Peppermint, but not so pungent. Its volatile oil, and its essence, made with spirit of wine, contain a similar stimulating principle, but are less intense, and therefore better adapted for children's maladies.

The Spearmint is called "Mackerel Mint," and in Germany "Lady's Mint," with a pun on the word *münze.* Its name, Spear, or Spire, indicates the spiry form of its floral blossoming. When the leaves of the herb are macerated in milk, this curdles much less quickly than it otherwise would; and therefore the essence is to be commended for use with milk diets by delicate persons, or for young children of feeble digestive powers, though not when feverishness is present. "Spearmint," says John Evelyn, "is friendly to the weak stomach, and powerful against all nervous crudities." "This is the Spearmint that steadies giddiness," writes Alfred Austin, Poet Laureate.

Our cooks employ it with vinegar for making the mint sauce which we eat with roast lamb, because of its condimentary virtues as a spice to the immature meat, whilst the acetic acid of the vinegar serves to help dissolve the crude albuminous fibre.

The oil is less used than that of Peppermint. From two to five drops may be given on sugar; or from half to one teaspoonful of the spirit of Spearmint with two tablespoonfuls of water. Also a distilled water of Spearmint is made, which will relieve hiccough, and flatulence, as well as the giddiness of indigestion. The tincture prepared from the dried herb looks of a bright dark green by day, but of a deep red colour by night. Martial called the Spearmint *Ructatrix mentha.* "*Nec deest ructatrix mentha.*"

The Calamint, or Basil Thyme, grows frequently in

our waysides and hedges, a labiate plant, with downy stems and leaves, whilst bearing light purple flowers. The whole herb has a sweet, aromatic odour, and makes a pleasant cordial tea. It is named from the Greek *kalos*, "excellent," because thought useful against serpents. "There is made hereof," said Galen, "an antidote marvellous good for young women that want their courses."

The stem of this pretty slender herb is seldom more than five or six inches high, and its blossoms are so inconspicuous as to be often overlooked. The flowers droop gracefully before expansion. In country places it is often called Mill Mountain, and its infusion is an old remedy for rheumatism. If bruised, and applied externally, it reddens the skin, and will sometimes even blister it. In this way it acts well when judiciously used for lumbago, and rheumatic pains. The Calamint contains a camphoraceous, volatile, stimulating oil, in common with the other mints; this is distilled by water, but its virtues are better extracted by rectified spirit. The lesser Calamint is a variety of the herb possessing almost superior virtues, with a stronger odour resembling that of Pennyroyal. "Apple Mint" is the "*Mentha rotundifolia.*"

"Many robust men and women among our peasantry," says Dr. George Moore, "from notions of their own, use infusions of Balm, Sage, or even a little Rue, or wild Thyme, as a common drink, with satisfaction to their stomachs, and advantage to their health, instead of infusing the Chinese herb." The Calamint is a favourite herb with such persons. About the Cat mint there is an old saying, "If you set it the cats will eat it: if you sow it the cats won't know it." This, the *Nepeta cataria*, or *herbe aux chats*, is as much beloved by cats as *Valerian*, and the common *Marum*, for which herbs they have a frenzied passion. They roll themselves over the plants, which they lick, tear with their teeth, and bathe with their urine. But the Cat mint is the detestation of rats, insomuch that with its leaves a small barricade may be constructed which the vermin will never pass however hungry they may be. It is sometimes called "Nep," as contracted from *Nepeta*. Hoffman said, "The root of the Cat mint, if chewed, will make the most gentle person fierce and quarrelsome"; and there is a legend of a certain hangman who could never find courage to exercise his gruesome task until he had masticated some of this aromatic root.

MISTLETOE.

THE Mistletoe, which we all associate so happily with the festivities of Christmas, is an evergreen parasite, growing on the branches of deciduous trees, and penetrating with simple roots through the bark into the wood. It belongs to the *Loranthaceæ*, and has the botanical name of *Viscum*, or "sticky," because of its glutinous juices. The Mistletoe contains mucilage, sugar, a fixed oil, resin, an odorous principle, some tannin, and various salts. Its most interesting constituent is the "viscin," or bird glue, which is mainly developed by fermentation, and becomes a yellowish, sticky, resinous mass, such as can be used with success as a bird-lime.

The dried young twigs, and the leaves, are chiefly the medicinal parts, though young children have been attacked with convulsions after eating freely of the berries.

The name (in Anglo-Saxon, *Mistiltan*) is derived, says Dr. Prior, from *mistil*, "different," and *tan*, "a twig," because so unlike the tree it grows upon; or, perhaps, *mist* may refer to excrement, and the adjective, *viscum*, bear some collateral reference to *viscera*, "entrails." Probably our *viscum* plant differs from that of the Latin writers in their accounts of the Druids, which would be the *Loranthus* growing on the *Quercus pubescens* (an oak indigenous to the south of France). They knew it by a name answering to "all-heal." It is of a larger and thicker sort than our common Mistletoe, which, however, possesses the same virtues in a lesser degree. The Germans call the plant *Vogellein*, and the French *Gui*, which is probably Celtic.

The plant is given powdered, or as an infusion, or made into a tincture (H.) with spirit of wine. From ten to sixty grains of the powder may be taken for a dose, or a decoction may be made by boiling two ounces of the bruised plant with half-a-pint of water, and giving one tablespoonful for a dose several times in the day; or from five to ten drops of the tincture (which is prepared almost exclusively by the homœopathic chemists) are a dose, with one or two tablespoonfuls of cold water.

Sir John Colebatch published in 1720 a pamphlet, on *The Treatment of Epilepsy by Mistletoe*, regarding it, and with much justice, as a specific. He procured the parasite from the lime trees at Hampton Court. The powdered leaves were ordered to be given (in black cherry water), as much of these as will lie on a sixpence every morning.

Sir John says, "This beautiful plant must have been designed by the Almighty for further and more noble purposes than barely to feed thrushes, or to be hung up superstitiously in houses to drive away evil spirits." His treatise was entitled, *A Dissertation concerning the Misseltoe—A most wonderful Specifick Remedy for the Cure of Convulsive Distempers.* The physiological effect of the plant is that of lessening, and temporarily benumbing such nervous action as is reflected to distant organs of the body from some central organ which is the actual seat of trouble. In this way the spasms of epilepsy and of other convulsive distempers, are allayed. Large doses of the plant, or of its berries, would, on the contrary, aggravate these convulsive disorders.

In a French "*Recueil de Remedes domestiques*," 1682, *Avec privilege du Roy*, we read, de l'epilepsie: "Il est certain que contre ce deplorable mal le veritablè Guy de Chêne (Mistletoe) est un remede excellent, curatif, preservatif, et qui soulage beaucoup dans l'accident. Il le faut secher au four apres qu'on aura tiré le pain: le mettre en poudre fort subtile; passer cette poudre par un tamis de foye, et la conserver pour le besoin. Il faut prendre les poids 'dun ecu d'or de cette poudre chaque matin dans vin blanc tous les trois derniers jours de la lune vieille. Il est encore bon que la personne affligée de ce mal porte toujours un morceau de Guy de Chêne pendu à son col; mais ce morceau doit etre toujours frais, et sans avoir eté mis au four." The active part of the plant is its resin (*viscin*), which is yielded to spirit of wine in making a tincture. This is prepared (H.) with proof spirit from the leaves and ripe berries of our Mistletoe in equal quantities, but it is difficult of manufacture owing to the viscidity of the sap. A special process is employed of passing the material twice through a sausage machine, and then mixing the mass with powdered glass before its percolation with the spirit. A trituration made from the leaves, berries, and tender twigs, is given for epilepsy, in doses of twenty grains, twice or three times a day.

Nowadays the berries are taken by country people when finding themselves troubled with severe stitches, and they obtain almost instantaneous relief. In accordance with which experience Johnson says it was creditably reported to him, "That a few of the berries of the Misseltoe, bruised and strained into oyle and drunken, hath presently and forthwith rid a grievous and sore stitch." The tincture, moreover, is put to a modern use as a heart tonic in place of the foxglove. It lessens reflex irritability, and strengthens the heart's beat, whilst raising the frequency of a slow pulse. Dr. J. Wilde has shown that the Mistletoe possesses a high repute in rural Hampshire for the cure of St. Vitus's dance, and similar spasmodic nervous complaints. In the United States the leaves have been successfully employed as an infusion to check female fluxes, and hæmorrhages, also to hasten childbirth by stimulating the womb when labour is protracted to the exhaustion of the mother. In Scotland the plant is almost unknown, and is restricted to one locality only.

The Druids regarded the Mistletoe as the soul of their sacred tree—the oak; and they taught the people to believe that oaks on which it was seen growing were to be respected, because of the wonderful cures which the priests were then able to effect with it, particularly of the falling sickness. The parasite was cut from the tree with a golden sickle at a high and solemn festival, using much ceremonial display, it being then credited with a special power of "giving fertility to all animals." Ovid said, "Ad viscum cantare Druidœ solebant."

Shakespeare calls it "The baleful Mistletoe," in allusion to the Scandinavian legend, that Balder, the god of peace, was slain with an arrow made of Mistletoe. He was restored to life at the request of the other gods and goddesses. The mistletoe was afterwards given to be kept by the goddess of love; and it was ordained in Olympus that every one who passed under it should receive a kiss, to show that the branch was the emblem of love, and not of death.

Persons in Sweden afflicted with epilepsy carry with them a knife having a handle of oak mistletoe, which plant they call Thunder-besom, connecting it with lightning and fire. The thrush is the great disseminator of the parasite. He devours the berries eagerly, and soils, or "missels" his feet with their viscid seeds, conveying them thus from tree to tree, and getting thence the name of missel thrush.

In Brittany the plant is named *Herbe de la croix*, and, because the crucifix was made from its wood when a tree, it is thought to have become degraded to a parasite.

When Norwood, in Surrey, was really a forest the Mistletoe grew there on the oak, and, being held as medicinal, it was abstracted for apothecaries in London. But the men who meddled with it were said to become lame, or to fall blind with an eye, and a rash fellow who ventured to cut down the oak itself broke his leg very shortly afterwards. One teaspoonful of the dried leaves, in powder, from the appletree Mistletoe, taken in acidulated water twice a day, will cure chronic giddiness. Sculptured sprays and berries, with leaves of Mistletoe, fill the spandrils of the tomb of one of the Berkeleys in Bristol Cathedral—a very rare adornment, because for some unknown reason the parasite has been always excluded from the decorations of churches. In some districts it is called Devil's-fuge, also the Spectre's Wand, from a belief that with due incantations a branch held in the hand will compel the appearance of a spectre, and require it to speak.

MOUNTAIN ASH.

A somewhat common and handsomely conspicuous tree in many parts of England, especially about high lands, is the Rowan, or Mountain Ash. In May and June it attracts attention by its bright green feathery foliage set off by cream-coloured bloom, whilst in September it bears a brilliant fruitage of berries, richly orange in colour at first, but presently of a clear ripe vermilion. Popularly this abundant fruit is supposed to be poisonous, but such is far from being the case. A most excellent and wholesome jelly may be prepared therefrom, which is slightly tonic by its salutary bitterness, and is an admirable antiseptic accompaniment to certain roast meats, such as venison and mutton. To make this jelly, boil the berries in water (cold at first) in an enamelled preserving pan; when the fruit has become sufficiently soft, run the contents of the pan through a flannel bag without pressure; tie the bag between two chairs, with a basin below, and let the juice strain leisurely through so as to come out clear. Then to each pint of the juice add a pound of sugar, and boil this from ten to twenty minutes; pour off into warm dry jars, and cover them securely when cool. After the juice has dripped off the fruit a pleasant refreshing drink may be made for children by pouring a kettleful of boiling water through the flannel bag. Some persons mix with the fruit an equal quantity of green apples when making the jelly. Birds, especially field fares, eat the berries with avidity; and a botanical designation of the tree is *aucuparia*, as signifying fruit used by the *auceps*, or bird catcher, with which to bait his snares.

"There is," says an old writer, "in every berry the exhilaration of wine, and the satisfying of old mead; and whosoever shall eat three berries of them, if he has completed a hundred years, he will return to the age of thirty years."

At the same time it must be noted that the *leaves* of the Mountain Ash are of a poisonous quality, and contain prussic acid like those of the laurel. But, as already shown, the berries, when ripe, may be eaten freely without fear. Chemically they contain tartaric acid when unripe, and both malic and citric acids when ripe. They also furnish sorbin, and parasorbic acid. The unripe fruit and the bark are extremely astringent, being useful in decoction, or infusion, to check diarrhœa; and externally in poultices or lotions, to constringe such relaxed parts as the throat, and lower bowel.

The title Rowan tree has affixed itself to the Mountain Ash, as derived from the Norse, *Runa* (a charm), because it is supposed to have the power of averting the evil eye.

> "Rowan tree and red thread
> Hold the witches a' in dread."

"Runa" was really a magician, or whisperer, from *ru*, to murmur, and in olden times *runes*, or mystical secrets, were carved exclusively on the Mountain Ash tree in Scandinavia and the British Isles.

Crosses made of the twigs, and tied with red thread were sewn by Highlandmen into their clothes. Dame Sludge fastened a piece of the wood into Flibbertigibbet's collar as a protection against Wayland Smith's sorceries.—(Kenilworth). Other folk-names of the tree are Quicken tree, Quick Beam, Wiggen, and Witcher.

The Mountain Ash is botanically a connecting link between the dog rose of our hedges and the apple tree of our orchards. Its flowers exactly resemble apple blossoms, and its thickly-clustered red berries are only small crabs dwarfed by the love of the tree for mountain heights and bleak windy situations. In the harsh cold regions of the north it is only a stunted shrub with leaves split up into many small leaflets, so as to suffer less by any breadth of resistance to the sharp driving blasts of icy winds.

Confusion has been often made between this tree and the Service tree (*Sorbus*, or *Pyrus domestica*), which is quite distinct, being more correctly called Servise tree, from *Cerevisia*, fermented beer. Formerly this Servise, or Checker-tree, was employed for making an intoxicating drink. Virgil says :—

> "Et pocula læti
> Fermento atque acidis imitantur vitea *sorbis*."

> "With acid juices from the Service Ash,
> And humming ale, they make their Lemon Squash."

The fruit of the Service tree (or Witten Pear-tree) resembles a small pear, and is considered in France very useful for dysentery because of its tannin ; but this *Pyrus domestica* is a rare tree in England. Sometimes mistaken for it is the *wild* Service tree (the *Pyrus torminalis*), much more common in our south country hedges. Its fruit is threaded on long strings, and carried in procession at village feasts in Northamptonshire, but is worthless. Evelyn says, "Ale and beer brewed from the berries, when ripe, of the true Service tree is an incomparable drink."

MUGWORT and WORMWOOD.

THE herb Mugwort (*Artemisia vulgaris*), a Composite plant, is frequent about hedgerows and waste ground throughout Britain ; and it chiefly merits a place among Herbal Simples because of a special medicinal use in certain female derangements. Its name Mugwort has been attributed to "moughte," a moth, or maggot, this title being given to the plant because Dioscorides commended it for keeping off moths. Its Anglo-Saxon synonym is *Wyrmwyrt*. Mugwort is named from Artemis the Greek goddess of the moon, and is also called Maidenwort or Motherwort (womb wort), being a plant beneficial to the womb.

Macer says, terming it by mistake "Mother of Worts":

> "Herbarum matrem justum puto ponere primo
> Præcipue morbis mulieribus illa medetur."

A decoction of the fresh tops acts famously to correct female irregularities when employed as a bath. *Uterina est, adeoque usus est creberrimus mulierculis quæ eam adhibent externe, atque interne ut vix balnea et lotiones parent in quibus artemisia non contineatur.* Thus writes Ray, quoting from Schroder. Or it may be that the term Mugwort became popularly applied because this herb was in demand for helping to preserve ale. The plant was formerly known as *Cingulum Sancti Johannis*, since a crown made from its sprays was worn on St. John's Eve, to gain security from evil possession; also as *Zona divi Johannis*, it being believed that John the Baptist bore a girdle of it in the wilderness. In Germany and Holland it has received the name of St. John's Plant, because, if gathered on St. John's Eve, it is thought protective against diseases and misfortunes. The Mugwort is also styled "Felon wort," or "Felon herb." If placed in the shoes, it will prevent weariness. A dram of the powdered leaves taken four times a day has cured chronic hysterical fits, which were otherwise intractable. "Mugwort," says Gerard, "cureth the shakings of the joynts inclining to the palsie."

The mermaid of the Clyde is said to have exclaimed,

when she beheld the funeral of a young maiden who had died from consumption and decline :—

> "If they wad drink nettles in March,
> And eat muggins [Mugwort] in May,
> Sae mony braw young maidens
> Wad na' be gang to clay."

Portions of old dead roots are found at the base of the herb, which go by the name of "coals," and are thought to be preventive of epilepsy when taken internally, or worn around the neck as an amulet. Parkinson says: "Mugwort is of wonderful help to women in risings of the mother, or hysteria." It is also useful against gout by boiling the tender parts of the roots in weak broth, and taking this frequently; whilst at the same time the affected limbs should be bathed and fomented with a hot decoction of the herb. The plant, without doubt, is decidedly anti-epileptic, its remedial effects being straightway followed by profuse and fetid perspirations. It is similarly useful against the convulsions of children in teething. For preventing disorders, as well as for curing rheumatism, the Japanese, young and old, rich and poor, indiscriminately, are said to be singed with a "moxa" made from the Mugwort. Its dried leaves are rubbed in the hands until the downy part becomes separated, and can be moulded into little cones. One of these having been placed over the site of the disease, is ignited and burnt down to the skin surface, which it blackens and scorches in a dark circular patch. This process is repeated until a small ulcer is formed when treating chronic diseases of the joints, which sore is kept open by issue peas retained within it so that they may constantly exercise a derivative effect.

The flesh of geese is declared to be more savoury when

stuffed with this herb, which contains "absinthin" as its active principle, and other chemical constituents in common with Wormwood; but the odour of Mugwort is not fragrant or aromatic, because it does not possess a volatile essential oil like that of the *Artemisia absinthium* (Wormwood).

This Wormwood is also a Composite plant of the same tribe and character, but with an intensely bitter taste; and hence its name, *Absinthium,* has been derived from the Greek privative, *a*, and *psinthos,* "delight," because the flavour is so bitterly distasteful. It is a bushy plant, which abounds in our rural districts, having silky stems and leaves, with small heads of dull yellow flowers, the whole plant being *amara et aromatica.*

The Mugwort, as an allied Wormwood of the same genus, is taller and more slender than the *Absinthium,* and is distinguished by being scentless, its leaves being green above, and white below. The bitter taste of the true Wormwood is also due to "absinthin," and each kind contains nitrate of potash, tannin, and resin, with succinic, malic, and acetic acids.

Old Tusser says:—

> "Where chamber is swept, and wormwood is strown,
> No flea for his life dare abide to be known."

And again:—

> "What savour is better, if physic be true,
> For places infected, than wormwood and rue."

The infusion of Wormwood makes a useful fomentation for inflammatory pains, and, combined with chamomile flowers and bay leaves, it formed the anodyne fomentation of the earlier dispensatories. This infusion, with a few drops of the essential oil of Wormwood, will serve as an astringent wash to prevent the hair from falling off when it is weak and thin.

Both Mugwort and Wormwood have been highly esteemed for overcoming epilepsy in persons of a feeble constitution, and of a sensitive nervous temperament, especially in young females. Mugwort tea, and a decoction of Wormwood, may be confidently given for the purposes just named, also to correct female irregularities.

For promoting the monthly flow, Chinese women make a confection of the leaves of Mugwort mixed with rice and sugar, which, when needed to overcome arrested monthly fluxes, or hysteria, they *instar bellaria ingerunt*, "eat as a sweetmeat."

A drachm of the powdered leaves of the Mugwort, taken four times a day, has cured chronic hysterical fits otherwise irrepressible. The true Wormwood (*Artemisia absinthium*) is used for preparing absinthe, a seductive liqueur, which, when taken to excess, induces epileptic attacks. Any habitual use of alcohol flavoured with this herb singularly impairs the mental and physical powers.

"An ointment," says Meyrick, "made of the juice of Mugwort with hogs' lard, disperses hard knots and kernels about the neck and throat."

MULBERRY.

THE Mulberry tree (*Morus nigra*) has been cultivated in England since the middle of the sixteenth century, being first planted at Sion house in 1548. It is now grown commonly in the garden, orchard, or paddock, where its well-known rich syrupy fruit ripens in September. This fruit, abounding with a luscious juice of regal hue, is used in some districts, particularly in Devonshire, for mixing with cider during fermentation, giving to the beverage a pleasant taste, and a deep red colour. The juice, made into syrup, is curative of sore throats, especially of the putrid sort, if it be used in gargles; also of thrush in the mouth, if applied thereto; and the ripe fruit is gently laxative.

Horace recommends that Mulberries be gathered before sunset:—

> "Æstatis peraget qui nigris prandia moris
> Finiet ante gravem quæ legerit arbore solem."

The generic name, *Morus*, is derived from the Celtic *mor*, "black." In Germany (at Iserlohn), mothers, in order to deter their children from eating Mulberries, tell them the devil requires the juicy berries for the purpose of blacking his boots. This fruit was fabled to have become changed from white to a deep red through absorbing the blood of Pyramus and Thisbe, who were slain beneath its shade.

It is thought by some that "morus" has been derived from the Latin word *mora*, delay, as shown in a tardy expansion of the buds. Because cautious not to burst into leaf until the last frost of spring is over, the Mulberry tree, as the wisest of its fellows, was dedicated by the ancients to Minerva, and the story of Pyramus and Thisbe owed its origin to the white and black fruited varieties:—

> "The Mulberry found its former whiteness fled,
> And, ripening, saddened into dusky red."

Shakespeare's famous Mulberry tree, planted in 1609, was of the black species. It was recklessly cut down at New Place, Stratford-on-Avon, in 1759. Ten years afterwards, when the freedom of the city was presented to Garrick, the document was enclosed in a casket made from the wood of this tree. Likewise a cup was wrought therefrom, and at the Shakespeare Jubilee, Garrick, holding the cup aloft, recited the following lines, composed by himself for the occasion :—

"Behold this fair goblet: 'twas carved from the tree
Which, oh, my sweet Shakespeare, was planted by thee!
As a relic I kiss it, and bow at thy shrine,
What comes from thy hand must be ever divine."

"All shall yield to the Mulberry tree;
Bend to the blest Mulberry:
Matchless was he who planted thee,
And thou, like him, immortal shall be."

A slip of it was grown by Garrick in his garden at Hampton Court. The leaves of the Mulberry tree are known to furnish excellent food for silk worms.

Botanically, each fruit is a collection of berries on a common pulpy receptacle, being, like the Strawberry, especially wholesome for those who are liable to heart-burn, because it does not undergo acetous fermentation in the stomach. In France Mulberries are served at the beginning of a meal. Among the Romans the fruit was famous for maladies of the throat and windpipe.

The tree does not bear until it is somewhat advanced in age. It contains in every part a milky juice, which will coagulate into a sort of Indian rubber, and this has been thought to give tenacity to the filament spun by the silkworm.

The juice of Mulberries contains malic and citric acids, with glucose, pectin, and gum. The bark of the root has been given to expel tapeworm; and the fruit is remarkable for its large quantity of sugar, being excelled in this respect only by the fig, the grape, and the cherry.

We are told in *Ivanhoe* that the Saxons made a favourite drink, "Morat," from the juice of Mulberries with honey. During the thirteenth century these berries were sometimes called "pynes."

In the memorable narrative of the Old Testament, 2 *Samuel*, v., 24, "When thou hearest the sound of a going in the tops of the Mulberry trees," the word used (*bekhaim*) has been mistranslated, really intending the Aspen (*Populus tremula*).

MULLEIN.

The great Mullein (*Verbascum thapsus*) grows freely in England on dry banks and waste places, but somewhat sparingly in Scotland. It belongs to the scrofula-curing order of plants, having a thick stalk, from eighteen inches to four feet high, with large woolly mucilaginous leaves, and with a long flower-spike bearing plain yellow flowers, which are nearly sessile on the stem. The name "Molayne" is derived from the Latin, *mollis*, soft.

In most parts of Ireland, besides growing wild, it is carefully cultivated in gardens, because of a steady demand for the plant by sufferers from pulmonary consumption. Constantly in Irish newspapers there are advertisements offering it for sale, and it can be had from all the leading local druggists. The leaves are best when gathered in the late summer, just before the plant flowers. The old Irish method of administering Mullein is to put an ounce of the dried leaves, or a corresponding quantity of the fresh ones, in a pint of milk, which is boiled for ten minutes, and then strained. This is afterwards given warm to the patient twice a day, with or without sugar. The taste of the decoction is bland, mucilaginous, and cordial. Dr. Quinlan, of Dublin, treated many cases of tubercular lung disease, even when some were far advanced in pulmonary consumption, with the Mullein, and with signal success as regards palliating the cough, staying the expectoration, and increasing the weight.

Mullein leaves have a weak, sleepy sort of smell, and rather a bitter taste. In Queen Elizabeth's time they were carried about the person to prevent the falling sickness; and distilled water from the flowers was said to be curative of gout.

The leaves and flowers contain mucilage, with a yellowish volatile oil, a fatty substance, and sugar, together with some colouring matter. Fish will become stupefied by eating the seeds. Gerard says "Figs do not putrifie at all that are wrapped in the leaves of Mullein. If worn under the feet day and night in the manner of a sock they bring down in young maidens their desired sicknesse."

The plant bears also the name of Hedge Taper, and used to be called Torch, because the stalks were dipped in suet, and burnt for giving light at funerals and other gatherings. "It is a plant," says the *Grete Herball*, "whereof is made a manner of lynke if it be tallowed."

According to Dodœus the Mullein was called "Candela." *Folia siquidem habet mollia hirsuta ad lucernarum funiculos apta.* "It was named of the Latines, *Candela Regia* and *Candelaria.*" The modern Romans style it the "Plant of the Lord." Other popular English names of the plant are "Adam's flannel," "Blanket," "Shepherd's club," "Aaron's rod," "Cuddie's lungs"; and in Anglo-Saxon, "Feldwode." Gower says of Medea:—

> "Tho' toke she feldwode, and verveine,
> Of herbes ben nought better tweine."

The name *Verbascum* is an altered form of the Latin *barbascum*, from *barba*, "a beard," in allusion to the dense woolly hairs on both sides of the leaves; and the appellation, Mullein, is got from the French *molène*, signifying the "scab" in cattle, and for curing which disease the plant is famous. It has also been termed Cow's Lung Wort, Hare's Beard, Jupiter's Staff, Ladies' Foxglove, and Velvet Dock from its large soft leaves. The Mullein bears the title "Bullock's lung wort," because of its supposed curative powers in lung diseases of this animal, on the doctrine of signatures, because its leaf resembles a dewlap; and the term "Malandre" was formerly applied to the lung maladies of cattle. Also the "Malanders" meant leprosy, whence it came about that the epithet "Malandrin" was attached to a brigand, who, like the leper, was driven from society and forced to lead a lawless life.

An infusion of the flowers was used by the Roman ladies to tinge their tresses of the golden colour once so much admired in Italy; and now in Germany, a hair wash made from the Mullein is valued as highly restorative. A decoction of the root is good for cramps and against the megrims of bilious subjects, which especially beset them in the dark winter months. The dried leaves of the Mullein plant, if smoked in an ordinary tobacco pipe, will completely control the hacking cough of consumption; and they can be employed with equal benefit, when made into cigarettes, for asthma, and for spasmodic coughs in general.

By our leading English druggists are now dispensed a *succus verbasci* (Mullein juice), of which the dose is from half to one teaspoonful; a tincture of *Verbascum* (Mullein), the dose of which is from half-a-teaspoonful to two teaspoonfuls; and an infusion of Mullein, in doses of from one to four tablespoonfuls. Also a tincture (H.) is made from the fresh herb with spirit of wine, which has been proved beneficial for migraine (sick head-ache) of long standing, with oppression of the ears. From eight to ten drops of this tincture are to be given as a dose, with cold water, and repeated pretty frequently whilst needed.

Mullein oil is a most valuable destroyer of disease germs. If fresh flowers of the plant be steeped for twenty-one days in olive oil whilst exposed to the sunlight, this makes an admirable bactericide; also by simply instilling a few drops two or three times a day into the ear, all pain therein, or discharges therefrom, and consequent deafness, will be effectually cured, as well as any itching eczema of the external ear and its canal. A conserve of the flowers is employed on the Continent against ringworm. Some of the most brilliant results have been obtained in suppurative inflammation of the inner ear by a single application of Mullein oil. In acute or chronic cases of this otorrhœa, two or three drops of the oil should be made fall into the ear twice or thrice in the day. And the same oil is an admirable remedy for children who "wet the bed" at night. Five drops should be put into a small tumblerful of cold water; and a teaspoonful of the mixture, first stirred, should be taken four times in the day.

Flowers of Mullein in olive oil, when kept near the fire for several days in a corked bottle, form a remedy popular in Germany for frost-bites, bruises, and piles. Also a poultice made with the leaves is a good application to these last named troublesome evils. For the cure of piles, sit for five minutes on a chamber vessel containing live coals, with crisp dry Mullein leaves over them, and some finely powdered resin.

MUSHROOMS.

WITHOUT giving descriptive attention to those Mushrooms (*Agarics*, *Boleti*, and others) which are edible, and of which over a hundred may be enumerated, as beyond our purpose when treating of curative Herbal Simples, notice will be bestowed here on two productions of the Mushroom nature—the Puff Ball and the Fly Agaric,—because of their medicinal qualities.

It may be first briefly stated that the *Agaricus campestris*, or field Mushroom, is the kind most commonly eaten in England, being highly nitrogenous, and containing much fat. This may be readily distinguished from any harmful fungus by the pink colour of its gills, the solidity of its stem, the fragrant anise-like odour which it possesses, and the separability of its outer skin. Other edible Mushrooms which grow with us, and are even of a better quality than the above, are the *Agaricus augustus* and the *Agaricus elvensis*, not to mention the *Chantarelle*, said to be unapproachable for excellence.

The Greeks were aware of edible fungi, and knew of injurious sorts which produced a sense of choking, whilst subsequent wasting of the body occurred. Athenæus quotes an author who said: "You will be choked like those who waste after eating mushrooms." The Romans also esteemed some fungi as of so exquisite a flavour that these would be stolen sooner than silver or gold by anyone entrusted with their delivery :—

> "Argentum, atque aurum facile est lænamque togamque.
> Mittere, boletos mittere difficile est."

Mushrooms were styled by Porphry *deorum filii*, and "without seed, as produced by the midwifery of autumnal thunderstorms, and portending the mischief which these cause." "They are generally reported to have something noxious in them, and not without reason; but they were exalted to the second course of the Cæsarean tables with the noble title "bromatheon," a dainty fit for the gods, to whom they sent the Emperor Claudius, as they have many since to the other world." "So true it is he who eats Mushrooms many times, *nil amplius edit*, eats no more of anything."

The poisonous kinds may be commonly recognised by their possessing permanently white gills which do not touch the stem; and a thin ring, or frill, is borne by the stem at some distance from the top, whilst the bottom of the stem is surrounded by a loose sheath, or volva. If "phalline" is the active poisonous principle, this is not rendered inert by heat in cooking; but the helvellic acid of other sorts disappears during the process, and its fungi are thus made non-poisonous. There is a popular belief that Mushrooms which grow near iron, copper, or other metals, are deadly; the same idea obtaining in the custom of putting a coin in the water used for boiling Mushrooms in order that it may attract and detach any poison, and so serve to make them wholesome.

In Essex there is an old saying:—

> "When the moon is at the full,
> Mushrooms you may freely pull;
> But when the moon is on the wane,
> Wait till you think to pluck again."

Even the most poisonous species may be eaten with impunity after repeated maceration in salt and water, or vinegar and water—which custom is generally adopted in the South of Europe, where the diet of the poorer classes largely includes the fungi which they gather; but when so treated the several Mushrooms lose much of their soluble nutritive qualities as well as their flavour. For the most part, *Agarics* with salmon-coloured spores are injurious, likewise fungi having a rancid or fetid odour, and an acrid, pungent, peppery taste. Celsus said: "If anyone shall have eaten noxious fungi, let him take radishes with vinegar and water, or with salt and vinegar."

Wholesome Mushrooms afford nourishment which is a capital substitute for butchers' meat, and almost equally sustaining. If a poisonous fungus has been eaten, its ill-effects may nowadays be promptly met by antidotes injected beneath the skin, and by taking small doses of strychnia in coffee.

Gerard says: "I give my advice to those that love such strange and new fangled meats to beware of licking honey among thorns, lest the sweetness of the one do not countervail the sharpness and pricking of the other." With regard to Mushrooms generally, Horace said:—

> "Pratensibus optima fungis
> Natura est; aliis male creditur."

> "The meadow Mushrooms are in kind the best;
> 'Tis ill to trust in any of the rest."

The St. George's Mushroom, an early one, takes, perhaps, the highest place as an agaric for the table. Blewits (formerly sold in Covent Garden market for Catsup), and Blue Caps, each an autumnal species, are savoury fungi to be fried. They may be served with bacon on toast.

A very old test as to the safety of Mushrooms is to stew with them in the saucepan a small carefully-peeled onion. If after boiling for a few minutes this comes out white, and clean-looking, the Mushrooms may all be confidently eaten: but if it has turned blue, or black, there are dangerous ones among them, and all should be rejected.

The Puff Ball (*Lycoperdon giganteum bovista*) grows usually on the borders of fields, in orchards, or meadows, also on dry downs, and occasionally in gardens. It should be collected as a Simple in August and September. This Puff Ball is smooth, globose, and yellowish-white when young, becoming afterwards brown. It contains, when ripe, a large quantity of extremely fine brown black powder, which is a capital application for stopping bleeding from slight wounds and cuts. This also makes a good drying powder for dusting on weeping eruptive sores between parts which approximate to one another, as the fingers, toes, and armpits. The powder is very inflammable, and when propelled in a hollow cone against lighted spirit of wine on tow at the other end by a sudden jerk, its flash serves to imitate lightning for stage purposes. It was formerly used as tinder for lighting fires with the flint and steel.

When the fungus is burnt, its fumes exercise a narcotic property, and will stupify bees, so that their honey may be removed. It has been suggested that these fumes may take the place of chloroform for minor surgical operations. The gas given off during combustion is carbonic oxide.

Puff Balls vary in size from that of a moderately large turnip to the bigness of a man's head. Their form is oval, depressed a little at the top, and the colour is a pure white both without and within. The surface is smooth at first, but at length cracking, and as the fungus ripens it becomes discoloured and dry; then the interior is resolved into a yellow mass of delicate threads, mixed with a powder of minute spores, about the month of September.

When young and pulpy the Puff Ball is excellent to be eaten, and is especially esteemed in Italy; but it deteriorates very rapidly after being gathered, and should not be used at table if it has become stained with yellow marks. When purely white it may be cut into thick slices of a quarter-of-an-inch, and fried in fresh butter, with pepper, salt, and pounded herbs, and each slice should be first dipped in the yolk of an egg; the Puff Ball will also make an excellent omelette. Small Puff Balls are common on lawns, heaths, and pastures. These are harmless, and eatable as long as their flesh remains quite white. The Society of Amateur Botanists, 1863, had its origin (as described by the president, Mr. M. C. Cooke), "over a cup of tea and fried Puff Balls," in Great Turnstile.

Pieces of its dried inner woolly substance, with a profusion of minute snuff-coloured spores, have been long kept by the wise old women of villages for use to staunch wounds and incisions; whilst a ready surgical appliance to a deep cut is to bind a piece of Puff Ball over it, and leave it until healing has taken place. In Norfolk large Puff Balls found at the margins of cornfields are known as Bulfers, or Bulfists, and are regarded with aversion.

In medicine a trituration (H.) is made of this fungus, and its spores, rubbed up with inert sugar of milk powdered, and it proves an effective remedy against dull, stupid, sleepy headache, with passive itchy pimples about the skin. From five to ten grains of the trituration, diluted to the third decimal strength, should be given twice a day, with a little water, for two or three weeks.

Sir B. Richardson found that even by smelling at a strong tincture of the fungus great heaviness of the head was produced; and he has successfully employed the same tincture for relieving an analogous condition when coming on of its own accord. But the Puff Ball, whether in tincture (H.) or in trituration, is chiefly of service for curing the itchy pimply skin of "tettery" subjects, especially if this is aggravated by washing. Likewise the remedy is of essential use in some forms of eczema, especially in what is known as bakers', or grocers' itch. Five drops of the diluted tincture may be given with a spoonful of water three times in the day; and the affected parts should be sponged equally often with a lotion made of one part of the stronger tincture to four parts of water, or thin strained gruel. Sometimes when a full meal of the Puff Ball fried in butter, or stewed in milk, has been taken, undoubted evidences of its narcotic effects have shown themselves.

Gerard said: "In divers parts of England, where people dwell far from neighbours, they carry the Puff Balls kindled with fire, which lasteth long." In Latin they were named *Lupi crepitum*, or Wolfs' Fists. "The powder of them is fitly applied to merigals, kibed heels, and such like; the dust or powder thereof is very dangerous for the eyes, for it hath been observed that divers have been poreblind even after when some small quantity thereof hath been blown into their eyes." This fungus has been called Molly Puff, from its resemblance to a powder puff; also Devil's Snuff Box, Fuss Balls, and Puck Fists (from *feist*, *crepitus ani*, and *Puck*, the impish king of the fairies). In Scotland the Puff Ball is the blind man's e'en, because it has been believed that its dust will cause blindness; and in Wales it is the "bag of smoke."

The Fly Agaric, or Bug Agaric (*Agaricus muscarius*) gives the name of Mushroom to all the tribe of Fungi as used for the destruction of flies (*mousches*). Albertus Magnus describes it as *Vocatus fungus muscarum eo quidem lacte pulverisatus interficit muscas*: and this seems to be the real source of the word, which has by caprice become transmitted from a poisonous sort to the wholesome kinds exclusively. The pileus of the Fly Agaric is broad, convex, and of a rich orange scarlet colour, with a striate margin and white gills. It gets its name, as also that of Flybane, from being used in milk to kill flies; and it is called Bug Agaric from having been formerly employed to smear over bedsteads so as to destroy bugs. It inhabits dry places, especially birchwoods, and pinewoods, having a bright red upper surface studded with brown warts; and when taken as a poisonous agent it causes intoxication, delirium, and death through narcotism. It is more common in Scotland than in England. This Mushroom is highly poisonous, and therefore the remedial preparations are only to be given in a diluted form. For medicinal purposes a tincture is made (H.) from the fresh fungus: and a trituration of the dried fungus powdered and mixed with inert sugar of milk also powdered. These preparations are kept specially by the homœopathic chemists: and the use of the Fly Agaric has been adopted by the school which they represent for curatively treating an irritable spinal cord, with soreness, twitching of the limbs, dragging of the legs, unsteadiness of the head, neuralgic pains in the arms and legs (as if caused by sharp ice), some giddiness, a coating of yellow fur on the lining mucous membranes, together with a crawling, or burning, and eruptive skin. In fact for a lamentably depraved condition of all the bodily health, such as characterises advanced locomotor ataxy, and allied spinal degradations leading to general physical failure. Just such a totality of symptoms has been recorded by provers after taking the fungus for some length of time in toxical quantities. The tincture should be used of the third decimal strength, five drops for a dose twice or three times a day with a spoonful of water; or the trituration of the third decimal strength, for each dose as much of the powder as will lie on the flat surface of a sixpence. Chilblains may be mitigated by taking the tincture of this Agaric, and by applying some of the stronger tincture on cotton wool over the swollen and itching parts at night.

"Muscarin" is the leading active principle of the Fly Agaric, in conjunction with agaricin, mycose, and mannite. It stimulates, when swallowed in strong doses, certain nerves which tend to retard the action of the heart. Both our Fly Agaric and the White Agaric of the United States serve to relieve the night sweats of advanced pulmonary consumption, and they have severally proved of supreme palliative use against the cough, the sleeplessness, and the other worst symptoms of this wasting disease, as also for drying up the milk in weaning. Each of these fungi when taken by mistake will salivate profusely, and provoke both immoderate, and untimely laughter. When the action of the heart is laboured and feeble through lack of nervous power, muscarin, or the tincture of Fly Agaric, in a much diluted potency will relieve this trouble. The dose of Muscarin, or Agaricin, is from a sixth to half a grain in a pill. These medicines increase the secretion of tears, saliva, bile, and sweating, but they materially lessen the quantity of urine. Belladonna is found to be the best antidote. From the Oak Agaric, "touchwood," or "spunk,"—when cut into thin slices and beaten with a hammer until soft,—is made "Amadou," or German tinder. This is then soaked in a solution of nitre and dried ; it afterwards forms an excellent elastic astringent application for staying bleedings and for bed sores. The Larch Agaric is powdered, and given in Germany as a purgative, its dose being from twenty to sixty grains.

In Belgium the *Polyporus Officinalis* is used medicinally

as an aperient, and to check profuse sweating. By the Malays the *Polyporus Sanguineus* is used outwardly for leprosy.

Truffles (*Tuber cibarium*) may receive a passing notice whilst treating of fungi, though they are really subterranean tubers of an edible sort found in the earth, especially beneath beech trees, and uprooted by dogs trained for the purpose. They somewhat resemble our English "earth nuts," which swine discover by their scent. The ancients called the Truffle *lycoperdon*, because supposing it to spring from the dung of wolves. In Athens the children of Cherips had the rights of citizenship granted them because their father had invented a choice ragout concocted of Truffles. But delicate and weak stomachs find them difficult to digest. Pliny said, "Those kinds which remain hard after cooking are injurious; whilst others, naturally harmful if they admit of being cooked thoroughly well, and if eaten with saltpetre, or, still better, dressed with meat, or with pear stalks, are safe and innocent.

In Italy these tubers are fried in oil and dusted with pepper. For epicures they are mixed with the liver of fattened geese in *paté de foie gras.* Also, greedy swine are taught to discover and root them out, "being of a chestnut colour and heavy rank hercline smell, and found not seldom in England." Black Truffles are chiefly used: but there are also red and white varieties, the best tubers being light of weight in proportion to their size, with an agreeable odour, and elastic to the touch.

They are stimulating and heating, insomuch, that for delicate children who are atrophied, and require a *multum in parvo* of fatty and nitrogenous food in a compact but light form, which is fairly easy of digestion, the *paté de foie gras* on bread is a capital prescription. Truffles grow in clusters several inches below the soil, being found commonly on the downs of Wiltshire, Hampshire and Kent; also in oak and chestnut forests. Dogs have been trained to discriminate their scent below the surface of the soil, and to assist in digging them out. There is a Garlic Truffle of a small inferior sort which is put into stews; and the best Truffles are frequently found full of perforations. The presence of the tubers beneath the ground is denoted by the appearance above of a beautiful little fly having a violet colour—this insect being never seen except in the neighbourhood of Truffles. They are subject to the depredations of certain animalcules, which excavate the tubers so that they soon become riddled with worms. These, after passing through a chrysalis state, develop into the violet flies. Gerard called Truffles "Spanish fussebals." They were not known to English epicures in Queen Elizabeth's day. Another appellation borne by them formerly was "Swines' bread," and they were supposed to be engendered by thunderbolts. In Northern France they were first popularised four hundred and fifty years ago, by John, Duke of Berry, a reprobate gambler, third son of John the Good. The Perigord Truffle has a dark skin, and smells of violets. Piedmontese truffles suggest garlic: those of Burgundy are a little resinous: the Neapolitan specimens are redolent of sulphur: and in the Gard Department (France) they have an odour of musk. The English truffle is white, and best used in salads. Dr. Warton, Poet Laureate, 1750, said "Happy the grotto'ed hermit with his pulse, who wants no truffles." A Girton girl under examination described the tuber as a "sort of sea-anemone on land." When once dug up truffles soon lose their perfume and aroma, so they are imported bedded in the very earth which produced them.

The Earth Nut (*Bunium flexuosum*) is also called Hog Nut, Pig Nut, Jur Nut, St. Anthony's Nut, Earth Chesnut, and Kipper Nut. Caliban says, in the *Tempest*, "I with my long nails will dig thee Pig Nuts." They are an excellent diuretic, serving to stimulate the kidneys.

Pliny talked of fungi in general as a great delicacy to be eaten with amber knives and a service of silver. But Seneca called them *voluptuaria venena*. The Russians take some which we think to be deleterious; but they first soak these in vinegar, which (adds Pliny), "being contrary to them neutralizes their dangerous qualities; also they are rendered still more safe if cooked with pear stalks; indeed it is good to eat pears immediately after all fungi." Almost every species except the common Mushroom is characterized by the majority of our countrymen as a toadstool; but this title really appertains to the large group bearing the subgeneric name of *Tricholoma*, which probably does not contain a single unwholesome species. Other rustic names given to this group are "Puckstools" and "Puckfists." They are further known as "Toad skeps" (toad's cap) in the Eastern counties.

Puck, the mischievous king of the fairies, has been commonly identified with *pogge*, the toad, which was believed to sit upon most of the unwholesome fungi; and the *Champignon* (or Paddock Stool) was said to owe its growth to "those wanton elves whose pastime is to make midnight mushrooms." One of the "toad stoo's" (the *Clathrus cancellatus*) is said to produce cancerous sores if handled too freely. It has an abominably disgusting odour, and is therefore named the "lattice stinkhorn." The toad was popularly thought to impersonate the devil; and the toad-stool, pixie stool, or paddock stool was believed to spring from the devil's droppings.

The word Mushroom may have been derived from the French *Moucheron*, or *Mousseron*, because of its growing among moss. The chief chemical constituents of wholesome Mushrooms are albuminoids, carbo-hydrates, fat, mineral matters, and water. When salted they yield what is known as catsup, or ketchup (from the Japanese *kitchap*). The second most edible fungus of this nature is the Parasol Mushroom (*Lepcota procera*).

Edible Mushrooms, if kept uncooked, become dangerous: they cannot be sent to table too soon. In Rome our favourite *Pratiola* is held in very small esteem, and the worst wish an Italian can express against his foe is "that he may die of a *Pratiola*." If this species were exposed for sale in the Roman markets it would be certainly condemned by the inspector of fungi.

Fairy rings are produced by the spawn, or *mycelium*, beginning to germinate where dropped by a bird or a beast, and exhausting the soil of carbon, nitrogen, phosphorus and potash, from the centre continuously outwards; whilst immediately within the enlarging ring there is constantly a band of coarse rank grass fed by the manure of the penultimate dead spawn. The innermost starved ground remains poor and barren. In this duplicate way the rings grow larger and larger.

Our edible Mushroom is a *Pratella* of the subgenus *Psalliota*, and the *Agaricus campestris* of English botanists. In common with the esculent Mushrooms of France it contains phosphate of potassium—a cell salt essentially reparative of exhausted nerve tissue and energy.

The old practice of testing Mushrooms with a silver

spoon, which is supposed to become tarnished only when the juices are of an injurious quality (*i.e.*, when sulphur is developed therein under decomposition) is not to be trusted. In cases of poisoning by injurious fungi after the most violent symptoms may have been relieved, and the patient rescued from immediate danger, yet great emaciation will often follow from the subsequent effects of the poison: and the skin may exhibit an abundant outbreak of a vesicular eruption, whilst the health will remain perhaps permanently injured. Strong alcoholic drinks should never be taken together with, or immediately after eating Mushrooms, or other innocent fungi. Experienced fungus eaters (mycophagists) have found themselves suffering from severe pains, and some swellings through taking whiskey and water shortly after the meal: whereas precisely the same fungus, minus the whiskey, could be eaten with impunity by these identical experimentalists.

MUSTARD.

THE wild Mustard (*Brassica Sinapistrum*), a Cruciferous herb commonly called Chedlock, from *leac*, a weed, and *kiede*, to annoy, grows abundantly as a product of waste places, and in newly disturbed ground.

The Field Mustard (*Arvensis*) is Charlock, or Brassock; its botanical term, *Sinapis*, being referable to the Celtic *nap*, as a general name for plants of the rape kind. Mustard was formerly known as "senvie" in English. It has been long cultivated and improved, especially in Durham.

Now we have for commercial and officinal purposes two varieties of the cultivated plant, the black Mustard (*Sinapis nigra*), and the white Mustard (*Brassica*, or *Sinapis alba*). There is also a plain plant of the hedges,

Hedge Mustard (*Sisymbrium officinale*) which is a mere rustic Simple.

It is the black Mustard which yields by its seeds the condiment of our tables, and the pungent yellow flour which we employ for the familiar stimulating poultice, or sinapism. This black Mustard is a tall smooth plant, having entire leaves, and smooth seed pods, being now grown for the market on rich alluvial soil chiefly in Lincolnshire and Yorkshire. In common with its kindred plants it gets its name from *mustum*, the "must," or newly fermented grape juice, and *ardens*, burning, because as a condiment, Mustard flour was formerly mixed with home-made wine and sugar. The virtues of black Mustard depend on the acrid volatile oil contained in its seeds. These when unbruised and macerated in boiling water yield only a tasteless mucilage which resides in their skin. But when bruised they develop a very active, pungent, and highly stimulative principle with a powerful penetrating odour which makes the eyes water. From thence is perhaps derived the generic name of the herb *Sinapis* (*Para tou sinesthai tous hopous*, "because it irritates the eyes"). This active principle contains sulphur abundantly, as is proved by the discoloration of a silver spoon when left in the mustard-pot, the black sulphuret of silver being formed. The chemical basis of black Mustard is "sinnigrin" and its acid myronic. The acridity of its oil is modified in the seeds by combination with another fixed oil of a bland nature which can be readily separated by pressure, then the cake left after the expression of this fixed oil is far more pungent than the seeds. The bland oil expressed from the hulls of the black seeds after the flour has been sifted away, promotes the growth of the hair, and may be used with benefit externally for rheumatism. Whitehead's noted Essence of Mustard is made with spirits of turpentine and rosemary, with which camphor and the farina of black Mustard seed are mixed. This oil is very little affected by frost or the atmosphere; and it is therefore specially prized by clock makers, and for instruments of precision.

A Mustard poultice from the farina of black Mustard made into a paste with, or without wheaten flour commingled, constitutes one of the most powerful external stimulating applications we can employ. It quickly induces a sharp burning pain, and it excites a destructive outward inflammation which enters much more into the true skin than that which is caused by an old fashioned blister of Spanish fly. This has therefore superseded the latter as more promptly and reliably effective for the speedy relief of all active internal congestions. If the application of Mustard has caused sores, these may be best soothed and healed by limewater liniment.

Mustard flour is an infallible antiseptic and sterilising agent. It is a capital deodoriser; and if rubbed thoroughly into the hands and nails will take away all offensive stink when corrupt or dead tissues have been manipulated.

If a tablespoonful of Mustard flour is added to a pint of tepid water, and taken at a draught it operates briskly as a stimulating and sure emetic. Hot water poured on bruised seeds of black Mustard makes a good stimulating footbath for helping to throw off a cold, or to dispel a headache; and meantime the volatile oil given out as an aroma, if not too strong, proves soporific. This oil contains erucic, and sinapoleic acids. When properly mixed with spirit of wine, twenty-four drops of the oil to an ounce of spirit, the essential oil forms, by reason of its stimulating properties and its contained sulphur, a capital liniment for use in rheumatism, or for determining blood to the surface from deeper parts. Caution should be used not to apply a plaster made altogether of Mustard flour to the delicate skin of young children, or females, because ulcers difficult to heal may be the result, or even gangrenous destruction of the deeper skin may follow. The effects of a Mustard bath, at about ninety degrees, are singular; decided chills are felt at first throughout the whole body, with some twitchings at times of the limbs; and later on, even after the skin surface has become generally red, this sense of coldness persists, until the person leaves the water, when reaction becomes quickly established, with a glowing heat and redness of the whole skin.

For obstinate hiccough a teacupful of boiling water should be poured on a teaspoonful of Mustard flour, and taken when sufficiently cool, half at first, and the other half in ten minutes if still needed. For congestive headache a small roll of Mustard paper or Mustard leaf may be introduced into one or both nostrils, and left there for a minute or more. It will relieve the headache promptly, and may perhaps induce some nose bleeding.

Admixture with vinegar checks the development of the pungent principles of Mustard. This used to be practised for the table in England, but is now discontinued, though some housewives add a little salt to their made Mustard.

Claims for the introduction of Mustard at Durham in 1720, have been raised in favour of a Mrs. Clements, but they cannot be substantiated. Shakespeare in the *Taming of the Shrew* makes Grumio ask Katherine "What say you to a piece of beef and Mustard?" and speaks, in *Henry IV.*, of Poins' wit being "as thick as Tewkesbury Mustard"; whilst Fuller in his *Worthies of England,* written only a very few years after Shakespeare's death, says "the best Mustard in England is made at Tewkesbury in the county of Gloucester." Coles observes (1657), "in Gloucestershire about Teuxbury they grind Mustard seed and make it up into balls, which are brought to London and other remote places as being the best that the world affords." George the First restored the popularity of Mustard by his approval of it. Prior to 1720 no such condiment as Mustard in its present form was used at table in this country. It is not improbable that the Romans, who were great eaters of Mustard-seed pounded and steeped in new wine, brought the condiment with them to our shores, and taught the ancient Britons how to prepare it. At Dijon in France where the best mixed continental Mustard is made, the condiment is seasoned with various spices and savouries, such as Anchovies, Capers, Tarragon, Catsup of Walnuts, or Mushrooms, and the liquors of other pickles. Philip the Bold granted armorial ensigns (1382) to Dijon, with the motto *moult me tarde* (I wish for ardently). The merchants of Sinapi copied this on their wares, the middle word of the motto being accidentally effaced. A well-known couplet of lines supposed to occur in *Hudibras* (but not to be found there), has long baffled the research of quotation hunters:

> "Sympathy without relief
> Is like to Mustard without beef."

Mustard flour moistened with a little water into a paste has the singular property of dispelling the odours of musk, camphor, and the fetid gum resins. For deodorising vessels which have contained the essences of turpentine, creasote, assafetida, or other such drugs, it will answer to introduce some bruised Mustard seed, and then a little water, shaking the vessel well for a minute or more, and afterwards rinsing it out with plenty of water.

The white Mustard grows when uncultivated on waste ground with large yellow flowers, and does not yield under any circumstances a pungent oil like the black Mustard. It is a hirsute plant, with stalked leaves and hairy seed pods; and when produced in our gardens its young leaves are eaten as a salad, or as "Mustard, with Cress."

"When in the leaf," says John Evelyn in his *Acetaria*, "Mustard, especially in young seedling plants, is of incomparable effect to quicken and revive the spirits, strengthening the memory, expelling heaviness, preventing the vertiginous palsy, and a laudable cephalic, besides being an approved antiscorbutic." He tells further that the Italians, in making Mustard as a condiment, mingle lemon and orange peel with the (black) seeds. "In the composition of a sallet the Mustard (a noble ingredient) should be of the best Tewkesbury or else of the soundest and weightiest Yorkshire seed, tempered a little by the fire to the consistence of a pap with vinegar, in which some shavings of the horse-radish have been steeped. Then, cutting an onion, and putting it into a small earthen gally-pot, pour the Mustard over it and close it very well with a cork. *Note.*—The seeds should have been pounded in a mortar, or bruised with a polished cannon bullet in a large wooden bowl dish."

The active principle of white Mustard is "Sinapin," and the seed germinates so rapidly that it has been said a salad of this may be grown while the joint of meat is being roasted for dinner. Seeds of the white Mustard have been employed medicinally from early times.

Hippocrates advised their use both internally, and as a counter-irritating poultice made with vinegar. When swallowed whole in teaspoonful doses three or four times a day, they exercise a laxative effect mechanically, and are voided without undergoing any perceptible change, only the outer skin being a little softened and mucilaginous. An infusion of the seed taken medicinally will relieve chronic bronchitis, and confirmed rheumatism: also for a relaxed sore throat a gargle of Mustard seed tea will be found of service.

A French expression for trifling one's time away is *s'amuser à la moutarde.* The essential oil is an admirable deodorant and disinfectant, especially on an emergency.

But the "grain of Mustard seed, the smallest of all seeds" (*Mark* iv., 31), "which when it is grown up is the greatest among herbs," was a tree of the East, very different from our Mustard, and bearing branches of real wood.

The Hedge Mustard (*Sisymbrium*, or *Erisymum*) grows by our roadsides, and on waste grounds, where it seems to possess a peculiar aptitude for collecting and retaining dust. The pods are downy, close pressed to the stem, and the leaves hairy with their points turned backwards. It is named by the French "St. Barbara's Hedge Mustard," and the Singer's Plant, "*herbe au chantre*," or "*herbe au chanteur.*" Up to the time of Louis XIV. it was considered an infallible remedy for loss of the voice. Racine writing to Boileau recommended the syrup of *Erysimum* to him when visiting the waters of Bourbonne in order to be cured of voicelessness. "Si les eaux de Bourbonne ne vous guerissent pas de votre extinction de voix, le sirop d'Erysimum vous guerirait infalliblement. Ne l'oubliez pas, et à l'occasion vingt grammes par litre d'eau en tisane matin et soir." It used to be called Flix, or Flux weed from being given with benefit in dysentery, a disease formerly known as the Flix. This herb has been commended for chronic coughs and hoarseness, using the juice mixed with an equal quantity of honey, or sugar. It has been designated "the most excellent of all remedies for diseases of the throat, especially in ulcerated sore throats, which it will serve to cure when all the advice of physicians and surgeons has proved ineffectual." A strong infusion of the herb is excellent in asthmas, and it may be made with sugar into a syrup which will keep all the year round. The Hedge Mustard contains chemically a soft resin, and a sulphuretted volatile oil. This herb with the vervain is supposed to form Count Mattæi's noted nostrum *Febrifugo.*

NETTLE.

No plant is more commonplace and plentiful in our fields and hedges throughout an English summer than the familiar stinging Nettle. And yet most persons unknowingly include under this single appellation several distinct herbs. Actually as Nettles are to be found: the annual *Urtica dioica*, or true Stinging Nettle; the perennial *Urtica urens* (burning); the White Dead Nettle; the Archangel, or Yellow Weasel Snout, and the Purple Hedge Nettle. This title "Urtica" comes *ab urendo*, "from burning."

The plant which stings has a round hairy stalk, and carries only a dull colourless bloom, whereas the others are labiate herbs with square stems, and conspicuous lipped flowers. As Simples only the great Stinging Nettle, the lesser Stinging Nettle, and the white Dead Nettle call for observation. Also another variety of our Stinging Nettle is the *Urtica pilulifera*, called by corruption the Roman Nettle, really because found abundantly at Romney in Kent. But a legend obtains belief with some that Roman soldiers first brought with them to England the seeds of this plant, and sowed it about for their personal uses. They heard before coming that the climate here was so cold that it might not be endured without some friction to warm the blood, and to stir up the natural heat; and they therefore bethought them to provide Nettles wherewith to chafe their limbs when "stiffe and much benummed." Or, again, Lyte says, "They do call al such strange herbes as be unknown of the common people Romish, or Romayne herbes, although the same be brought direct from Sweden or Norweigh." The cure for Nettle stings has been from early times to rub the part with a dock leaf. The dead Nettles are so named as having no sting, but possessing nettle-like leaves. The stinging effect of the true Nettle is caused by an acrid secretion contained in minute vesicles at the base of each of the stiff hairs; and *urtication*, or flogging with Nettles, is an old external remedy, which was long practised for chronic rheumatism, and loss of muscular power. *Tacta quod exuret digitos urtica tenentis.*—Macer. Tea made from the young tops is a Devonshire cure for Nettle-rash. Gerard says, "the Nettle is a good medicine for them that cannot breathe unless they hold their necks upright: and being eaten boiled with periwinkles it makes the body soluble."

The word Nettle is derived from *net*, meaning something spun, or sewn; and it indicates the thread made from the hairs of the plant, and formerly used among Scandinavian nations. This was likewise employed by Scotch weavers in the seventeenth century. Westmacott, the historian, says, "Scotch cloth is only the housewifery of the Nettle." And the poet Campbell writes in one of his letters, "I have slept in Nettle sheets, and dined off a Nettle table cloth: and I have heard my mother say she thought Nettle cloth more durable than any other linen." Goldsmith has recorded the "rubbing of a cock's heart with stinging Nettles to make it hatch hen's eggs." Some think the word "Nettle" an alteration of the Anglo-Saxon "Needl," with reference to the needle-like stings. Spun silk is now made in England from "Ramie" the decorticated fibre of Nettles after washing away the glutinous juice from under their bark.

The seeds (*dioica*) contain a fine oil, and powerfully stimulate the sexual functions.

In Russia, as a recent mode of treatment, *urtication* is now enthusiastieally commended, that is, slapping, or pricking with a bundle of fresh Nettle twigs for one or more minutes, once, or several times in the day. It is a superlative method of cure because harmless (neither irritating the kidneys nor disfiguring the skin), cleanly, simple in application, rapid in its effects, and cheap, though perhaps somewhat rude.

For sciatica, for incipient wasting, for the difficult breathing of some heart troubles (where such stimulation along the backbone affords more prompt and complete relief than any other treatment), for some coughs palsy, suppression of the monthly flow in women, rheumatism, and for lack of muscular energy, this *urtication* is said to be an invaluable resuscitating measure which has been successfully resorted to by the peasantry of Russia from time immemorial. It will sometimes produce a crop of small harmless blisters.

The analysis of the fresh Nettle shows a presence of formic acid (the irritating principle of the stinging hairs), with mucilage, salts, ammonia, carbonic acid, and water. A strong decoction of Nettles drunk too freely by mistake has produced severe burning over the whole body, with general redness, and a sense of being stung. The features became swollen, and minute vesicles appeared on the skin, which burst, and discharged a limpid fluid. No fever accompanied the attack, and after five or six days the eruption dried up. A medicinal tincture (H.) is made from the entire plant with spirit of wine: and this, as taught by the principle of similars, may be confidently given in small diluted doses to mitigate such a totality of symptoms as now described, whether coming on as an attack of severe Nettle rash, or assuming some more pronounced eruptive aspect, such as chicken pox. The same tincture also acts admirably in cases of burns, when the deep skin is not destructively involved. And again for relieving the itching of the fundament caused by the presence of threadworms.

"Burns," says Lucomsky, "may be rapidly cured by applying over them linen cloths well wetted with an alcoholic tincture of the Stinging Nettle prepared from the fresh plant, this being diluted with an equal, or a double quantity of cold water. The cloths should be frequently re-wetted, but without removing them, so as to prevent pain from exposure." Dr. Burnett has shown conclusively that Nettle tea, and Nettle tincture (ten drops for a dose in water), are curative of feverish gout, as well as of intermittent fever and ague. Either remedy will promote a speedy extrication of gravel through the kidneys. Again the Nettle was a favourite old English remedy for consumption, as already mentioned (see *Mugwort*), with reference to the mermaid of the Clyde, when she beheld with regret the untimely funeral of a young Glasgow maiden.

Fresh Nettle juice given in doses of from one to two tablespoonfuls is a most serviceable remedy for all sorts of bleeding, whether from the nose, the lungs, or some internal organ. Also the decoction of the leaves and stalks taken in moderate quantities is capital for many of the minor skin maladies.

An alcoholic extract is made officinally from the entire young plant gathered in the spring, and some of this if applied on cotton wool will arrest bleeding from the nose, or after the extraction of a tooth, when persistent. If a leaf of the plant be put upon the tongue and pressed against the roof of the mouth, it will stop a bleeding from the nose. Taken as a fresh young vegetable in the spring, or early summer, Nettle tops make a very wholesome and succulent dish of greens, which is slightly laxative; but during Autumn they are hurtful. In Italy where herb soups are in high favour, "herb knodel" (or round balls made like a dumpling in size and consistency) of Nettles are esteemed as nourishing and medicinal. The greater Nettle (*Urtica dioica*), and the lesser Nettle (*Urtica urens*) possess stinging properties in common.

A crystalline alkaloid which is fatal to frogs in a dose of one centigramme, has been isolated from the common Stinging Nettle. The watery extract has but little effect on mammals: but in the frog it causes paralysis, beginning in the great nervous centres and finally stopping the action of the heart. If planted in the neighbourhood of beehives, the Nettle will serve to drive away frogs.

The expressed seeds yield an oil which may be used for burning in lamps. Nettle leaves, rubbed into wooden vessels, such as tubs, &c., will prevent their leaking. The juice of the leaves coagulates, and fills up the interstices of the wood. When dried the leaves will often relieve asthma and similar bronchial troubles by inhalation, although other means have failed. Eight or ten grains should be burnt, and the fumes inspired at bed-time.

The *Lamium album* (white dead Nettle), a labiate plant, though not of the stinging Nettle order, is likewise of special use for arresting hæmorrhage, as in spitting of blood, dysentery, and female fluxes. Its name *Lamium* is got from the Greek *laimos*, the throat, because of the shape of its corollæ. If the plant be macerated in alcohol for a week, then cotton wool dipped in the liquid is as efficacious for staying bleeding, when applied to the spot, as the strongly astringent muriate of iron. Also, a tincture of the flowers is made (H.) for internal use in similar cases. From five to ten drops of this tincture should be given for a dose with a tablespoonful of cold water. The Red Nettle, another *Lamium*, is also called Archangel, because it blossoms on St. Michael's day, May 8th. If made into a tea and sweetened with honey, it promotes perspiration, and acts on the kidneys. The white dead Nettle is a degenerate form of this purple herb as shown by still possessing on its petals the same brown markings. Nevertheless, having disobeyed the laws of its growth, it has lost its original colour, and, like the Lady of Shalott, it is fain to complain "the curse has come upon me." Count Mattæi's nostrum *Pettorale* is thought to be got from the *Galeopsis* (hemp Nettle), another of the labiate herbs, with Nettle-like leaves, but no stinging hairs, named from *galee*, a cat, or weazel, and *opsis*, a countenance, because supposed to have a blossom resembling the face of the animal specified.

NIGHT SHADE, DEADLY (*Belladonna*).

THIS is a Solanaceous plant found native in Great Britain, and growing generally on chalky soil under hedges, or about waste grounds. It bears the botanical name of *Atropa*, being so called from one of the classic Fates,—she who held the shears to cut the thread of human life :—

"Clotho velum retinet, Lachesis net, et atropos occit."

Its second title, *Belladonna*, was bestowed because the Spanish ladies made use of the plant to dilate the pupils of their brilliant black eyes. In this way their orbs appeared more attractively lustrous : and the *donna* became *bella* (beautiful). The plant is distinguished by a large leaf growing beside a small one about its stems, whilst the solitary flowers, which droop, have a dark full purple border, being paler downwards, and without scent. The berries (in size like small cherries) are of a rich purplish black hue, and possess most dangerously narcotic properties. They are medicinally useful, but so deadly that only the skilled hands of the apothecary should attempt to manipulate them ; and they should not be prescribed for a patient except by the competent physician. When taken by accident their mischievous effects may be prevented by swallowing as soon as possible a large glass of warm vinegar.

A tincture of allied berries was used of old by ladies of fashion in the land of the Pharaohs, as discovered among the mummy graves by Professor Baeyer, of Munich. This had the property of imparting a verdant sheen to the human iris ; and, perhaps by the quaint colour-effect it produced on the transparent cornea of some wily Egyptian belle, it gave rise to the saying, 'Do you see any green in the white of my eye ?"

At one time *Belladonna* leaves were held to be curative of cancer when applied externally as a poultice, either fresh, or dried, and powdered. It is remarkable that sheep, rabbits, goats, and swine can eat these leaves with impunity, though (as Boerhaave tells) a single berry has been known to prove fatal to the human subject; and a gardener was once hanged for neglecting to remove plants of the deadly Night Shade from certain grounds which he knew. A peculiar symptom in those poisoned by *Belladonna* berries is the complete loss of voice, together with frequent bending forward of the trunk, and continual movements of the hands and fingers. The Scotch under Macbeth sent bread and wine treacherously impregnated with this poison to the troops of Sweno.

The plant bears other titles, as "Dwale" (death's herb), "Great Morel," and "Naughty Man's Cherry." The term "Morel" is applied to the plant as a diminutive of *mora*, a Moor, on account of the black-skinned berries. The *Belladonna* grows especially near the ruins of monasteries, and is so abundant around Furness Abbey that this locality has been styled the "Vale of Night Shade."

Hahnemann taught that, acting on the law of similars, *Belladonna* given in very small doses of its tincture will protect from the infection of scarlet fever. He confirmed this fact by experiments on one hundred and sixty children. When taken by provers in actual toxic doses the tincture, or the fresh juice, has induced sore throat, feverishness, and a dry, red, hot skin, just as if symptomatic of scarlet fever. The plant yields atropine and hyoscyamine from all its parts. As a drug it specially affects the brain and the bladder. The berries are known in Buckinghamshire as "Devil's cherries."

NUTMEG, CINNAMON, GINGER, and CLOVES.

THE spice box is such a constant source of ready domestic comforts of a medicinal sort in every household that the more important, and best known of its contents may well receive some consideration when treating of Herbal Simples; though it will, of course, be understood these spices are of foreign growth, and not indigenous products.

Cinnamon, Nutmeg, Ginger, and Cloves, claim particular notice in this respect.

> "Sinament, Ginger, Nutmeg, and Cloves,
> And that gave me my jolly red nose."
>
> *Beaumont and Fletcher.*

Cinnamon possesses positive medicinal as well as aromatic virtues. What we employ as this spice consists of the inner bark of shoots from the stocks of a Ceylon tree, first cultivated here in 1768.

Such bark chemically contains cinnamic acid, tannin, a resin, and sugar, so that its continued use will induce constipation. The aromatic and stimulating effects of Cinnamon have been long known. It was freely given in England during the epidemic scourges of the early and middle centuries, nearly every monastery keeping a store of the cordial for ready use. The monks administered it in fever, dysentery, and contagious diseases. And recent discovery in the laboratory of M. Pasteur, the noted French bacteriologist, has shown that Cinnamon possesses the power of absolutely destroying all disease germs. Our ancestors, it would appear, had hit upon a valuable preservative against microbes, when they infused Cinnamon with other spices in their mulled drinks. Mr. Chamberland says, "no disease germ can long resist the antiseptic powder of essence of Cinnamon, which is as effective to destroy microbes as corrosive sublimate."

By its warming astringency, it exercises cordial properties which are most useful in arresting passive diarrhœa, and in relieving flatulent indigestion.

Its volatile oil is procured from the bark, and likewise a tincture, as well as an aromatic water of Cinnamon. For a sick qualmish stomach either preparation is an excellent remedy, as the virtue of the bark rests in this essential volatile oil. When obtained from the *fruit* it is extremely fragrant, of thick consistence, and sometimes made into candles at Ceylon, for the sole use of the king. The doses are of the powdered bark from ten to twenty grains ; of the oil from one to five drops ; of the tincture from half to one teaspoonful, and of the distilled water from one to two tablespoonfuls. Our Queen is known to be partial to the use of Cinnamon. Keats, the poet, wrote of "lucent syrups tinct. with Cinnamon." And Saint Francis of Sales says in his *Devout Life*: "With respect to the labour of teaching, it refreshes and revives the heart by the sweetness it brings to those who are engaged in it, as the Cinnamon does in *Arabia Felix* to them who are laden with it." In toxic quantities of an injurious amount, Cinnamon bark has produced hæmorrhage from the bowels, and nose bleeding. Therefore small doses of the diluted tincture are well calculated to obviate these symptoms when presenting themselves through illness.

The bark was formerly thought to stimulate the functions of the womb, and of late it has come again into medical use for this purpose. To check fluxes from that organ, a teaspoonful of the bruised bark should be infused in half a pint of boiling water, and a tablespoonful given frequently when cool. Lozenges made with the essential oil are also medicinally available for the speedy relief of sickness, and as highly useful against influenza. It is well known that persons who live in Cinnamon districts have an immunity from malaria.

Ginger (*Zingiberis radix*) is the root-stock of a plant grown in the East and West Indies, and is scraped before importation. Its odour is due to an essential oil, and its pungent hot taste to a resin. It was known in Queen Elizabeth's reign, having been introduced by the Dutch about 1566. "Grene Gynger of almondes" is mentioned in the Paston Letters, 1444. "When condited," says Gerard, "it provoketh veneric."

This Green Ginger, which consists of the young shoots of the *rhizome*, when boiled in syrup makes an excellent preserve. Officinally from the dried and scraped rhizome are prepared a tincture, and a syrup. If a piece of the root is chewed it causes a considerable flow of saliva, and an application of powdered Ginger, made with water into paste, against the skin will produce intense tingling and heat. To which end it may be spread on paper and applied to the forehead as a means for relieving a headache from passive fulness. In India, Europeans who suffer from languid indigestion drink an infusion of Ginger as a substitute for tea. For gouty dyspepsia the root may be powdered in a mortar: and a heaped teaspoonful of it should be then infused in boiling milk; to be taken when sufficiently cool, for supper or at breakfast.

The dose of the powder is from ten to twenty grains; of the tincture from a third of a teaspoonful to a teaspoonful, in water hot or cold; of the syrup from one to two teaspoonfuls in water. Either preparation is of service to correct diarrhœa, and to relieve weakly chronic bronchitis. Also as admirably corrective of chronic constipation through general intestinal sluggish ness, a vespertine slice of good, old-fashioned Gingerbread made with brown treacle and grated ginger may be eaten with zest, and reliance. There is a street in Hull called "The land of Ginger."

The habitat of the tree from which our Nutmeg comes is the Molucca Islands, and the part of the nut which constitutes the Spice is the kernel. This is called generically *Nux moschata*, or Mugget (French *Musqué*) a diminutive of musk, from its aromatic odour, and properties. The Nutmeg is oval, or nearly round, of a brown wrinkled aspect, with an aromatic smell, and a bitter fragrant taste. Officinally the tree is named *Myristica officinalis*, and the oil distilled from the Nutmeg in Britain is much superior to foreign oil.

Ordinarily as a condiment of a warming character the Nutmeg is employed to correct cold indigestible food, or as a cordial addition to negus: and medicinally for languid digestion, with giddiness and flatulence, causing oppressed breathing. Its activity depends on the volatile oil, contained in the proportion of six per cent. in the nut. This when given at all largely is essentially narcotic. Four Nutmegs have been known to completely paralyse all nervous sensibility, and have produced a sort of wakeful unconsciousness for three entire days, with loss of memory afterwards, and with more or less paralysis until after eight days.

The Banda, or Nutmeg Islands in the Indian Ocean, are twelve in number, and the strength of the Nutmeg in its season is said to overcome birds of Paradise so that they fall helplessly intoxicated.

When taken to any excess, whether as a spice, or as a medicine, the Nutmeg and its preparations are apt to cause giddiness, oppression of the chest, stupor, and delirium. A moderate dose of the powdered Nutmeg is from five to twenty grains, but persons with a tendency to apoplexy should abstain from any free use of this spice. From two to six drops of the essential oil may be taken on sugar to relieve flatulent oppression and dyspepsia, or from half to one teaspoonful of the spirit of Nutmeg made by mixing one part of the oil with forty parts of spirit of wine; this dose being had with one or two tablespoonfuls of hot water, sweetened if desired.

A medicinal tincture is prepared (H.) from the kernel with spirit of wine (not using the oil, nor the essenee). This in small diluted doses is highly useful for drowsiness connected with flatulent indigestion, and a disposition to faintness: also for gout retrocedent to the stomach. The dose is from five to ten drops with a spoonful of water every half hour, or every hour until the symptoms are adequately relieved. Against diarrhœa Nutmeg grated into warm water is very helpful, and will prove an efficient substitute for opium in mild cases. Externally the spirit of Nutmeg is a capital application to be rubbed in for chronic rheumatism, and for paralysed limbs. The "butter of Nutmegs," or their concrete oil, is used in making plasters of a warming, and stimulating kind. A drink that was concocted by our grandmothers was Nutmeg tea. One Nutmeg would make a pint of this tea, two or three cupfuls of which would produce a sleep of many hours' duration. The worthy old ladies were wont to carry a silver grater and Nutmeg case suspended from the waist on their chatelaines. But in any large quantity the Nutmeg may produce sleep of such a profundity as to prove really dangerous. Two drachms of the powder have brought on a comatose sleep with some delirium.

The Nutmeg contains starch, protein, and other simple constituents, in addition to its stimulating principles. Mace is the aromatic envelope of the Nutmeg, and possesses the same qualities in a minor degree. Its infusion is a good warming medicine against chronic cough, and moist bronchial asthma in an old person. Mace is a membranaceous structure enveloping the Nutmeg, having a fleshy texture, and being of a light yellowish-brown colour. It supplies an allied essential volatile principle, which is fragrant and cordial. If given three or four times during the twenty-four hours, in a dose of from eight to twelve grains, crushed, or powdered Mace will prove serviceable against long-continued looseness of the bowels ; but this dose should not be exceeded for fear of inducing narcotism.

Cloves (from *clavus*, a nail), also found in the kitchen spice-box, and owning certain medicinal resources of a cordial sort, which are quickly available, belong to the Myrtle family of plants, and are the unexpanded flower buds of an aromatic tree (*Caryophyllus*), cultivated at Penang and elsewhere. They contain a volatile oil which, like that of Chamomile, although cordial, lowers nervous sensibility, or irritability: also tannin, a gum resin, and woody fibre. This volatile oil consists principally of "eugenin" with a camphor, "caryophyllin." The "eugenic acid," with a strong odour of cloves, is powerfully antiseptic and anti-putrescent. It reduces the sensibility of the skin: and therefore the oil with lanolin is a useful application for eczema.

Dr Burnett has lately taught (1895) that a too free use of Cloves will bring on albuminuria ; and that when this disease has supervened from other causes, the dilute tincture of Cloves, third decimal strength, will frequently do much to lessen the quantity of albumen excreted by the kidneys. From five to ten drops of this tincture should be given with water three times a day.

Used in small quantities as a spice the Clove stimulates digestion, but when taken more freely it deadens the susceptibility of the stomach, lessens the appetite, and induces constipation. An infusion of Cloves, made with half an ounce to a pint of water, and drank in doses of a small wineglassful, will relieve the nausea and coldness of flatulent indigestion. The oil put on cotton wool into the hollow of a decayed tooth is a useful means for giving ease to toothache. The dose of the oil is from one to five drops, on sugar, or in a spoonful of milk. The odour of Cloves is aromatic, and the taste pleasantly hot, but acrid. Half a tumbler of quite hot water poured over half a dozen Cloves (which are to brew for a few minutes on the hob, and then to be taken out), will often secure a good night to a restless dyspeptic patient, if taken just before getting into bed. Or if given cold before breakfast this dose will obviate constipation. In Holland the oil of Cloves is prescribed with cinchona bark for ague. Arthur Cecil's German medico in the Play advises his patient to "rub your pelly mit a Clove."

All-Spice (*Pimento*) is another common occupant of the domestic spice box. It is popular as a warming cordial, of a sweet odour, and a grateful aromatic taste; but being a native of South America, grows with us only as a stove plant. The leaves and bark are full of inflammable particles, whilst walks between Pimento trees are odorous with a delicious scent. The name All-Spice is given because the berries afford in smell and taste a combination of Cloves, Juniper berries, Cinnamon and Pepper. The special qualities of the Pimento reside in the rind of these berries; and this tree is the *Bromelia ananas*, named in Brazil *Nana*. An extract made from the crushed berries by boiling them down to a thick liquor, is, when spread on linen, a capital stimulating plaster for neuralgic or rheumatic parts. About the physician in "les Francais" it was said admiringly "c'est lui qui a inventé la salade d'Ananas." The essential oil, as well as the spirit and the distilled water of Pimento, are useful against flatulent indigestion and for hysterical paroxysms. This Spice was formerly added to our syrup of buckthorn to prevent it from griping. The berries are put into curry powder, and added to mulled wines.

OAT.

THE Oat is a native of Britain in its wild and uncultivated form, and is distinguished by the spikelets of its ears hanging on slender pedicels. This is the *Avena fatua*, found in our cornfields, but not indigenous in Scotland. When cultivated it is named *Avena sativa.* As it needs less sunshine and solar warmth to ripen the grain than wheat, it furnishes the principal grain food of cold Northern Europe. With the addition of some fat this grain is capable of supporting life for an indefinite period. Physicians formerly recommended highly a diet-drink made from Oats, about which Hoffman wrote a treatise at the end of the seventeenth century; and Johannis de St. Catherine, who introduced the drink, lived by its use to a hundred years free from any disease. Nevertheless the Oat did not enjoy a good reputation among the old Romans; and Pliny said "Primum omnis frumenti vitium avena est."

American doctors have taken of late to extol the Oat (*Avena sativa*) when made into a strong medicinal tincture with spirit of wine, as a remarkable nervine stimulant and restorative: this being "especially valuable in all cases where there is a deficiency of nervous power, for instance, among over-worked lawyers, public speakers, and writers."

The tincture is ordered to be given in a dose of from ten to twenty drops, once or twice during the day, in hot water to act speedily; and a somewhat increased dose in cold water at bedtime so as to produce its beneficial effects more slowly then. It proves an admirable remedy for sleeplessness from nervous exhaustion, and as prepared in New York may be procured from any good druggist in England. Oatmeal contains two per cent. of protein compounds, the largest portion of which is avenin. A yeast poultice made by stirring Oatmeal into the grounds of strong beer is a capital cleansing and healing application to languid sloughing sores.

Oatmeal supplies very little saccharine matter ready formed. It cannot be made into light bread, and is therefore prepared when baked in cakes; or, its more popular form for eating is that of porridge, where the ground meal becomes thoroughly soft by boiling, and is improved in taste by the addition of milk and salt. "The halesome parritch, chief of Scotia's food," said Burns, with fervid eloquence. Scotch people actually revel in their parritch and bannocks. "We defy your wheaten bread," says one of their favourite writers, "your home-made bread, your bakers' bread, your baps, rolls, scones, muffins, crumpets, and cookies, your bath buns, and your sally luns, your tea cakes, and slim cakes, your saffron cakes, and girdle cakes, your shortbread, and singing hinnies: we swear by the Oat cake, and the parritch, the bannock, and the brose." Scotch beef brose is made by boiling Oatmeal in meat liquor, and kail brose by cooking Oatmeal in cabbage-water.

Crushed Oatmeal, from which the husk has been removed, is known as "groats," and is employed for making gruel. At the latter end of the seventeenth century this was a drink asked-for eagerly by the public at London taverns. "Grantham gruel," says quaint old Fuller, in his *History of the Worthies of England*, "consists of nine grits and a gallon of water." When "thus made, it is wash rather, which one will have little heart to eat, and yet as little heart by eating." But the better gruel concocted elsewhere was "a wholesome spoon meat, though homely; physic for the sick, and food for persons in health; grits the form thereof: and giving the being thereunto." In the border forays of the twelfth and thirteenth centuries all the provision carried by the Scotch was simply a bag of Oatmeal. But as a food it is apt to undergo some fermentation in the stomach, and to provoke sour eructations. Furthermore, it is somewhat laxative, because containing a certain proportion of bran which mechanically stimulates the intestinal membranes: and this insoluble bran is rather apt to accumulate. Oatmeal gruel may be made by boiling from one to two ounces of the meal with three pints of water down to two pints, then straining the decoction, and pouring off the supernatant liquid when cool. Its flavour may be improved by adding raisins towards the end of boiling, or by means of sugar and nutmeg. Because animals of speed use up, by the lungs, much heat-forming material, Oats (which abound in carbonaceous constituents) are specially suitable as food for the horse.

ONION (*see* **Garlic,** *page* 209).

ORANGE.

THOUGH not of native British growth, except by way of a luxury in the gardens of the wealthy, yet the Orange is of such common use amongst all classes of our people as a dietetic fruit, when of the sweet China sort, and for tonic medicinal purposes when of the bitter Seville kind, that some consideration may be fairly accorded to it as a Curative Simple in these pages.

The *Citrus aurantium*, or popular Orange, came originally from India, and got its distinctive title of *Aurantium*, either (*ab aureo colore corticis*) from the golden colour of its peel, or (*ab oppido Achæiæ Arantium*) from Arantium, a town of Achaia. It now comes to us chiefly from Portugal and Spain. This fruit is essentially a product of cultivation extending over many years. It began in Hindustan as a small bitter berry with seeds; then about the eighth century it was imported into Persia, though held somewhat accursed. During the tenth century it bore the name "Bigarade," and became better known. But not until the sixteenth century was it freely grown by the Spaniards, and brought into Mexico. Even at that time the legend still prevailed that whoever partook of the luscious juice was compelled to embrace the faith of the prophet. Spenser and Milton tell of the orange as the veritable golden apple presented by Jupiter to Juno on the day of their nuptials: and hence perhaps arose its more modern association with marriage rites.

Of the varieties the China Orange is the most juicy, being now grown in the South of Europe; whilst the St. Michael Orange (a descendant of the China sort, first produced in Syria), is now got abundantly from the Azores, whence it derives its name.

John Evelyn says the first China Orange which appeared in Europe, was sent as a present to the old Condé Mellor, then Prime Minister to the King of Portugal, when only one plant escaped sound and useful of the whole case which reached Lisbon, and this became the parent of all the Orange trees cultivated by our gardeners, though not without greatly degenerating.

The Seville Orange is that which contains the medicinal properties, more especially in its leaves, flowers, and fruit, though the China sort possesses the same virtues in a minor degree. The leaves and the flowers have been esteemed as beneficial against epilepsy, and other convulsive disorders; and a tea is infused from the former for hysterical sufferers.

Two delicious perfumes are distilled from the flowers—oil of neroli, and napha water,—of which the chemical hydro-carbon "hesperidin," is mainly the active principle. This is secreted also as an aromatic attribute of the leaves through their minute glands, causing them to emit a fragrant odour when bruised. A scented water is largely prepared in France from the flowers, *l'eau de fleur d'oranger*, which is frequently taken by ladies as a gentle sedative at night, when sufficiently diluted with sugared water. Thousands of gallons are drunk in this way every year. As a pleasant and safely effective help towards wooing sleep, from one to two teaspoonfuls of the French *Eau de fleur d'oranger*, if taken at bedtime in a teacupful of hot water, are to be highly commended for a nervous, or excitably wakeful person.

Orange buds are picked green from the trees in the gardens of the Riviera, and when dried they retain the sweet smell of the flowers. A teaspoonful of these buds is ordered to be infused in a teacupful of quite hot water, and the liquid to be drunk shortly before going to bed. The effect is to induce a refreshing sleep, without any subsequent headache or nausea. The dried berries may be had from an English druggist.

A peeled Orange contains some citric acid, with citrate of potash; also albumen, cellulose, water, and about eight per cent. of sugar. The white lining pith of the peel possesses likewise the crystalline principle "hesperidin." Dr. Cullen showed that the acid juice of oranges, by uniting with the bile, diminishes the bitterness of that secretion; and hence it is that this fruit is of particular service in illnesses which arise from a redundancy of bile, chiefly in dark persons of a fibrous, or bilious temperament. But if the acids of the Orange are greater in quantity than can be properly corrected by the bile (as in persons with a small liver, and feeble digestive powers), they seem, by some prejudicial union with that liquid, to acquire a purgative quality, and to provoke diarrhœa, with colicky pains.

The rind or peel of the Seville Orange is darker in colour, and more bitter of taste than that of the sweet China fruit. It affords a considerable quantity of fragrant, aromatic oil, which partakes of the characters exercised by the leaves and the flowers as affecting the nervous system. Pereira records the death of a child which resulted from eating the rind of a sweet China Orange.

The small green fruits (windfalls) from the Orange trees of each sort, which become blown off, or shaken down during the heats of the summer, are collected and dried, forming the "orange berries" of the shops. They are used for flavouring curacoa, and for making issue peas. These berries furnish a fragrant oil, the *essence de petit grain*, and contain citrates, and malates of lime and potash, with "hesperidin," sulphur, and mineral salts. The Orange flowers yield a volatile, odorous oil, acetic acid, and acetate of lime. The juice of the Orange consists of citric and malic acids, with sugar, citrate of lime, and water. The peel furnishes hesperidin, a volatile oil, gallic acid, and a bitter principle.

By druggists, a confection of bitter orange peel is sold; also a syrup of this orange peel, and a tincture of the same, made with spirit of wine, to be given in doses of from one to two teaspoonfuls with water, as an agreeable stomachic bitter. *Eau de Cologne* contains oil of neroli, oil of citron, and oil of orange.

The fresh juice of Oranges is antiseptic, and will prevent scurvy if taken in moderation daily. Common Oranges cut through the middle while green, and dried in the air, being afterwards steeped for forty days in oil, are used by the Arabs for preparing an essence famous among their old women because it will restore a fresh dark, or black colour to grey hair. The custom of a bride wearing Orange blossoms, is probably due to the fact that flowers and fruit appear together on the tree, in token of a wish that the bride may retain the graces of maidenhood amid the cares of married life. This custom has been derived from the Saracens, and was originally suggested also by the fertility of the Orange tree.

The rind of the Seville Orange has proved curative of ague, and powerfully remedial to restrain the monthly flux of women when in excess. Its infusion is of service also against flatulency. A drachm of the powdered leaves may be given for a dose in nervous and hysterical ailments. Finally, "the Orange," adds John Evelyn, "sharpens appetite, exceedingly refreshes, and resists putrefaction."

With respect to the fruit, it is said that workpeople engaged in the orange trade enjoy a special immunity from influenza, whilst a free partaking of the juice given largely, has been found preventive of pneumonia as complicating this epidemic. The benefit is said to occur through lessening the fibrin of the blood.

In the time of Shakespeare, it was the fashion to carry "pomanders," these being oranges from which all the pulp had been scooped out, whilst a circular hole was made at the top. Then after the peel had become dry, the fruit was filled with spices, so as to make a sort of scent-box. Orange lilies, Orangemen, and William of Orange, are all more or less associated with this fruit. The Dutch Government had no love for the House of Orange: and many a grave burgomaster went so far as to banish from his garden the Orange lily, and Marigold; also the sale of Oranges and Carrots was prohibited in the markets on account of their aristocratic colour.

There exists at Brighton a curious custom of bowling or throwing Oranges along the high road on Boxing day. He whose Orange is hit by that of another, forfeits the fruit to the successful hitter.

In Henry the Eighth's reign Oranges were made into pies, or the juice was squeezed out, and mixed with wine. This fruit when peeled, and torn into sections, after removing the white pith, and the pips, and sprinkling over it two or three spoonfuls of powdered loaf sugar, makes a most wholesome salad. A few candied orange-flower petals will impart a fine flavour to tea when infused with it.

ORCHIDS.

Our common English Orchids are the "Early Purple," which is abundant in our woods and pastures; the "Meadow Orchis"; and the "Spotted Orchis" of our heaths and commons. Less frequent are the "Bee Orchis," the "Butterfly Orchis," "Lady's Tresses," and the "Tway blade."

Two roundish tubers form the root of an Orchid, and give its name to the plant from the Greek *orchis*, testicle. A nutritive starchy product named Salep, or Saloop, is prepared from the roots of the common Male Orchis, and its infusion or decoction was taken generally in this country as a beverage before the introduction of tea and coffee. Sassafras chips were sometimes added for giving the drink a flavour. Salep obtained from the tubers of foreign Orchids was specially esteemed; and even now that sold in Indian bazaars is so highly valued for its fine qualities that most extravagant prices are paid for it by wealthy Orientals. Also in Persia and Turkey it is in great repute for recruiting the exhausted vitality of aged, and enervated persons. In this country it may be purchased as a powder, but not readily miscible with water, so that many persons fail in making the decoction. The powder should be first stirred with a little spirit of wine: then the water should be added suddenly, and the mixture boiled. One dram by weight of the salep powder in a fluid dram and a half of the spirit, to half-a-pint of water, are the proper proportions. Sometimes amber, cloves, cinnamon, and ginger are added.

Dr. Lind, in the middle of the last century, strongly advised that ships, and soldiers on long marches, should be provided with Salep made into a paste or cake. This (with a little portable soup added) will allay hunger and thirst if made liquid. An ounce in two quarts of boiling water will sufficiently sustain a man for one day, being a combination of animal and vegetable foods. Among the early Romans the Orchis was often called "Satyrion," because it was thought to be the food of the Satyrs, exciting them to their sexual orgies. Hence the Orchis root became famous as an aphrodisiac medicine, and has been so described by all herbalists from the time of Dioscorides.

A tradition is ascribed to the English Orchis Mascula (early Purple), of which the leaves are usually marked with purple spots. It is said that these are stains of the precious blood which flowed from our Lord's body on the cross at Calvary, where this species of Orchis is reputed to have grown. Similarly in Cheshire, the plant bears the name of Gethsemane. This early Orchis is the "long Purples," mentioned by Shakespeare in Hamlet: and it is sometimes named "Dead men's fingers," from the pale colour, and the hand-like shape of its tubers.

> "That liberal shepherds give a grosser name,
> But our cold maids do 'dead men's fingers' call them."

It is further styled "Cain and Abel" and "Rams' horns," the odour being offensive, especially in the evening. It thrives wherever the wild hyacinth flourishes, and is believed by some to grow best where the earth below is rich in metal. Country people in Yorkshire call it "Crake feet," and in Kent "Keat legs," or "Neat legs." The roots of this Orchis abound with a glutinous sweetish juice, of which a Salep may be made which is quite equal to any brought from the Levant. The new root should be washed in hot water, and its thin brown skin rubbed off with a linen cloth. Having thus prepared a sufficient number of roots, the operator should spread them on a tin plate in a hot oven for eight or ten minutes, until they get to look horny, but without shrinking in size: and being then withdrawn, they may be dried with more gentle heat, or by exposure to the air. Their concocted juice can be employed with the same intentions and in the same complaints as gum arabic,—about which we read that not only has it served to sustain whole negro towns during a scarcity of other provisions, but the Arabs who collect it by the river Niger have nothing else to live upon for months together.

Salep is a most useful article of diet for those who suffer from chronic diarrhœa.

PARSLEY.

PARSLEY is found in this country only as a cultivated plant, having been introduced into England from Sardinia in the sixteenth century. It is an umbelliferous herb, which has been long of garden growth for kitchen uses. The name was formerly spelt "Percely," and the herb was known as March, or Merich (in Anglo-Saxon, Merici). Its adjective title, *Petro-selinum*, signifies "growing on a rock." The Greeks held Parsley in high esteem, making therewith the victor's crown of dried and withered Parsley, at their Isthmian games, and the wreath for adorning the tombs of their dead. Hence the proverb, *Deeisthai selinon* (to need only Parsley) was applied to persons dangerously ill, and not expected to live. The herb was never brought to table of old, being held sacred to oblivion and the defunct.

It is reputed to have sprung from the blood of a Greek hero, Archemorus, the fore-runner of death; and Homer relates that chariot horses were fed by warriors with this herb. Greek gardens were often bordered with Parsley and Rue: and hence arose the saying when an undertaking was in contemplation but not yet commenced, "Oh! we are only at the Parsley and Rue."

Garden Parsley was not cultivated in England until the second year of Edward the Sixth's reign, 1548. In our modern times the domestic herb is associated rather with those who come into the world than with those who go out of it. Proverbially the Parsley-bed is propounded to our little people who ask awkward questions, as the fruitful source of new-born brothers and sisters when suddenly appearing within the limits of the family circle. In Suffolk there is an old belief that to ensure the herb coming up "double," Parsley seed must be sown on Good Friday.

The root is faintly aromatic, and has a sweetish taste. It contains a chemical principle, "apiin," sugar, starch, and a volatile oil. Likewise the fruit furnishes the same volatile oil in larger abundance, this oil comprising parsley-camphor, and "apiol," the true essential oil of parsley, which may be now had from all leading druggists. Apiol exercises all the virtues of the entire plant, and is especially beneficial for women who are irregular as to their monthly courses because of ovarian debility. From three to six drops should be given on sugar, or in milk (or as a prepared capsule) twice or three times in the day for some days together, at the times indicated, beginning early at the expected date of each period. If too large a dose of apiol be taken it will cause headache, giddiness, staggering, and deafness; and if going still further, it will induce epileptiform convulsions. For which reason, in small diluted doses, the same medicament will curatively meet this train of symptoms when occurring as a morbid state. And it is most likely on such account Parsley has been popularly said to be "poison to men, and salvation to women." Apiol was first obtained in 1849, by Drs. Joret and Homolle, of Brittany, and proved an excellent remedy there for a prevailing ague. It exercises a singular influence on the great nervous centres within the head and spine. Bruised Parsley seeds make a decoction which is likewise beneficial against ague and intermittent fever. They have gained a reputation in America as having a special tendency to regulate the reproductive functions in either sex. Country folk in many places think it unlucky to sow Parsley, or to move its roots; and a rustic adage runs thus: "Fried parsley brings a man to his saddle, and a woman to her grave." Taking Parsley in excess at table will impair the eyesight, especially the tall Parsley; for which reason it was forbidden by Chrysippus and Dionysius.

The root acts more readily on the kidneys than other parts of the herb; therefore its decoction is useful when the urine becomes difficult through a chill, or because of gravel. The bruised leaves applied externally will serve to soften hard breasts early in lactation, and to resolve the glands in nursing, when they become knotty and painful, with a threatened abscess. Sheep are fond of the plant, which protects them from foot-rot; but it acts as a deadly poison to parrots.

In France a rustic application to scrofulous swellings is successfully used, which consists of Parsley and snails pounded together in a mortar to the thickness of an ointment. This is spread on coarse linen and applied freely every day. Also on the Continent, and in some parts of England, snails as well as slugs are thought to be efficacious medicinally in consumption of the lungs, even more so than cod-liver oil. The *Helix pomatia* (or Apple Snail) is specially used in France, being kept for the purpose in a snaillery, or boarded-in space of which the floor is covered half-a-foot deep with herbs.

The Romans were very partial to these Apple Snails, and fattened them for the table with bran soaked in wine until the creatures attained almost a fabulous size. Even in this country shells of Apple Snails have been found which would hold a pound's worth of silver. The large Snail was brought to England in the sixteenth century, to the South downs of Surrey, and Sussex, and to Box Hill by an Earl of Arundel for his Countess, who had them dressed, and ate them because of her consumptive disease. Likewise in Pliny's time Snails beaten up with warm water were commended for the cure of coughs. Gipsies are great Snail eaters, but they first starve the creatures, which are given to devour the deadly Night Shade, and other poisonous plants. It is certain that Snails retain the flavour and odour of the vegetables which they consume.

The chalky downs of the South of England are literally covered with small snails, and many persons suppose that the superior flavour of South Down mutton is due to the thousands of these snails which the sheep consume together with the pasture on which they feed. In 1854 a medical writer set forth the curative virtues of *Helicin*, a glutinous constituent principle derived from the Snail, and to be given in broth as a remedy for pulmonary consumption. In France the Apple Snail is known as the "great Escargot"; and the Snail gardens in which the gasteropods are fattened, and reared, go by the name of "Escargotoires." Throughout the winter the creatures hybernate, shutting themselves up by their operculum whilst lying among dead leaves, or having fixed themselves by their glutinous secretion to a wall or tree. They are only taken for use whilst in this state. According to a gipsy, the common English Snail is quite as good to be eaten, and quite as beneficial as an Apple Snail, but there is less of him. In Wiltshire, when collected whilst hybernating, snails are soaked in salted water, and then grilled on the bars of the grate. About France the Escargots are dried, and prepared as a lozenge for coughs. Our common garden Snail is the *Helix aspersa*. On the Continent for many years past the large Apple Snail, together with a reddish-brown slug, the Arion Rufus, has been employed in medicine for colds, sore throats, and a tendency to consumption of the lungs. These contain "limacine," and eight per cent. of emollient mucilage, together with "helicin," and uric acid just under the shell. Many quarts of cooked garden snails are sold every week to the labouring classes in Bristol; and an annual Feast of Snails is held in the neighbourhood of Newcastle. Mrs. Delaney in 1758, recommended that "two or three snails should be boiled in the barley-water which Mary takes who coughs at night. She must know nothing of it; they give no manner of taste. Six or eight boiled in water, and strained off, and put in a bottle would be a good way of adding a spoonful of the same to every liquid thing she takes. They must be fresh done every two or three days, otherwise they grow too thick." The *London Gazette*, of March 23rd, 1739, tells that Mrs. Joanna Stephens received from the Government five thousand pounds for revealing the secret of her famous cure against stone in the bladder, and gravel. This consisted chiefly of eggshells, and snails, mixed with soap, honey and herbs. It was given in powders, decoctions, and pills. To help weak eyes in South Hampshire, snails and bread crust are made into a poultice.

A moderate dose of Parsley oil when taken in health, induces a sense of warmth at the pit of the stomach, and of general well-being. The powdered seeds may be taken in doses of from ten to fifteen grains. The bruised leaves have successfully resolved tumours of hard (scirrhous) cancer when cicuta, and mercury had failed.

Though used so commonly at table, facts have proved

that the herb, especially when uncooked, may bring on epilepsy in certain constitutions, or at least aggravate the fits in those who are subject to them. Alston says: "I have observed after eating plentifully of raw Parsley, a fulness of the vessels about the head, and a tenderness of the eyes (somewhat inflamed) and face, as if the cravat were too tight."

The victors at the old Grecian games were crowned with chaplets of Parsley leaves; and it is more than probable our present custom of encircling a joint, and garnishing a dish with the herb had its origin in this practice. The Romans named Parsley *Apium*, either because their bee (*apis*) was specially fond of the herb, or from *apex*, the head of a conqueror, who was crowned with it. The tincture has a decided action on the lining membrane of the urinary passages, and may be given usefully when this is inflamed, or congested through catarrh, in doses of from five to ten drops three times in the day with a spoonful or two of cold water.

Wild Parsley is probably identical with our garden herb. It is called in the Western counties Eltrot, perhaps because associated with the gambols of the elves.

The Fool's Parsley (*Œthusa cynapium*) is a very common wayside weed, and grows wild in our gardens. It differs botanically from all other parsleys in having no bracts, but three narrow leaves at the base of each umbel. This is a more or less poisonous herb, producing, when eaten in a harmful quantity, convulsive and epileptic symptoms; also an inflamed state of the eyelids, just such as is seen in the scrofulous ophthalmia of children, the condition being accompanied with swelling of glands and eruptions on the skin. Therefore the tincture which is made (H.) of Fool's Parsley, when given in small doses, and diluted, proves very useful for such ophthalmia, and for obviating the convulsive attacks of young children, especially if connected with derangement of the digestive organs. Also as a medicine it has done much good in some cases of mental imbecility. And this tincture will correct the Summer diarrhœa of infants, when the stools are watery, greenish, and without smell. From three to ten drops of the tincture diluted to the third decimal strength, should be given as a dose, and repeated at intervals, for the symptoms just recited.

This variety is named Œthusa, because of its acridity, from the Greek verb *aitho* (to burn). "It has faculties," says Gerard, "answerable to the common Hemlock," the poisonous effects being inflamed stomach and bowels, giddiness, delirium, convulsions, and insensibility. It is called also "Dog's Parsley" and "Kicks."

The leaves of the Fool's Parsley are glossy beneath, with lanceolate lobes, whereas the leaflets of other parsleys are woolly below. Gerard calls it Dog's Parsley, and says: "The whole plant is of a naughty smell." It contains a peculiar alkaloid "cynapina." The tincture, third decimal strength, in half-drop doses, with a teaspoonful of water, will prevent an infant from vomiting the breast milk in thick curds.

Another variety which grows in chalky districts, the Stone Parsley, *Sison*, or breakstone, was formerly known as the "Hone-wort," from curing a "hone," or boil, on the cheek. It was believed at one time to break a glass goblet or tumbler if rubbed against this article.

PARSNIP.

THE Wild Parsnip (*Pastinaca sativa*) grows on the borders of ploughed fields and about hedgerows, being generally hairy, whilst the Garden Parsnip is smooth, with taller stems, and leaves of a yellowish-green colour. This cultivated Parsnip has been produced as a vegetable since Roman times. The roots furnish a good deal of starch, and are very nutritious for warming and fattening, but when long in the ground they are called in some places "Madnip," and are said to cause insanity.

Chemically, they contain also albumen, sugar, pectose, dextrin, fat, cellulose, mineral matters, and water, but less sugar than turnips or carrots. The volatile oil with which the cultivated root is furnished causes it to disagree with persons of delicate stomach; otherwise it is highly nutritive, and makes a capital supplement to salt fish, in Lent. The seeds of the wild Parsnip (quite a common plant) are aromatic, and are kept by druggists. They have been found curative in ague, and for intermittent fever, by their volatile oil, or by its essence given as a medicine. But the seeds of the garden Parsnip, which are easier to get, though not nearly so efficacious, are often substituted at the shops. A decoction of the wild root is good for a sluggish liver, and in passive jaundice.

In Gerard's time, Parsnips were known as Mypes. Marmalade made with the roots, and a small quantity of sugar, will improve the appetite, and serve as a restorative to invalids.

From the mashed roots of the wild Parsnip in some parts of Ireland, when boiled with hops, the peasants brew a beer. In Scotland a good dish is prepared from Parsnips and potatoes, cooked and beaten together, with butter. Parsnip wine, when properly concocted, is particularly exhilarating and refreshing.

The Water Parsnip (spelt also in old *Herbals*, Pasnep, and Pastnip, and called Sium) is an umbelliferous plant, common by the sides of rivers, lakes, and ditches, with tender leaves which are "a sovereign remedy against gravel in the kidney, and stone in the bladder." It is known also as *Apium nodiflorum*, from *apon*, water, and contains "pastinacina," in common with the wild Parsnip. This is a volatile alkaloid which is not poisonous, and is thought to be almost identical with ammonia. The fresh juice, in doses of one, two, or three tablespoonfuls, twice a day, is of curative effect for scrofulous eruptions on the face, neck, and other parts of children. Dr. Withering tells of a child, aged six years, who was thus cured of an obstinate and otherwise intractable skin disease. The juice may be readily mixed with milk, and does not disagree in any way.

PEA and BEAN.

TYPICAL of leguminous plants (so called because they furnish legumin, or vegetable cheese), whilst furthermore possessing certain medicinal properties, the Bean and the Pea have a claim to be classed with Herbal Simples.

The common Kidney Bean (*Phaseolus vulgaris*) is a native of the Indies, but widely cultivated all over Europe, and so well known as not to need any detailed description as a plant. Because of the seed's close resemblance to the kidney, as well as to the male testis, the Egyptians made it an object of sacred worship, and would not partake of it as food. They feared lest by so doing they should eat what was human remaining after death in the Bean, or should consume a soul. The Romans celebrated feasts (Lemuria) in honour of their departed, when Beans were cast into the fire on the altar; and the people threw black Beans on the graves of the deceased, because the smell was thought disagreeable to any hostile Manes. In Italy at the present day it is customary to eat Beans, and to distribute them among the poor, on the anniversary of a death. Because of its decided tendency to cause sleepiness the Jewish High Priest was forbidden to partake of Beans on the day of Atonement; and there is now a common saying in Leicestershire that for bad dreams, or to be driven crazy, one has only to sleep all night in a Bean field. The philosopher, Pythagoras, warned his pupils against eating Beans, the black spot thereon being typical of death; and the disciples were ever mindful: "*Jurare in verba magistri.*" When bruised and boiled with garlic, Beans have been known to cure coughs which were past other remedies. But the roots of the Kidney Bean have proved themselves dangerously narcotic.

The Pea (*Pisum sativum*) is a native of England, first taking its botanical name from Pisa, a town of Elis, where Peas grew in plenty. The English appellation was formerly Peason, or Pease, and the plant has been cultivated in this country from time immemorial; though not commonly, even in Elizabeth's day, when (as Fuller informs us) "Peas were brought from Holland, and were fit dainties for ladies, they came so far, and cost so dear." In Germany Peas are thought good for many complaints, especially for wounds and bruises; children affected with measles are washed there systematically with water in which peas have been boiled. These, together with Beans and lentils, etc., are included under the general name of pulse, about which Cowper wrote thus :—

> "Daniel ate pulse by choice: example rare!
> Heaven blest the youth, and made him fresh and fair."

Grey Peas were provided in the pits of the Greek and Roman theatres, as we supply oranges and a bill of the Play.

"Hot Grey Pease and a suck of bacon" (tied to a string of which the stall-keeper held the other end), was a popular street cry in the London of James the First.

Peas and Beans contain sulphur, and are richer in mineral salts, such as potash and lime, than wheat, barley, or oats; but their constituents are apt to provoke indigestion, whilst engendering flatulence through sulphuretted hydrogen. They best suit persons who take plenty of out-door exercise, but not those of sedentary habits. The skins of parched Peas remain undigested when eaten cooked, and are found in the excrements. These leguminous plants are less easily assimilated than light animal food by persons who are not robust, or laboriously employed, though vegetarians assert to the contrary. Lord Tennyson wrote to such effect as the result of his personal experience (in his dedication of *Tiresias* to E. Fitzgerald):—

> "Who live on meal, and milk, and grass:—
> And once for ten long weeks I tried
> Your table of Pythagoras,
> And seem'd at first 'a thing enskied'
> (As Shakespeare has it)—airylight,
> To float above the ways of men:
> Then fell from that half spiritual height,
> Until I tasted flesh again.
> One night when earth was winter black,
> And all the heavens were flashed in frost,
> And on me—half asleep—came back
> That wholesome heat the blood had lost."

But none the less does a simple diet foster spirituality of mind. "In milk"—says one of the oldest Vedas—"the finer part of the curds, when shaken, rises and becomes butter. Just so, my child, the finer part of food rises when it is eaten, and becomes mind."

Old Fuller relates "In a general dearth all over

England (1555), plenty of Pease did grow on the sea-shore, near Dunwich (Suffolk), never set or sown by human industry, which being gathered in full ripeness much abated the high prices in the markets, and preserved many hungry families from famishing." "They do not grow" says he, "among the bare stones, neither did they owe their original to shipwrecks, or Pease cast out of ships." The Sea-side Pea *(pisum maritimum)* is a rare plant.

PEACH.

THE Peach (*Amygdalus Persica*), the apple of Persia, began to be cultivated in England about 1562, or perhaps before then. Columella tells of this fatal gift conveyed treacherously to Egypt in the first century :—

> "Apples, which most barbarous Persia sent,
> With native poison armed."

The Peach tree is so well known by its general characteristics as not to need any particular description. Its young branches, flowers, and seeds, after maceration in water, yield a volatile oil which is chemically identical with that of the bitter almond. The flowers are laxative, and have been used instead of manna. When distilled, they furnish a white liquor which communicates a flavour resembling the kernels of fruits. An infusion made from one drachm of the dried flowers, or from half an ounce of the fresh flowers, has a purgative effect. The fruit is wholesome, and seldom disagrees if eaten when ripe and sound. Its quantity of sugar is only small, but the skin is indigestible.

The leaves possess the power of expelling worms if applied outside a child's belly as a poultice, but in any medicinal form they must be used with caution, as they contain some of the properties of prussic acid, as found also in the leaves of the laurel. A syrup of Peach flowers was formerly a preparation recognised by apothecaries. The leaves infused in white brandy, sweetened with barley sugar, make a fine cordial similar to noyeau. Soyer says the old Romans gave as much for their peaches as eighteen or nineteen shillings each.

Peach pie, owing to the abundance of the fruit, is as common fare in an American farm-house, as apple pie in an English homestead. Our English King John died at Swinestead Abbey from a surfeit of peaches, and new ale.

A tincture made from the flowers will allay the pain of colic caused by gravel; but the kernels of the fruit, which yield an oil identical with that of bitter almonds, have produced poisonous effects with children.

Gerard teaches "that a syrup or strong infusion of Peach flowers doth singularly well purge the belly, and yet without grief or trouble." Two tablespoonfuls of the infusion for a dose.

In Sicily there is a belief that any one afflicted with goitre, who eats a Peach on the night of St. John, or the Ascension, will be cured, provided only that the Peach tree dies at the same time. In Italy Peach leaves are applied to a wart, and then buried, so that they and the wart may perish simultaneously.

Thackeray one day at dessert was taken to task by his colleague on the *Punch* staff, Angus B. Reach, whom he addressed as Mr. Reach, instead of as Mr. (*Scotticé*) Re-ack. With ready promptitude, Thackeray replied: "Be good enough Mr. Rē-ack to pass me a pē-ack."

PEAR.

THE Pear, also called Pyrrie, belongs to the same natural order of plants (the *Rosaceæ*) as the Apple. It is sometimes called the Pyerie, and when wild is so hard and austere as to bear the name of Choke-pear. It grows wild in Britain, and abundantly in France and Germany. The Barland Pear, which was chiefly cultivated in the seventeenth century, still retains its health and vigour, "the identical trees in Herefordshire which then supplied excellent liquor, continuing to do so in this, the nineteenth century."

This fruit caused the death of Drusus, a son of the Roman Emperor Claudius, who caught in his mouth a Pear thrown into the air, and by mischance attempted to swallow it, but the Pear was so extremely hard that it stuck in his throat, and choked him.

Pears gathered from gardens near old monasteries were formerly held in the highest repute for flavour, and it was noted that the trees which bore them continued fruitful for a great number of years. The secret cause seems to have been, not the holy water with which the trees were formally christened, but the fact that the sagacious monks had planted them upon a layer of stones so as to prevent the roots from penetrating deep into the ground, and so as thus to ensure their proper drainage.

The cellular tissue of which a Pear is composed differs from that of the apple in containing minute stony concretions which make it, in many varieties of the fruit, bite short and crisp; and its specific gravity is therefore greater than that of the apple, so much so that by taking a cube of each of equal size, that of the Pear will sink when thrown into a vessel of water, while that of the apple will float. The wood of the wild Pear is strong, and readily stained black, so as to look like ebony. It is much employed by wood-engravers. Gerard says "it serveth to be cut up into many kinds of moulds: not only such fruits as those seen in my Herbal are made of, but also many sorts of pretty toies for coifes, breast plates, and such like; used among our English gentlewomen."

The good old black Pear of Worcester is represented in the civic arms, or rather in the second of the two shields belonging to the faithful city: Argent, a fesse between three Pears, sable. The date of this shield coincides with that of the visit of Queen Elizabeth to Worcester.

Virgil names three kinds of Pears which he received as a present from Cato:—

> "Nec surculus idem,
> Crustaneis, Syriisque pyris, gravibusque volemis."

The two first of these were Bergamots and Pounder Pears, whilst the last-named was called *a volemus*, because large enough to fill the hollow of the hand, (*vola*).

Mural paintings which have been disclosed at Pompeii represent the Pear tree and its fruit. In Pliny's time there were "proud" Pears, so called because they ripened early, and would not keep; and "winter" pears for baking, etc. Again, in the time of Henry the Eighth, a "warden" Pear, so named (Anglo-Saxon "wearden") from its property of long keeping, was commonly cultivated.

> "Her cheek was like the Catherine Pear,
> The side that's next the sun,"

says one of our old poets concerning a small fruit seen often now-a-days in our London streets, handsome, but hard, and ill-flavoured.

The special taste of Pears is chemically due for the most part to their containing amylacetate; and a solution of this substance in spirit is artificially prepared for making essence of Jargonelle Pears, as used for flavouring Pear drops and other sweetmeats. The acetate amyl is a compound ether got from vinegar and potato oil. Pears contain also malic acid, pectose, gum, sugar, and albumen, with mineral matter, cellulose, and water. Gerard says wine made of the juice of Pears, called in English, Perry, purgeth those that are not accustomed to drinke thereof, especially when it is new; notwithstanding, it is as wholesome a drink (being taken in small quantity) as wine; it comforteth and warmeth the stomacke, and causeth good digestion."

Perry contains about one per cent. alcohol over cider, and a slightly larger proportion of malic acid, so that it is rather more stimulating, and somewhat better calculated to produce the healthful effects of vegetable acids in the economy. How eminently beneficial fruits of such sort are when ripe and sound, even to persons out of health, is but little understood, though happily the British public is growing wiser to-day in this respect. For instance, it has been lately discovered that there is present in the juice of the Pine-apple a vegetable digestive ferment, which, in its action, imitates almost identically the gastric juices of the stomach; and a demand for Bananas is developing rapidly in London since their wholesome virtues have become generally recognised. It is a remarkable fact that the epidemics of yellow fever in New Orleans have declined in virulence almost incredibly since the Banana began to be eaten there in considerable quantities. If a paste of its ripe pulp dried in the sun be made with spice, and sugar, this will keep well for years.

At Godstone, as is related in *Bray's Survey*, the water

from a well sunk close to a wild Pear tree (which bore fruit as hard as iron) proved so curative of gout, that large quantities of it were sent to London and sold there at the rate of sixpence a quart. Pears were deemed by the Romans an antidote to poisonous fungi; and for this reason, which subsequent experience has confirmed, Perry is still reckoned the best thing to be taken after eating freely of mushrooms, as also Pear stalks cooked therewith.

There is an old Continental saying: *Pome, pere, ed noce guastano la voce*—"Apples, pears, and nuts spoil the voice." And an ancient rhymed distich says:—

> "For the cough take Judas eare,
> With the parynge of a pear;
> And drynke them without feare,
> If ye will have remedy."

All Pears are cold, and have a binding quality, with an earthy substance in their composition.

It should be noted that Pears dried in the oven, and kept without syrup, will remain quite good, and eatable for a year or more.

Most Pears depend on birds for the dispersion of their seeds, but one striking variety prefers to attract bees, and the larger insects for cross-fertilization, and it has therefore assumed brilliant crimson petals of a broadly expanded sort, instead of bearing a succulent edible fruit. This is the highly ornamental *Pyrus Japonica*, which may so often be seen trained on the sunny walls of cottages.

PELLITORY.

A PLANT belonging to the order of Nettles, the Pellitory of the Wall, or Paritory—*Parietaria*, from the Latin *parietes*, walls—is a favourite Herbal Simple in many rural districts. It grows commonly on dry walls, and is in flower all the summer. The leaves are narrow, hairy, and reddish ; the stems are brittle, and the small blossoms hairy, in clusters. Their filaments are so elastic that if touched before the flower has expanded, they suddenly spring from their incurved position, and scatter the pollen broadcast.

An infusion of the plant is a popular medicine to stimulate the kidneys, and promote a large flow of watery urine. The juice of the herb acts in the same way when made into a thin syrup with sugar, and given in doses of two tablespoonfuls three times in the day. Dropsical effusions caused by an obstructed liver, or by a weak dilated heart, may be thus carried off with marked relief. The decoction of *Parietaria*, says Gerard, "helpeth such as are troubled with an old cough." All parts of the plant contain nitre abundantly. The leaves may be usefully applied as poultices.

But another Pellitory, which is more widely used because of its pungent efficacy in relieving toothache, and in provoking a free flow of saliva, is a distinct plant, the *Pyrethrum*, or Spanish Chamomile of the shops, and not a native of Great Britain, though sometimes cultivated in our gardens. The title "Purethron" is from *pur*, fire, because of its burning ardent taste. Its root is scentless, but when chewed causes a pricking sensation (with heat, and some numbness) in the mouth and tongue. Then an abundant flow of saliva, and of mucus within the cheeks quickly ensues. These effects are due to "pyrethrin" contained in the plant, which is an acid fixed resin ; also there are present a second resin, and a yellow, acrid oil, whilst the root contains inulin, tannin, and other substances. When sliced and applied to the skin it induces heat, tingling, and redness. A patient seeking relief from rheumatic or neuralgic affections of the head and face, or for palsy of the tongue, should chew the root of this *Pyrethrum* for several minutes.

The "Pelleter of Spain" (*Pyrethrum Anacyclus*), was so styled, not because of being brought from Spain, but because it is grown there.

A gargle of *Pyrethrum* infusion is prescribed for relaxed uvula, and for a partial paralysis of the tongue and lips. The tincture made from the dried root may be most helpfully applied on cotton wool to the interior of a decayed tooth which is aching, or the milder tincture of the wall Pellitory may be employed for the same purpose. To make a gargle, two or three tea-spoonfuls of the tincture of *Pyrethrum*, which can be had from any druggist, should be mixed with a pint of cold water, and sweetened with honey, if desired. The powdered root forms a good snuff to cure chronic catarrh of the head and nostrils, and to clear the brain by exciting a free flow of nasal mucus and tears—*Purgatur cerebrum mansâ radice Pyrethri.*

Incidentally, as a quaint but effective remedy for carious toothache, may be mentioned the common lady bird insect, Coccinella, which when captured secretes from its legs a yellow acrid fluid having a disagreeable odour. This fluid will serve to ease the most violent toothache, if the creature be placed alive in the cavity of the hollow tooth.

Gerard says this *Pyrethrum* (Pellitory of Spain, or Pelletor) "is most singular for the surgeons of the hospitals to put into their unctions *contra Neapolitanum morbum*, and such other diseases that are cousin germanes thereunto." The *Parietaria*, or Pellitory of the wall, is named Lichwort, from growing on stones.

Sir William Roberts, of Manchester, has advised jujubes, made of gum arabic and pyrethrum, to be slowly masticated by persons who suffer from acid fermentation in the stomach, a copious flow of alkaline saliva being stimulated thereby in the mouth, which is repeatedly swallowed during the sucking of one or more of the jujubes, and which serves to neutralise the acid generated within the stomach. Distressing heartburn is thus effectively relieved without taking injurious alkalies, such as potash and soda.

PENNYROYAL, *see* MINT.

PERIWINKLE.

THERE are two British Periwinkles growing wild; the one *Vinca major*, or greater, a doubtful native, and found only in the neighbourhood of dwelling-houses; the other *Vinca minor*, lesser, abounding in English woods, particularly in the Western counties, and often entirely covering the ground with its prostrate evergreen leaves. The common name of each is derived from *vincio*, to bind, as it were by its stems resembling cord; or because bound in olden times into festive garlands and funeral chaplets. Their title used also to be Pervinca, and Pervinkle, Pervenkle, and Pucellage (or virgin flower).

This generic name has been derived either from *pervincire*, to bind closely, or from *pervincere*, to overcome. Lord Bacon observes that it was common in his time for persons to wear bands of green Periwinkle' about the calf of the leg to prevent cramp. Now-a-days we use for the same purpose a garter of small new corks strung on worsted. In Germany this plant is the emblem of immortality. It bears the name "Penny-winkles" in Hampshire, probably by an inland confusion with the shell fish "winkles."

Each of the two kinds possesses acrid astringent properties, but the lesser Periwinkle, *Vinca minor* or Winter-green, is the Herbal Simple best known of the pair, for its medicinal virtues in domestic use. The Periwinkle order is called *Apocynaceæ*, from the Greek *apo*, against, and *kunos*, a dog; or dog's bane.

The flowers of the greater Periwinkle are gently purgative, but lose their effect by drying. If gathered in the Spring, and made into a syrup, they will impart all their virtues, and this is excellent to keep the bowels of children gently open, as well as to overcome habitual constipation in grown persons. But the leaves are astringent, contracting and strengthening the genitals if applied thereto either as a decoction, or as the bruised leaves themselves. An infusion of the greater Periwinkle, one part of the fresh plant to ten of water, may be used for staying female fluxes, by giving a wine-glassful thereof when cool, frequently; or of the liquid extract, half a teaspoonful for a dose in water. On account of its striking colour, and its use for magical purposes, the plant, when in bloom, has been named the Sorcerer's Violet, and in some parts of Devon the flowers are known as Cut Finger or Blue Buttons. The Italians use it in making garlands for their dead infants, and so call it Death's flower.

Simon Fraser, whose father was a faithful adherent of Sir William Wallace, when on his way to be executed (in 1306) was crowned in mockery with the Periwinkle, as he passed through the City of London, with his legs tied under the horse's belly. In Gloucestershire, the flowers of the greater Periwinkle are called Cockles.

The lesser Periwinkle is perennial, and is sometimes

cultivated in gardens, where it has acquired variegated leaves. It has no odour, but gives a bitterish taste which lasts in the mouth. Its leaves are strongly astringent, and therefore very useful to be applied for staying bleedings. If bruised and put into the nostrils, they will arrest fluxes from the nose, and a decoction made from them is of service for the diarrhœa of a weak subject, as well as for chronic looseness of the bowels; likewise for bleeding piles, by being applied externally, and by being taken internally. Again, the decoction makes a capital gargle for relaxed sore throat, and for sponginess of the mouth, of the tonsils, and the gums.

This plant was also a noted Simple for increasing the milk of wet nurses, and was advised for such purpose by physicians of repute. Culpeper gravely says: "The leaves of the lesser Periwinkle, if eaten by man and wife together, will cause love between them."

A tincture is made (H.) from the said plant, the *Vinca minor*, with spirit of wine. It is given medicinally for the milk-crust of infants, as well as for internal hæmorrhages, the dose being from two to ten drops three or four times in the day, with a spoonful of water.

PIMPERNEL.

THE "Poor Man's Weather Glass" or "Shepherd's Dial," is a very well-known and favourite little flower, of brilliant scarlet hue, expanding only in bright weather, and closing its petals at two o'clock in the day. It occurs quite commonly in gardens and open fields, being the scarlet Pimpernel, or *Anagallis arvensis*, and belonging to the Primrose tribe of plants. Old authors called it Burnet; which is quite a distinct herb, cultivated now for kitchen use, the *Pimpinella Saxifraga*, of so cheery and exhilarating a quality, and so generally commended, that its excellence has passed into a proverb, "*l'insolata non buon, ne betta ove non é Pimpinella.*" But this Burnet Pimpinella is of a different (Umbelliferous) order, though similarly styled because its leaves are likewise bipennate.

The Scarlet Pimpernel is named *Anagallis*, from the Greek *anagelao*, to laugh ; either because, as Pliny says, the plant removes obstructions of the liver, and spleen, which would engender sadness, or because of the graceful beauty of its flowers :—

> "No ear hath heard, no tongue can tell
> The virtues of the Pimpernell."

The little plant has no odour, but possesses a bitter taste, which is rather astringent. Doctors used to consider the herb remedial in melancholy, and in the allied forms of mental disease, the decoction, or a tincture being employed. It was also prescribed for hydrophobia, and linen cloths saturated with a decoction were kept applied to the bitten part.

Narcotic effects were certainly produced in animals by giving considerable doses of an extract made from the herb. The flowers have been found useful in epilepsy, twenty grains dried being given four times a day. A medicinal tincture (H.) is prepared with spirit of wine. It is of approved utility for irritability of the main urinary passage, with genital congestion, erotism, and dragging of the loins, this tincture being then ordered of the third decimal strength, in doses of from five to ten drops every three or four hours, with a spoonful of water.

A decoction of the plant is held in esteem by countryfolk as checking pulmonary consumption in its early stages. Hill says there are many authenticated cases of this dire disease being absolutely cured by the herb.

The infusion is best made by pouring boiling water on the fresh plant. It contains "saponin," such as the Soapwort also specially furnishes.

In France the Pimpernel (*Anagallis*) is thought to be a noxious plant of drastic narcotico-acrid properties, and called *Mouron—qui tue les petits oiseaux, et est un violent drastique pour l'homme, et les grands animaux; à dose tres elevée le mouron peut meme leur donner la mort.* In California a fluid extract of the herb is given for rheumatism, in doses of one teaspoonful with water three times a day.

The *Burnet Pimpinella* is more correctly the Burnet Saxifrage, getting its first name because the leaves are brown, and the second because supposed to break up stone in the bladder. It grows abundantly in our dry chalky pastures, bearing terminal umbels of white flowers. It contains an essential oil and a bitter resin, which are useful as warmly carminative to relieve flatulent indigestion, and to promote the monthly flow in women. An infusion of the herb is made, and given in two tablespoonfuls for a dose. Cows which feed on this plant have their flow of milk increased thereby. Small bunches of the leaves and shoots when tied together and suspended in a cask of beer impart to it an agreeable aromatic flavour, and are thought to correct tart, or spoiled wines. The root, when fresh, has a hot pungent bitterish taste, and may be usefully chewed for toothache, or to obviate paralysis of the tongue. In Germany a variety of this Burnet yields a blue essential oil which is used for colouring brandy. Again the herb is allied to the Anise (*Pimpinella Anisum*). The term Burnet was formerly applied to a brown cloth. Smaller than this Common Burnet is the Salad Burnet, *Poterium sanguisorba, quod sanguineos fluxus sistat,* a useful styptic, which is also cordial, and promotes perspiration. It has the smell of cucumber, and is, therefore, an ingredient of the salad bowl, or often put into a cool tankard, whereto, says Gerard, "it gives a grace in the drynkynge." Another larger sort of the Burnet Pimpinella (*Magna*), which has broad upper leaves less divided, grows in our woods and shady places.

A bright blue variety of the true Scarlet Pimpernel (*Anagallis*) is less frequent, and is thought by many to be a distinct species. Gerard says, "the Pimpernel with the blue flower helpeth the fundament that is fallen down: and, contrariwise, red Pimpernel being applied bringeth it down."

The Water Pimpernel (*Anagallis aquatica*) is more commonly known as Brooklime, or Beccabunga, and belongs to a different order of plants, the *Scrophulariaceæ* (healers of scrofula).

It grows quite commonly in brooks and ditches, as a succulent plant with smooth leaves, and small flowers of bright blue, being found in situations favourable to the growth of the watercress. It is the *brok lempe* of old writers, *Veronica beccabunga*, the syllable *bec* signifying a beck or brook; or perhaps the whole title comes from the Flemish *beck pungen*, mouth-smart, in allusion to the pungent taste of the plant.

"It is eaten," says Gerard, "in salads, as watercresses are, and is good against that *malum* of such as dwell near the German seas, which we term the scurvie, or skirby, being used after the same manner that watercress and scurvy-grass is used, yet is it not of so great operation and virtue." The leaves and stem are slightly acid and astringent, with a somewhat bitter taste, and frequently the former are mixed by sellers of watercresses with their stock-in-trade.

A full dose of the juice of fresh Brooklime is an easy purge; and the plant has always been a popular Simple for scrofulous affections, especially of the skin. Chemically, this Water Pimpernel contains some tannin, and a special bitter principle; whilst, in common with most of the Cruciferous plants, it is endowed with a pungent volatile oil, and some sulphur. The bruised plant has been applied externally for healing ulcers, burns, whitlows, and for the mitigation of swollen piles.

The Bog Pimpernel (*Anagallis tenella*), is common in boggy ground, having erect rose-coloured leaves larger than those of the Poor Man's Weather Glass.

PINK.

THE Clove Pink, or Carnation of our gardens, though found apparently wild on old castle walls in England, is a naturalised flower in this country. It is, botanically, the *Dianthus Caryophyllus*, being so named as *anthos*, the flower, *dios*, of Jupiter: whilst redolent of *Caryophylli*, Cloves. The term Carnation has been assigned to the Pink, either because the blossom has the colour, *carnis*, of flesh: or, as more correctly spelt by our older writers, Coronation, from the flowers being employed in making chaplets, *coronæ*. Thus Spenser says:—

> "Bring Coronations, and Sops in Wine,
> Worn of paramours."—*Shepherd's Kalendar*.

This second title, Sops in Wine, was given to the plant because the flowers were infused in wine for the sake of their spicy flavour; especially in that presented to brides after the marriage ceremony. Further, this Pink is the Clove Gilly (or *July*) flower, and gives its specific name to the natural order *Caryophyllaceæ*. The word Pink is a corruption of the Greek Pentecost (fiftieth), which has now come to signify a festival of the Church. In former days the blossoms were commended as highly cordial: their odour is sweet and aromatic, so that an agreeable syrup may be made therefrom. The dried petals, if powdered, and kept in a stoppered bottle, are of service against heartburn and flatulence, being given in a dose of from twenty to sixty grains. Gerard says, "a conserve made of the flowers with sugar is exceeding cordiall, and wonderfully above measure doth comfort the heart, being eaten now and then. A water distilled from Pinks has been commended as excellent for curing epilepsy, and if a conserve be composed of them, this is the life and delight of the human race." The flower was at one time called *ocellus*, from the eye-shaped markings of its corolla. It is nervine and antispasmodic. By a mistake Turner designated the Pink Incarnation.

PLANTAIN.

THE Plantains (*Plantaginaceæ*), from *planta*, the sole of the foot, are humble plants, well known as weeds in fields and by roadsides, having ribbed leaves and spikes of flowers conspicuous by their long stamens. As Herbal Simples, the Greater Plantain, the Ribwort Plantain, and the Water Plantain, are to be specially considered.

The Greater Plantain of the waysides affords spikes of seeds which are a favourite food of Canaries, and which, in common with the seeds of other sorts, yield a tasteless mucilage, answering well as a substitute for linseed. The leaves of the Plantains have a bitter taste, and are somewhat astringent.

The generic name *Plantago* is probably derived from the Latin *planta*, the sole of the foot, in allusion to the broad, flat leaves lying close on the ground, and *ago*, the old synonym for *wort*, a cultivated plant.

This greater Plantain (*Plantago major*) is also termed Waybred, Waybread, or Waybroad, "spread on the way," and has followed our colonists to all parts of the globe, being therefore styled "The Englishman's Foot" and "Whiteman's Foot." The shape of the leaf in the larger species resembles a footprint. The root has a sweet taste, and gives the saliva a reddish tinge.

Dioscorides advised that it should be applied externally for sores of every kind, and taken internally against hæmorrhages. In the *Romeo and Juliet* of Shakespeare, Romeo says, "Your Plantain leaf is excellent for broken shin." Country persons apply these leaves to open sores and wounds, or make a poultice of them, or give fomentations with a hot decoction of the same, or prepare a gargle from the decoction when cold.

The expressed juice of the greater Plantain has proved of curative effect in tubercular consumption, with spitting of blood. This herb is said to furnish a cure for the venomous bite of the rattlesnake, as discovered by the negro Cæsar in South Carolina.

It is of excellent curative use against the intermittent fevers of Spring, but for counteracting autumnal (*septic*) fevers it is of no avail.

The virtues of the greater Plantain as an application to wounds and sores were known of old. It possesses a widespread repute in Switzerland as a local remedy for toothache, the root or leaves being applied against the ear of the affected side. Those persons who proved the plant by taking it experimentally in various doses, suffered much pain in the teeth and jaws. Accordingly, Dr. Hale found that, of all his remedies for the toothache, none could compare with the *Plantago major*.

It gives rise to an active flow of urine when taken in considerable doses, and when administered in small doses of the diluted tincture, it has proved curative of bed wetting in young children. Gerard tells that "Plantain leaves stuped stayeth the inordinate flux of the terms, though it hath continued many years." For inflamed protruding piles, a broad-leaved Plantain reduced to a pulp, and kept bound to the parts by a compress, will give sure and speedy relief. Highlanders call it *Slanlus*, the healing plant.

The Ribwort Plantain (*Plantago lanceolata*), Ribgrass, Soldiers, or Cocks and Hens, is named from the strong parallel veins in its leaves. The flower stalks are termed *Kemps*, from *campa*, a warrior. The leaves are astringent, and useful for healing sores when applied thereto, and for dressing wounds. This Plantain is also named Hardheads, Fighting Cocks, and in Germany, Devil's Head, being used in divination. Children challenge one another to a game of striking off the heads.

Toads are thought to cure themselves of their ailments by eating its leaves. In Sussex, it is known as Lamb's Tongue. The powdered root of the Ribwort Plantain is of use for curing vernal ague, a dessertspoonful being given for a dose, two or three times in a day.

The Water Plantain (*Alisma Plantago*), belonging to a different natural order, is common on the margins of our rivers and ditches, getting its name from the Celtic *alos*, water, and being called also the greater Thrumwort, from *thrum*, the warp end of a weaver's web. The root and leaves contain an acrid juice, dispersed by heat, which is of service for irritability of the bladder. After the root is boiled so as to dissipate this medicinal juice it makes an edible starchy vegetable.

This plant is commonly classed with the Plantains because its leaves resemble theirs; but in general characteristics and qualities it more properly belongs to the *Ranunculaceæ.*

Its fresh leaves applied to the skin will raise a blister, and may be used for such a purpose, especially to relieve the swollen legs of dropsical subjects when the vesicles should be punctured and the serum drawn off. They contain a pungent butyraceous volatile oil. The seeds dislodged from the dry, ripe plant, by striking it smartly on a table, are good in decoction against bleedings, and are employed by country people for curing piles. About the Russian Empire the Water Plantain is still regarded as efficacious against hydrophobia. Dr. George Johnston says: "In the Government of Isola it has never failed of a cure for the last twenty-five years." Reduced to powder it is spread over bread and butter, and is eaten. Likewise, cures of rabid dogs by this plant are reported; and in America it is renowned as a remedy against the bite of the rattlesnake. The tubers contain a nutritious substance, and are eaten by the Tartars.

Apropos of this "Water Plantain" a Teesdale proverb says: "He's nar a good weaver that leaves lang *thrums.*"

The small seeds of a Plantain grass which grows commonly in Southern Europe, the Fleawort, or *Plantago Psyllium,* have been known from time immemorial as an easy and popular aperient. In France these Psyllium seeds, given in a dessertspoonful dose, are widely prescribed as a laxative in lieu of mineral aperient waters, or the morning Seidlitz. They act after being soaked for some hours in cold water, by their mucilage, and when swallowed, by virtue of a laxative oil set free within the intestines. The grass is well known in some parts as "Clammy Plantain," and it has leafless heads with toothed leaves. These seeds are dispensed by the London druggists who supply French medicines.

POPPY.

THE Scarlet Poppy of our cornfields (*Papaver Rhœas*) is one of the most brilliant and familiar of English wild flowers, being strikingly conspicuous as a weed by its blossoms rich in scarlet petals, which are black at the base. The title *Papaver* has been derived from *pap*, a soft food given to young infants, in which it was at one time customary to boil Poppy seeds for the purpose of inducing sleep. Provincially this plant bears the titles of "Cop Rose" (from its rose-like flowers, and the button-like form of its cop, or capsule) and "Canker Rose," from its detriment to wheat crops.

The generic term *Rhœas* comes from *reo*, to fall, because the scarlet petals have so fragile a hold on their receptacles; and the plant has been endowed with the sobriquet, "John Silver Pin, fair without and foul within." In the Eastern counties of England any article of finery brought out only occasionally, and worn with ostentation by a person otherwise a slattern, is called "Joan Silver Pin." After this sense the appellation has been applied to the Scarlet Poppy. Its showy flower is so attractive to the eye, whilst its inner juice is noxious, and stains the hands of those who thoughtlessly crush it with their fingers.

> "And Poppies a sanguine mantle spread,
> For the blood of the dragon St. Margaret shed."

Robert Turner naively says, "The Red Poppy Flower (*Papaver erraticum*) resembleth at its bottom the settling of the 'Blood in pleurisie'"; and, he adds, "how excellent is that flower in diseases of the pleurisie with similar surfeits hath been sufficiently experienced."

It is further called Blindy Buff, Blind Eyes, Headwarke, and Headache, from the stupefying effects of smelling it. Apothecaries make a syrup of a splendid deep colour from its vividly red petals; but this does not exercise any soporific action like that concocted from the white Poppy, which is a sort of modified opiate, suitable for infants under certain conditions, when sanctioned by a doctor. Otherwise, all sedatives of a narcotic sort are to be strongly condemned for use by mothers, or nurses:—

> "But a child that bids the world 'Good-night'
> In downright earnest, and cuts it quite,
> (A cherub no art can copy),
> 'Tis a perfect picture to see him lie,
> As if he had supped on dormouse pie,
> An ancient classical dish, by-the-bye,
> With a sauce of syrup of Poppy."

Petronius, in the time of Nero, A.D. 80, "delivered an odd receipt for dressing dormouse sausages, and serving them up with Poppies and honey, which must have been a very soporiferous dainty, and as good as owl pye to such as want a nap after dinner."

The white Poppy is specially cultivated in Britain for the sake of its seed capsules, which possess attributes similar to opium, but of a weaker strength. These capsules are commonly known as Poppyheads, obtained from the druggist for use in domestic fomentations to allay pain. Also from the capsules, without their seeds, is made the customary syrup of White Poppies, which is so familiar as a sedative for childhood; but it should be always remembered that infants of tender years are highly susceptible to the influence even of this mild form of opium. The true gum opium, and laudanum, which is its tincture, are derived from Eastern Poppies (*Papaver somniferum*) by incisions made in the capsules at a proper season of the year. The cultivated Poppy of the garden will afford English opium in a like manner, but it is seldom used for this purpose. A milky juice exudes when the capsules of these cultivated flowers are cut, or bruised. They are familiar to most children as drumsticks, plucked in the garden after the gaudy petals of the flowers have fallen off. The leaves and stems likewise afford some of the same juice, which, when inspissated, is known as English opium. The seeds of the white Poppy yield by expression a bland nutritive oil, which may be substituted for that of olives, or sweet almonds, in cooking, and for similar uses. Dried Poppy-heads, formerly in constant request for making hot soothing stupes, or for application directly to a part in pain, are now superseded for the most part by the many modern liquid preparations of opium handy for the purpose, to be mixed with hot water, or applied in poultices.

For outward use laudanum may be safely added to stupes, hot or cold, a teaspoonful being usually sufficient for the purpose, or perhaps two, if the pain is severe; and powdered opium may be incorporated with one or another ointment for a similar object. If a decoction of Poppy capsules is still preferred, it should be made by adding to a quarter-of-a-pound of white Poppy heads (free from seeds, and broken up in a mortar) three pints of boiling water; then boil for ten or fifteen minutes, and strain off the decoction, which should measure about two pints.

Dr. Herbert Snow, resident physician at the Brompton Cancer Hospital, says (1895) he has found: "after a long experience, Opium exhibits a strong inhibitive influence on the cancer elements, retarding and checking the cell growth, which is a main feature of the disease. Even when no surgical operation has been performed, Opium is the only drug which markedly checks cancer growth: and the early employment of this medicine will usually add years of comfortable life to the otherwise shortened space of the sufferer's existence." Opium gets its name from the Greek *apos*, juice.

The seeds of the white Poppy are known as mawseed, or balewort, and are given as food to singing birds. In old Egypt these seeds were mixed with flour and honey, and made into cakes.

Pliny says: "The rustical peasants of Greece glazed the upper crust of their loaves with yolks of eggs, and then bestrewed them with Poppy seeds," thus showing that the seeds were then considered free from narcotic properties. And in Queen Elizabeth's time these seeds were strewn over confectionery, whilst the oil expressed from them was "delightful to be eaten when taken with bread."

White Poppy capsules, when dried, furnish papaverine and narcotine, with some mucilage, and a little waxy matter. The seeds contained within the capsules yield Poppy seed oil, with a fixed oil, and a very small quantity of morphia—about five grains in a pound of white Poppy seeds. In some parts of Russia the seeds are put into soups.

The Poppy was cultivated by the Greeks before the time of Hippocrates. It has long been a symbol of death, because sending persons to sleep. Ovid says, concerning the Cave of Somnus:—

> "Around whose entry nodding Poppies grow,
> And all cool Simples that sweet rest bestow."

The common scarlet Poppy was called by the Anglo-Saxons "Chesebolle," "Chebole," or "Chybolle," from the ripe capsule resembling a round cheese.

There is a Welsh Poppy, with yellow flowers; and a horned Poppy, named after Glaucus, common on our sea coasts, with sea-green leaves, and large blossoms of golden yellow. Glaucus, a fisherman of Bœotia, observed that all the fishes which he caught received fresh vigour when laid on the ground, and were immediately able to leap back into the sea. He attributed these effects to some herb growing in the grass, and upon tasting the leaves of the Sea Poppy he found himself suddenly moved with an intense desire to live in the sea; wherefore he was made a sea-god by Oceanus and Tethys. Borlase says: "That in the Scilly Islands the root of the Sea Poppy is so much valued for removing all pains in the breast, stomach, and intestines, as well as so good for disordered lungs, whilst so much better there than in other places, that the apothecaries of Cornwall send thither for it; and some persons plant these roots in their gardens in Cornwall, and will not part with them under sixpence a root." The scarlet petals of the wild Poppy, very abundant in English cornfields, when treated with sulphuric acid make a splendid red dye. With gorgeous tapestry cut from these crimson petals, the clever "drapery bee" (*Apis papaveris*) upholsters the walls of her solitary cell. Bruised leaves of the wild, or the garden Poppy, if applied to a part which has been stung by a bee or a wasp, will give prompt relief.

POTATO.

OUR invaluable Potato, which enters so largely into the dietary of all classes, belongs to the Nightshade tribe of dangerous plants, though termed "solanaceous" as a natural order because of the sedative properties which its several genera exercise to lull pain.

This Potato, the *Solanum tuberosum*, is so universally known as a plant that it needs no particular description. It is a native of Peru, and was imported in 1586 by Thomas Heriot, mathematician and colonist, being afterwards taken to Ireland from Virginia by Sir Walter Raleigh, and passing from thence over into Lancashire. He knew so little of its use that he tried to eat the fruit, or poisonous berries, of the plant. These of course proved noxious, and he ordered the new comers to be rooted out. The gardener obeyed, and in doing so first learnt the value of their underground wholesome tubers. But not until the middle of the eighteenth century, were they common in this country as an edible vegetable. "During 1629," says Parkinson, "the Potato from Virginia was roasted under the embers, peeled and sliced: the tubers were put into sack with a little sugar, or were baked with cream, marrow, sugar, spice, etc., in pies, or preserved and candied by the comfit makers." But he most probably refers here to the Batatas, or sweet Potato, a *Convolvulus*, which was a popular esculent vegetable at that date, of tropical origin, and to which our Potato has since been thought to bear a resemblance.

This Batatas, or sweet Potato, had the reputation, like Eringo root, of being able to restore decayed vigour, and so Falstaff is made by Shakespeare to say: "Let the sky rain potatoes, hail kissing comfits, and snow eringoes." For a considerable while after their introduction the Potato tubers were grown only by men of fortune as a delicacy; and the general cultivation of this vegetable was strongly opposed by the public, chiefly by the Puritans, because no mention of it could be found in the Bible.

Also in France great opposition was offered to the recognised use of Potatoes: and it is said that Louis the Fifteenth, in order to bring the plant into favour, wore a bunch of its flowers in the button hole of his coat on a high festival. Later on during the Revolution quite a mania prevailed for Potatoes. Crowds perambulated the streets of Paris shouting for "la liberté, et des Batatas"; and when Louis the Sixteenth had been dethroned the gardens of the Tuileries were planted with Potatoes. Cobbett, in this country, exclaimed virulently against the tuber as "hogs' food," and hated it as fiercely as he hated tea. The stalks, leaves, and green berries of the plant share the narcotic and poisonous attributes of the nightshades to which it belongs; and the part which we eat, though often thought to be a root, is really only an underground stem, which has not been acted on by light so as to develop any poisonous tendencies, and in which starch is stored up for the future use of the plant.

The stalks, leaves, and unripe fruit yield an active principle apparently very powerful, which has not yet been fully investigated. There are two sorts of tubers, the red and the white. A roasted Potato takes two hours to digest; a boiled one three hours and a half. "After the Potato," says an old proverb, "cheese."

Chemically the Potato contains citric acid, like that of the lemon, which is admirable against scurvy: also potash, which is equally antiscorbutic, and phosphoric acid, yielding phosphorus in a quantity less only than that afforded by the apple, and by wheat. It is of the first importance that the potash salts should be retained by the Potato during cooking: and the tubers should therefore be steamed with their coats on; else if peeled, and then steamed, they lose respectively seven and five per cent. of potash, and phosphoric acid. If boiled after peeling they lose as much as thirty-three per cent. of potash, and twenty-three per cent. of phosphoric acid.

"The roots" says Gerard, "were forbidden in Burgundy, for that they were persuaded the too frequent use of them causeth the leprosie." Nevertheless it is now believed that the Potato has had much to do with expelling leprosy from England. The affliction has become confined to countries where the Potato is not grown.

Boiled or steamed Potatoes should turn out floury, or mealy, by reason of the starch granules swelling up and filling the cellular tissue, whilst absorbing the albuminous contents of its cells. Then the albumen coagulates, and forms irregular fibres between the starch grains. The most active part of the tuber lies just beneath the skin, as may be shown by pouring some tincture of guaiacum over the cut surface of a Potato, when a ring of blue forms close to the skin, and is darkest there while extending over the whole cut surface. Abroad there is a belief the Potato thrives best if planted on Maundy Thursday. Rustic names for it are: Taiders, Taities, Leather Coats, Leather Jackets, Lapstones, Pinks, No Eyes, Flukes, Blue Eyes, Red Eyes, and Murphies; in Lancashire Potatoes are called Spruds, and small Potatoes, Sprots.

The peel or rind of the tuber contains a poisonous substance called "solanin," which is dissipated and rendered inert when the whole Potato is boiled, or steamed. Stupes of hot Potato water are very serviceable in some forms of rheumatism. To make the decoction for this purpose, boil one pound of Potatoes (not peeled, and divided into quarters,) in two pints of water slowly down to one pint ; then foment the swollen and painful parts with this as hot as it can be borne. Similarly some of the fresh stalks of the plant, and its unripe berries, as well as the unpeeled tubers cut up as described, if infused for some hours in cold water, will make a liquor in which the folded linen of a compress may be loosely rung out, and applied most serviceably under waterproof tissue, or a double layer of dry flannel. The carriage of a small raw Potato in the trousers' pocket has been often found preventive of rheumatism in a person predisposed thereto, probably by reason of the sulphur, and the narcotic principles contained in the peel. Ladies in former times had their dresses supplied with special bags, or pockets, in which to carry one or more small raw Potatoes about their person for avoiding rheumatism.

If peeled and pounded in a mortar, uncooked Potatoes applied cold make a very soothing cataplasm to parts that have been scalded, or burnt. In Derbyshire a hot boiled Potato is used against corns ; and for frost-bites the mealy flour of baked potatoes, when mixed with sweet oil and applied, is very healing.

The skin of the tuber contains *corky* wood which swells in boiling with the jackets on, and which thus serves to keep in all the juices so that the digestibility of the Potato is increased ; at the same time water is prevented from entering and spoiling the flavour of the vegetable. The proportion of muscle-forming food (nitrogen) in the Potato is very small, and it takes ten and a half pounds of the tubers to equal one pound of butcher's meat in nutritive value.

The Potato is composed mainly of starch, which

affords animal heat and promotes fatness. The Irish think that these tubers foster fertility; they prefer them with the jackets on, and somewhat hard in the middle—"with the bones in." A potato pie is believed to invigorate the sexual functions.

New Potatoes contain as yet no citric acid, and are hard of digestion, like sour crude apples; their nutriment, as Gerard says, "is sadly windy," the starch being immature, and not readily acted on by the saliva during mastication. "The longer I live," said shrewd Sidney Smith, "the more I am convinced that half the unhappiness in the world proceeds from a vexed stomach, or vicious bile: from small stoppages, or from food pressing in the wrong place. Old friendships may be destroyed by toasted cheese; and tough salted meat has led a man not infrequently to suicide."

A mature Potato yields enough citric acid even for commercial purposes; and there is no better cleaner of silks, cottons, and woollens, than ripe Potato juice. But even of ripe Potatoes those that break into a watery meal in the boiling are always found to prove greatly diuretic, and to much increase the quantity of urine.

By fermentation mature Potatoes, through their starch and sugar, yield a wine from which may be distilled a Potato spirit, and from it a volatile oil can be extracted, called by the Germans, *Fuselöl*. This is nauseous, and causes a heavy headache, with indigestion, and biliary disorders together with nervous tremors. Chemically it is amylic ether.

Also when boiled with weak sulphuric acid, the Potato starch is changed into glucose, or grape sugar, which by fermentation yields alcohol: and this spirit is often sold under the name of British brandy.

A luminosity strong enough to enable a bystander to

read by its light issues from the common Potato when in a state of putrefaction. In Cumberland, to have "taities and point to dinner," is a figurative expression which implies scanty fare. At a time when the duty on salt made the condiment so dear that it was scarce in a household, the persons at table were fain to point their Potatoes at the salt cellar, and thus to cheat their imaginations. Carlyle asks in *Sartor Resartus* about "an unknown condiment named 'point,' into the meaning of which I have vainly enquired; the victuals *potato and point* not appearing in any European cookery book whatever."

German ladies, at their five o'clock tea, indulge in Potato talk (*Kartoffel gesprach*) about table dainties, and the methods of cooking them. Men likewise, from the four quarters of the globe, in the days of our childhood, were given to hold similar domestic conclaves, when :—

> "Mr. East made a feast,
> Mr. North laid the cloth,
> Mr. West brought his best,
> Mr. South burnt his mouth
> Eating a cold Potato."

With pleasant skill of poetic alliteration, Sidney Smith wrote in ordering how to mix a sallet :—

> "Two large Potatoes passed through kitchen sieve,
> Unwonted softness to a salad give."

And Sir Thomas Overbury wittily said about a dolt who took credit for the merits of his ancestors: "Like the Potato, all that was good about him was underground."

PRIMROSE.

The Common Primrose (*Primula veris*) is the most widely known of our English wild flowers, and appears in the Spring as its earliest herald.

It gets its name from the Latin *primus*, first, being named in old books and M.S. *Pryme rolles*, and in the *Grete Herball*, Primet, as shortened from Primprint.

In North Devon it is styled the Butter Rose, and in the Eastern counties it is named (in common with the Cowslip) Paigle, Peagle, Pegyll, and Palsy plant.

Medicinally also it possesses similar curative attributes, though in a lesser degree, to those of the Cowslip. Both the root and the flowers contain a volatile oil, and "primulin" which is identical with mannite: whilst the acrid principle is "saponin." Alfred Austin, Poet Laureate, teaches to "make healing salve with early Primroses."

Pliny speaks of the Primrose as almost a panacea: *In aquâ potam omnibus morbis mederi tradunt.* An infusion of the flowers has been always thought excellent against nervous disorders of the hysterical sort. It should be made with from five to ten parts of the petals to one hundred of water. "Primrose tea" says Gerard, "drunk in the month of May, is famous for curing the phrensie."

The whole plant is sedative and antispasmodic, being of service by its preparations to relieve sleeplessness, nervous headache, and muscular rheumatism. The juice if sniffed up into the nostrils will provoke violent sneezing, and will induce a free flow of water from the lining membranes of the nostrils for the mitigation of passive headaches: though this should not be tried by a person of full habit with a determination of blood to the head. A teaspoonful of powdered dry Primrose root will act as an emetic. The whole herb is somewhat expectorant.

When the petals are collected and dried they become of a greenish colour: whilst fresh they have a honey-like odour, and a sweetish taste.

Within the last few years a political significance and popularity have attached themselves to the Primrose beyond every other British wild flower. It arouses the patriotism of the large Conservative party, and enlists the favour of many others who thoughtlessly follow an attractive fashion, and who love the first fruits of early Spring. Botanically the Primrose has two varieties of floral structure: one "pin-eyed," with a tall pistil, and short stamens; the other "thrum-eyed," showing a rosette of tall stamens, whilst the short pistil must be looked for, like the great Panjandrum himself, "with a little round button at the top," half way down the tube. Darwin was the first to explain that this diversity of structure ensures cross fertilisation by bees and allied insects. Through advanced cultivation at the hands of the horticulturist the Primula acquires in some instances a noxious character. For instance, the *Primula biconica*, which is often grown in dwelling rooms as a window plant, and commonly sold as such, will provoke an erysipelatous vesicular eruption of a very troublesome and inflamed character on the hands and face of some persons who come in contact with the plant by manipulating it to take cuttings, or in other ways. A knowledge of this fact should suggest the probable usefulness of the said Primula, when made into a tincture, and given in small diluted doses thereof, to act curatively for such an eruption if attacking the sufferer from idiopathic causes.

The Latins named the Ligustrum (our Privet) Primrose. Coles says concerning it (17th century): "This herbe is called Primrose; it is good to 'Potage.'" They also applied the epithet, "Prime rose" to a lady.

The Evening Primrose (*Œnothera biennis*, or *odorata*) is found in this country on sand banks in the West of England and Cornwall; but it is then most probably a garden scape, and an alien, its native habitat being in Canada and the United States of America. We cultivate it freely in our parterres as a brilliant, yellow, showy flower. It belongs to the natural order, *Onagraceœ*, so called because the food of wild asses; and was the "vini venator" of Theophrastus, 350 B.C. The name signifies having the odour of wine, *oinos* and *theera.* Pliny said: "It is an herbe good as wine to make the heart merrie. It groweth with leaves resembling those of the almond tree, and beareth flowers like unto roses. Of such virtue is this herbe that if it be given to drink to the wildest beast that is, it will tame the same and make it gentle." The best variety of this plant is the *Œnothera macrocarpa.*

The bark of the Evening Primrose is mucilaginous, and a decoction made therefrom is of service for bathing the skin eruptions of infants and young children. To answer such purpose a decoction should be made from the small twigs, and from the bark of the larger branches, retaining the leaves. This has been found further of use for diarrhœa associated with an irritable stomach, and asthma. The infusion, or the liquid extract, acts as a mild but efficient sedative in nervous indigestion, from twenty to thirty drops of the latter being given for a dose. The ascertained chemical principle of the plant, *Œnotherin,* is a compound body. Its flowers open in the evening, and last only until the next noon; therefore this plant is called the "Evening Primrose," or "Evening Star."

Another of the Primrose tribe, the Cyclamen, or Sowbread (*Panis porcinus*), is often grown in our gardens, and for ornamenting our rooms as a pot plant. Its name means (Greek) "a circle," and refers to the reflected corolla, or to the spiral fruit-stalks; and again, from the tuber being the food of wild swine. Gerard said it was reported in his day to grow wild on the Welsh mountains, and on the Lincolnshire hills: but he failed to find it. Nevertheless it is now almost naturalised in some parts of the South, and East of England. As the petals die, the stalks roll up and carry the capsular berries down to the surface of the ground. A medicinal tincture is made (H.) from the fresh root when flowering. The ivy-leaved variety is found in England, with nodding fresh-coloured blossoms, and a brown intensely acrid root. Besides starch, gum, and pectin, it yields chemically, "cyclamin," or "arthanatin," with an action like "saponin," whilst the juice is poisonous to fish. When applied externally as a liniment over the bowels, it causes them to be purged. Gerard quaintly and suggestively declares "It is not good for women with childe to touch, or take this herbe, or to come neere unto it, or to stride over the same where it groweth: for the natural attractive vertue therein contained is such that, without controversie, they that attempt it in manner above said, shall be delivered before their time; which danger and inconvenience to avoid, I have fastened sticks in the ground about the place in my garden where it groweth, and some other sticks also crosswaies over them, lest any woman should by lamentable experiment find my words to be true by stepping over the same. Again, the root hanged about women in their extreme travail with childe, causeth them to be delivered incontinent: and the leaves put into the place hath the like effect." Inferentially a tincture of the plant should be good for falling and displacement of the womb. "Furthermore, Sowbread, being beaten, and made into little flat cakes, is reputed to be a good amorous medicine, to make one in love."

In France, another Primula, the wild Pimpernel, occurs as a noxious herb, and is therefore named *Mouron.*

QUINCE.

THE Quince (*Cydonia*) is cultivated sparingly in our orchards for the sake of its highly fragrant, and strong-smelling fruit, which as an adjunct to apples is much esteemed for table uses.

It may well be included among remedial Herbal Simples because of the virtues possessed by the seeds within the fruit. The tree is a native of Persia and Crete ; bearing a pear-shaped fruit, golden yellow when gathered, and with five cells in it, each containing twelve closely packed seeds. These are mucilaginous when unbroken, and afford the taste of bitter almonds.

When immersed in water they swell up considerably, and the mucilage will yield salts of lime with albumen.

Bandoline is the mucilage of Quince seeds to which some Eau de Cologne is added: and this mixture is employed for keeping the hair fixed when dressed by the *Coiffeur*.

The mucilage of Quince seeds is soothing and protective to an irritated or inflamed skin ; it may also be given internally for soreness of the lining mucous membranes of the stomach and bowels, as in gastric catarrh, and for cough with a dry sore throat. One dram of the seeds boiled slowly in half-a-pint of fresh water until the liquor becomes thick, makes an excellent mucilage as a basis for gargles and injections ; or, one part of the seeds to fifty parts of rosewater, shaken together for half-an-hour.

From growing at first in Cydon, now Candia, the tree got its name *Cydonia*: its old English title was Melicotone ; and in ancient Rome it was regarded as a sacred fruit, being hung upon statues in the houses of the great. Now we banish the tree, because of its strong pene trating odour, to a corner of the garden.

Lord Bacon commended "quiddemy," a preserve of Quinces, for strengthening the stomach; and old Fuller said of this fruit, "being not more pleasant to the palate than restorative to the health, they are accounted a great cordiall." Jam made from the Quince (*Marmelo*) first took the name of Marmalade, which has since passed on to other fruit conserves, particularly to that of the Seville Orange. In France the Quince is made into a *compôte* which is highly praised for increasing the digestive powers of weakly persons. According to Plutarch Solon made a law that the Quince should form the invariable feast of the bridegroom (and some add likewise of the bride) before retiring to the nuptial couch. Columella said: "Quinces yield not only pleasure but health." The Greeks named the Quince "Chrysomelon," or the Golden Apple; so it is asserted that the golden fruit of the Hesperides were Quinces, and that these tempted Hercules to attack their guardian dragon. Shakespeare makes Lady Capulet when ordering the wedding feast,

> "Call for dates, and Quinces in the pastry."

In Persia the fruit ripens, and is eaten there as a dessert delicacy which is much prized. If there be but a single Quince in a caravan, no one who accompanies it can remain unconscious of its presence.

In Sussex at one time a popular wine was made of Quinces. They are astringent to stay diarrhœa; and a syrup may be concocted from their juice to answer this purpose. For thrush and for excoriations within the mouth and upper throat, one drachm of the seeds should be boiled in eight fluid ounces of water until it acquires a proper demulcent mucilaginous consistence. "Simon Sethi writeth," says Gerard: "that the woman with child that eateth many Quinces during the time of her breeding, shall bring forth wise children, and of good understanding." Gerard says again: "The marmalad, or Cotiniat made of Quinces and sugar is good and profitable to strengthen the stomach that it may retain and keep the meat therein until it be perfectly digested. It also stayeth all kinds of fluxes both of the belly, and of other parts, and also of blood. Which cotiniat is made in this manner. Take four Quinces, pare them, cut them in pieces, and cast away the core: then put into every pound of Quinces a pound of sugar, and to every pound of sugar a pint of water. These must be boiled together over a still fire till they be very soft: next let it be strained, or rather rubbed through a strainer, or a hairy sieve, which is better. And then set it over the fire to boil again until it be stiff: and so box it up: and as it cooleth, put thereto a little rose water, and a few grains of musk mingled together, which will give a goodly taste to the cotiniat. This is the way to make marmalad." "The seed of Quinces tempered with water doth make a mucilage, or a thing like jelly which, being held in the mouth is marvellous good to take away the roughness of the tongue in hot burning fevers." Lady Lisle sent some cotiniat of Quinces to Henry the Eighth by her daughter Katharine. They were reputed a sexual stimulant. After being boiled and preserved in syrup, Quinces give a well known pleasant flavour to apple pie. As the fruit is free from acid, or almost so, its marmalade may be eaten by the goutily disposed with more impunity than that made with the Seville orange. An after taste suggestive of garlic is left on the palate by masticating Quince marmalade.

In the modern treatment of chronic dysentery the value of certain kinds of fresh fruit has come to be medically recognised. Of these may be specified strawberries, grapes, fresh figs, and tomatoes, all of which are seed fruits as distinguished from stone fruit. It is essential that they shall be absolutely sound, and in good condition. Dr. Saumaurez Lacy, of Guernsey, has successfully practised this treatment for many years, and it has been recently employed by others for chronic dysentery, and diarrhœa, with most happy results.

RADISH.

THE common garden Radish (*Raphanus sativus*) is a Cruciferous plant, and a cultivated variety of the Horse Radish. It came originally from China, but has been grown all over Europe from time immemorial. Radishes were celebrated by Dioscorides and Pliny as above all roots whatsoever, insomuch, that in the Delphic temple there was a Radish of solid gold, *raphanus ex auro dicatus*: and Moschinus wrote a whole volume in their praise; but Hippocrates condemned them as *vitiosas, innatantes, ac œgre concoctiles.*

Among the oblations offered to Apollo in his temple at Delphi, turnips were dedicated in lead, beet in silver, and radishes in wrought gold. The wild Radish is *Raphanus raphanistrum.* The garden Radish was not grown in England before 1548.

Later on John Evelyn wrote in his *Acetaria*: "And indeed (besides that they decay the teeth) experience tells us that, as the Prince of Physicians writes, it is hard of digestion, inimicous to the stomach, causing nauseous eructations, and sometimes vomiting, though otherwise diuretic, and thought to repel the vapours of wine when the wits were at their genial club." "The Radish" says Gerard, "provoketh urine, and dissolveth cluttered sand."

The roots, which are the edible part, consist of a watery fibrous pulp, which is comparatively bland, and of an external skin furnished with a pungent volatile aromatic oil which acts as a condiment to the phlegmatic pulp. "Radishes are eaten with salt alone as carrying their pepper in them." The oil contained in the roots, and likewise in the seeds, is sulphuretted, and disagrees with persons of weak digestion. A young Radish, which is quickly grown and tender, will suit most stomachs, especially if some of the leaves are masticated together with the root; but a Radish which is tough, strong, and hollow, "*fait penser à l'ile d'Elbe: il revient.*"

The pulp is chemically composed chiefly of nitrogenous substance, being fibrous and tough unless when the roots are young and quickly grown. On this account they should not be eaten when at all old and hard by persons of slow digestion, because apt to lodge in the intestines, and to become entangled in their cæcal pouch, or in its appendix. But boiled Radishes are almost equal to asparagus when served at table, provided they have been cooked long enough to become tender, that is, for almost an hour. The syrup of Radishes is excellent for hoarseness, bronchial difficulty of breathing, whooping cough, and other complaints of the chest.

For the cure of corns, if after the feet have been bathed, and the corns cut, a drop or two of juice be squeezed over the corn from the fresh pulp of a Radish on several consecutive days, this will wither and disappear. Also Radish roots sliced when fresh, and applied to a carbuncle will promote its healing. An old Saxon remedy against a woman's chatter was to "taste at night a root of Radish when fasting, and the chatter will not be able to harm him." In some places the Radish is called Rabone.

From the fresh plant, choosing a large Spanish Radish, with a turnip-shaped root, and a black outer skin, and collected in the autumn, a medicinal tincture (H.) is made with spirit of wine. This tincture has proved beneficial in cases of bilious diarrhœa, with eructations, and mental depression, when a chronic cough is also liable to be present. Four or five drops should be given with a tablespoonful of cold water, twice or three times in the day. The Black Radish is found useful against whooping cough, and is employed for this purpose in Germany, by cutting off the top, and then making a hole in the root. This is filled with treacle, or honey, and allowed to stand for a day or two; then a teaspoonful of the medicinal liquid is given two or three times in the day. Roman physicians advised that Radishes should be eaten raw, with bread and salt in the morning before any other food. And our poet Thomson describes as an evening repast:—

> "A Roman meal
> Such as the mistress of the world once found
> Delicious, when her patriots of high note,
> Perhaps by moonlight at their humble doors,
> Under an ancient Oak's domestic shade,—
> Enjoy'd spare feast, a Radish and an Egg."

RAGWORT.

The Ragwort (*Senecio Jacobœa*) is a very common plant in our meadows, and moist places, closely allied to the

Groundsel, and well known by its daisy-like flowers, but of a golden yellow colour, with rays in a circle surrounding the central receptacle, and with a strong smell of honey.

This plant goes popularly by the name of St. James's wort, or Canker wort, or (near Liverpool) Fleawort, and in Yorkshire, Seggrum; also Jacoby and Yellow Top. The term Ragwort, or Ragweed, is a corruption of Ragewort, as expressing its supposed stimulating effects on the sexual organs. For the same reason the *pommes d'amour* (Love Apples, or Tomatoes) are sometimes called Rage apples. The Ragwort was formerly thought to cure the staggers in horses, and was hence named Stagger wort, or because, says Dr. Prior, it was applied to heal freshly cut young bulls, known as Seggs, or Staggs. So also it was called St. James's wort, either because that great warrior and saint was the patron of horses, or because it blossoms on his day, July 25th: sometimes also the plant has been styled Stammer wort. Furthermore it possesses a distinct reputation for the cure of cancer, and is known as Cankerwort, being applied when bruised, either by itself, or combined with Goosegrass.

Probably the lime which the whole plant contains in a highly elaborated state of subdivision has fairly credited it with anti-cancerous powers. For just such a reason Sir Spencer Wells commended powdered egg shells and powdered oyster shells as efficacious in curing certain cases under his immediate observation of long-standing cancer, when steadily given for some considerable time.

A poultice made of the fresh leaves, and applied externally two or three times in succession "will cure, if ever so violent, the old ache in the hucklebone known as sciatica." Chemically the active principle of the

Ragwort is "senecin," a dark resinous substance, of which two grains may be given twice or three times in the day.

Also the tincture, made with one part of the plant to ten parts of spirit of wine (tenuior), may be taken in doses of from five to fifteen drops, with a spoonful of water three times in the day.

Either form of medicine will correct monthly irregularities of women where the period is delayed, or difficult, or arrested by cold. It must be given steadily three times a day for ten days or a fortnight before the period becomes re-established. In suitable cases the Senecio not only anticipates the period, but also increases the quantity: and where the monthly time has never been established the Ragwort is generally found useful.

This herb—like its congener, the common Groundsel—has lancinated, juicy leaves, which possess a bitter saline taste, and yield earthy potash salts abundantly. Each plant is named "Senecio" because of the grey woolly pappus of its seeds, which resemble the silvered hair of old age. In Ireland the Ragwort is dedicated to the fairies, and is known as the Fairies' Horse, on the golden blossoms of which the good little people are thought to gallop about at midnight.

RASPBERRY.

The Raspberry (*Rubus Idæus*) occurs wild plentifully in the woods of Scotland, where children gather the fruit early in summer. It is also found growing freely in some parts of England—as in the Sussex woods—and bearing berries of as good a quality as that of the cultivated Raspberry, though not so large in size.

Another name for the fruit is *Framboise*, which is

a French corruption of the Dutch word *brambezie*, or brambleberry.

Again, the Respis, or Raspberry, was at one time commonly known in this country as Hindberry, or the gentler berry, as distinguished from one of a harsher and coarser sort, the Hartberry. "Respberry" signifies in the Eastern Counties of England a shoot, or sucker, this name being probably applied because the fruit grows on the young shoots of the previous year.

Raspberry fruit is fragrant and cooling, but sugar improves its flavour. Like the strawberry, if eaten without sugar and cream, it does not undergo any acetous fermentation in the stomach, even with gouty or strumous persons. When combined with vinegar and sugar it makes a liqueur which, if diluted with water, is most useful in febrile disorders, and which is an excellent addition to sea stores as preventive of scurvy.

The Latins named this shrub "the bramble of Ida," because it grew in abundance on that classic mountain where the shepherd Paris adjudged to Venus the prize for beauty—a golden apple—on which was divinely inscribed the words, *Detur pulchriori*—"Let this be awarded to the fairest of womankind."

The fresh leaves of the Raspberry are the favourite food of kids. There are red, white, yellow, and purple varieties of this fruit. Heat develops the richness of its flavour; and Raspberry jam is the prince of preserves.

Again, a wine can be brewed from the fermented juice, which is excellent against scurvy because of its salts of potash—the citrate and malate.

Raspberry vinegar, made by pouring vinegar repeatedly over successive quantities of the fresh fruit, is a capital remedy for sore throat from cold, or of the relaxed kind; and when mixed with water it furnishes a most refreshing drink in fevers. But the berries should be used immediately after being gathered, as they quickly spoil, and their fine flavour is very evanescent. The vinegar can be extemporised by diluting Raspberry jelly with hot vinegar, or by mixing syrup of the fruit with vinegar.

In Germany a conserve of Raspberries which has astringent effects is concocted with two parts of sugar to one of juice expressed from the fruit. Besides containing citric and malic acids, the Raspberry affords a volatile oil of aromatic flavour, with crystallisable sugar, pectin, colouring matter, mucus, some mineral salts, and water.

Gerard says: "The fruit is good to be given to them that have weake, and queasie stomackes."

A playful example of the declension of a Latin substantive is given thus:—

> "*Musa, Musæ,*
> The Gods were at tea:
> *Musæ, Musam,*
> Eating Raspberry jam:
> *Musa, Musāh,*
> Made by Cupid's mamma."

RHUBARB (Garden), *see* **Dock,** *page* 159.

RICE.

Rice, or Ryse, the grain of *Oryza sativa*, a native cereal of India, is considered here scarcely as a Herbal Simple, but rather as a common article of some medicinal resource in the store cupboard of every English household, and therefore always at hand as a vegetable remedy.

Among the Arabs Rice is considered a sacred food:

and their tradition runs that it first sprang from a drop of Mahomet's perspiration in Paradise.

Being composed almost exclusively of starch, and poorer in nitrogen, as well as in phosphoric acid, than other cereals, it is less laxative, and is of value as a demulcent to palliate irritative diarrhœa, and to allay intestinal distress.

A mucilage of Rice made by boiling the well-washed grain for some time in water, and straining, contains starch and phosphate of lime in solution, and is therefore a serviceable emollient. But when needed for food the grain should be steamed, because in boiling it loses the little nitrogen, and the greater part of the lime phosphate which it has scantily contained.

Rice bread and Rice cakes, simply made, are very light and easy of digestion. The gluten confers the property of rising on dough or paste made of Rice flour. But as an article of sustenance Rice is not well suited for persons of fermentative tendencies during the digestion of their food, because its starch is liable to undergo this chemical change in the stomach.

Dr. Tytler reported in the *Lancet* (1833), cases resembling malignant cholera from what he termed the *morbus oryzæus*, as provoked by the free and continued use of Rice as food. And Boutins, in 1769, published an account of the diseases common to the East Indies, in which he stated that when Rice is eaten more or less exclusively, the vision becomes impaired. But neither of these allegations seems to have been afterwards authoritatively confirmed.

Chemically, Rice consists of starch, fat, fibrin, mineral matter such as phosphate of lime, cellulose, and water.

A spirituous liquor is made in China from the grain of Rice, and bears the name "arrack."

Rice cannot be properly substituted in place of succulent green vegetables dietetically for any length of time, or it would induce scurvy. The Indians take stewed Rice to cure dysentery, and a decoction of the grain for the purpose of subduing inflammatory disorders.

Paddy, or Paddee, is Rice from which the husk has not been removed before crushing. It has been said by some that the cultivation of Rice lowers vitality, and shortens life.

In Java a special Rice-pudding is made by first putting some raw Rice in a conical earthen pot wide at the top, and perforated in its body with holes. This is placed inside another earthen pot of a similar shape but not perforated, and containing boiling water. The swollen Rice soon stops up the holes of the inner pot, and the Rice within becomes of a firm consistence, like pudding, and is eaten with butter, sugar, and spices.

An ordinary Rice-pudding is much improved by adding some rosewater to it before it is baked.

This grain has been long considered of a pectoral nature, and useful for persons troubled with lung disease, and spitting of blood, as in pulmonary consumption. The custom of throwing a shower of Rice after and over a newly married couple is very old, though wheat was at first the chosen grain as an augury of plenty. The bride wore a garland of ears of corn in the time of Henry the Eighth.

ROSES.

CERTAIN curative properties are possessed both by the Briar, or wild Dog Rose of our country hedges, and by the cultivated varieties of this queen of flowers in our Roseries. The word Rose means red, from the Greek *rodon*, connected also with *rota*, a wheel, which resembles the outline of a Rose. The name Briar is from the Latin *bruarium*, the waste land on which it grows. The first Rose, of a dark red colour, is held to have sprung from the blood of Adonis. The fruit of the wild Rose, which is so familiar to every admirer of our hedgerows in the summer, and which is the common progenitor of all Roses, is named Hips. "Heps maketh," says Gerard, "most pleasant meats or banquetting dishes, as tarts and suchlike, the concoction whereof I commit to the cunning cook, and teeth to eat them in the rich man's mouth."

Hips, derived from the old Saxon, *hiupa*, *jupe*, signifies the Briar rather than its fruit. They are called in some parts, "choops," or "hoops." The woolly down which surrounds the seeds within the Hips serves admirably for dispelling round worms, on which it acts mechanically without irritating the mucous membrane which lines the bowels.

When fully ripe and softened by frost, the Hips, after removal of their hard seeds, and when plenty of sugar is added, make a very nice confection, which the Swiss and Germans eat at dessert, and which forms an agreeable substitute for tomato sauce. Apothecaries employ this conserve in the preparing of electuaries, and as a basis for pills. They also officinally use the petals of the Cabbage Rose (*Centifolia*) for making Rose water, and the petals of the Red Rose (*Gallica*) for a cooling infusion, the brilliant colour of which is much improved by adding some diluted sulphuric acid; and of these petals they further direct a syrup to be concocted.

Next in development to the Dog Rose, or Hound's Rose, comes the Sweetbriar (Eglantine), with a delicate perfume contained under its glandular leaves. "*Frag-*

rantia ejus olei omnia alia odoramenta superest." This (*Rosa rubiginosa*) grows chiefly on chalk as a bushy shrub. Its poetic title, Eglantine, is a corruption of the Latin *aculeius*, prickly. A legend tells that Christ's crown of thorns was made from the Rose-briar, about which it has been beautifully said :—

> " Men saw the thorns on Jesus' brow,
> But Angels saw the Roses."

Pliny tells a remarkable story of a soldier of the Prætorian guard, who was cured of hydrophobia, against all hope, by taking an extract of the root of the *Kunoroddon*, Dog Rose, in obedience to the prayer of his mother, to whom the remedy was revealed in a dream ; and he says further, that it likewise restored whoever tried it afterwards. Hence came the title *Canina.* '*Parceque elle a longtemps été en vogue pour guerir de la rage.*"

But the term, Dog Rose, is generally thought to merely signify a flower of lower quality than the nobler Roses of garden culture.

The five graceful fringed leaflets which form the special beauty of the Eglantine flower and bud, have given rise to the following Latin enigma (translated):—

> " Of us five brothers at the same time born,
> Two from our birthday always beards have worn :
> On other two none ever have appeared,
> While our fifth brother wears but half a beard."

From Roses the Romans prepared wine and confections, also subtle scents, sweet-smelling oil, and medicines. The petals of the crimson French Rose, which is grown freely in our gardens, have been esteemed of signal efficacy in consumption of the lungs since the time of Avicenna, A.D. 1020, who states that he cured many patients by prescribing as much of the conserve as they could manage to swallow daily. It was combined with milk, or with some other light nutriment; and generally from thirty to forty pounds of this medicine had to be consumed before the cure was complete. Julius Cæsar hid his baldness at the age of thirty with Roman Roses.

"Take," says an old MS. recipe of Lady Somerset's, "Red Rose buds, and clyp of the tops, and put them in a mortar with ye waight of double refined sugar; beat them very small together, then put it up; must rest three full months, stirring onces a day. This is good against the falling sickness."

It is remarkable that while the blossoms of the Rose Order present various shades of yellow, white, and red, *blue* is altogether foreign to them, and unknown among them.

As the Thistle is symbolical of Scotland, the Leek of Wales, and the Shamrock of Ireland: so the sweet, pure, simple, honest Rose of our woods is the apt-chosen emblem of Saint George, and the frank, bonny, blushing badge of Merrie England.

The petals of the Cabbage Rose (*Centifolia*), which are closely folded over each other like the leaves of a cabbage, have a slight laxative action, and are used for making Rose-water by distillation, whether when fresh, or after being preserved by admixture with common salt. This perfumed water has long enjoyed a reputation for the cure of inflamed eyes, more commonly when combined with zinc, or with sugar of lead. Hahnemann quotes the same established practice as a tacit avowal that there exists in the leaves of the Rose some healing power for certain diseased conditions of the eyes, which virtue is really founded on the homœopathic property possessed by the Rose, of exciting a species of ophthalmia in healthy persons; as was observed by Echtius, Ledelius, and Rau.

It is recorded also in his *Organon of Medicine*, that persons are sometimes found to faint at the smell of Roses (or, as Pope puts it, to "die of a rose in aromatic pain"); whereas the Princess Maria cured her brother, the Emperor Alexius, who suffered from faintings, by sprinkling him with Rose-water, in the presence of his aunt Eudoxia.

The wealthy Greeks and Romans strewed Roses on the tombs of departed friends, whilst poorer persons could only afford a tablet at the grave bearing the prayer:

> "Sparge, precor, rosas super mea busta, viator."
>
> "Scatter Roses, I beseech you, over my ashes, O pitiful passer-by."

But nowadays many persons have an aversion to throwing a Rose into a grave, or even letting one fall in.

Roses and reticence of speech have been linked together since the time of Harpocrates, whom Cupid bribed to silence by the gift of a golden Rose-bud; and therefore it became customary at Roman feasts to suspend over the table a flower of this kind as a hint that the convivial sayings which were then interchanged were not to be talked of outside. What was spoken "sub vino" was not to be published "sub divo":

> "Est rosa flos veneris, cujus quo facta laterent
> Harpocrati, matris dona, dicavit amor;
> Inde rosam mensis hospes suspendit amicis,
> Conviva ut sub eâ dicta tacenda sciat."

For the same reason the Rose is found sculptured on the ceilings of banqueting rooms; and in 1526 it began to be placed over Confessionals. Thus it has come about that the Rose is held to be the symbol of secrecy, as well as the flower of love, and the emblem of beauty: so that the significant phrase "sub rosa,"—under the Rose,—conveys a recognised meaning, understood, and respected by everyone. The bed of Roses is not altogether a poetic fiction. In old days the Sybarites slept upon mattresses which were stuffed with Rose petals: and the like are now made for persons of rank on the Nile.

A memorial brass over the tomb of Abbot Kirton, in Westminster Abbey, bears testimony to the high value he attached during life to Roses curatively:—

"Sis, Rosa, flos florum, morbis medicina meorum."

Many country persons believe, that if Roses and Violets are plentiful in the autumn, some epidemic may be expected presently. But this conclusion must be founded like that which says, "a green winter makes a fat churchyard," on the fact that humid warmth continued on late in the year tends to engender putrid ferments, and to weaken the bodily vigour.

Attar of Roses is a costly product, because consisting of the comparatively few oil globules found floating on the surface of a considerable volume of Rose-water thrice distilled It takes five hundredweight of Rose petals to produce one drachm by weight of the finest Attar, which is preserved in small bottles made of rock crystal. The scent of the minutest particle of the genuine essence is very powerful and enduring:—

"You may break, you may ruin, the vase if you will,
But the scent of the Roses will hang round it still."

The inscription, *Rosamundi, non Rosa munda*, was graven on the tomb of fair Rosamund, the inamorata of Henry the Seventh :—

> "Hic jacet in tombâ Rosa Mundi, non Rosa munda;
> Non redolet, sed olet quæ redolere solet."

> "Here Rose the graced, not Rose the chaste, reposes;
> The smell that rises is no smell of Roses."

In Sussex, the peculiar excrescence which is often found on the Briar, as caused by the puncture of an insect, and which is known as the canker, or "robin redbreast's cushion," is frequently worn round the neck as a protective amulet against whooping cough. This was called in the old Pharmacopeias "Bedeguar," and was famous for its astringent properties. Hans Andersen names it the "Rose King's beard."

The Rosary was introduced by St. Dominick to commemorate his having been shown a chaplet of Roses by the Blessed Virgin. It consisted formerly of a string of beads made of Rose leaves tightly pressed into round moulds and strung together, when real Roses could not be had. The use of a chaplet of beads for recording the number of prayers recited is of Eastern origin from the time of the Egyptian Anchorites.

The Rock Rose (a *Cistus*), grows commonly in our hilly pastures on a soil of chalk, or gravel, bearing clusters of large, bright, yellow flowers, from a small branching shrub. These flowers expand only in the sunshine, and have stamens which, if lightly touched, spread out, and lie down on the petals. The plant proves medicinally useful, particularly if grown in a soil containing magnesia. A tincture is prepared (H.) from the whole plant, English or Canadian, which is useful for curing shingles, on the principle of its producing, when taken by healthy provers in doses of various potencies, a cutaneous outbreak on the trunk of the body closely resembling the characteristic symptoms of shingles, whilst attended with nervous distress, and with much burning of the affected skin. The plant has likewise a popular reputation for healing scrofula, and its tincture is beneficial for reducing enlarged glands, as of the neck and throat ; also for strumous swelling of the knee joint, as well as of other joints. It is a "helianthemum" of the Sunflower tribe.

The Canadian Rock Rose is called Frostwort and Frostweed, because crystals of ice shoot from the cracked bark below the stem during freezing weather in the autumn.

A decoction of our plant has proved useful in prurigo (itching), and as a gargle for the sore throat of scarlet fever. For shingles, from five to ten drops of the tincture, third decimal strength, should be given with a spoonful of water three times a day.

ROSEMARY.

The Rosemary is a well-known, sweet-scented shrub, cultivated in our gardens, and herb beds on account of its fragrancy and its aromatic virtues. It came originally from the South of Europe and the Levant, and was introduced into England before the Norman Conquest. The shrub (*Rosmarinus*) takes its compound name from *ros*, dew, *marinus*, belonging to the sea ; in allusion to the grey, glistening appearance of the plant, and its natural locality, as well as its odour, like that of the sea. It is ever green, and bears small, pale, blue flowers.

Rosemary was thought by the ancients to refresh the memory and comfort the brain. Being a cordial herb it was often mentioned in the lays, or amorous ballads, of the Troubadours ; and was called "Coronaria" because women were accustomed to make crowns and garlands thereof.

> "What flower is that which regal honour craves?
> Adjoin the Virgin: and 'tis strewn o'er graves."

In some parts of England Rosemary is put with the corpse into the coffin, and sprigs of it are distributed among the mourners at a funeral, to be thrown into the grave. Gay alludes to this practice when describing the burial of a country lass who had met with an untimely death:—

> "To show their love, the neighbours far and near
> Followed, with wistful looks, the damsel's bier;
> Sprigged Rosemary the lads and lasses bore,
> While dismally the Parson walked before;
> Upon her grave the Rosemary they threw,—
> The Daisy, Butter flower, and Endive blue."

In *Romeo and Juliet*, Father Lawrence says:—

> "Dry up your tears, and stick your Rosemary
> On this fair corse."

The herb has a pleasant scent and a bitter, pungent taste, whilst much of its volatile, active principle resides in the calices of the flowers; therefore, in storing or using the plant these parts must be retained. It yields its virtues partially to water, and entirely to rectified spirit of wine.

In early times Rosemary was grown largely in kitchen gardens, and it came to signify the strong influence of the matron who dwelt there:—

> "Where Rosemary flourishes the woman rules."

The leaves and tops afford an essential volatile oil, but not so much as the flowers.

A spirit made from this essential oil with spirit of wine will help to renovate the vitality of paralyzed limbs, if rubbed in with brisk friction. The volatile oil includes a special camphor similar to that possessed by the myrtle. The plant also contains some tannin, with a resin and a bitter principle. By old writers it was said to increase the flow of milk.

The oil is used officinally for making a spirit of Rosemary, and is added to the compound tincture of Lavender, as well as to Soap liniment. By common consent it is agreed that the volatile oil (or the spirit) when mixed in washes will specially stimulate growth of the hair. The famous Hungary water, first concocted for a Queen of Hungary who, by its continual use, became effectually cured of paralysis, was prepared by putting a pound and a half of the fresh tops of Rosemary, when in full flower, into a gallon of proof spirit, which had to stand for four days, and was then distilled.

Hungary water (*l'eau de la reine d'Hongrie*) was formerly very famous for gout in the hands and feet. Hoyes says, the formula for composing this water, written by Queen Elizabeth's own hand in golden characters, is still preserved in the Imperial Library at Vienna.

An ounce of the dried leaves and flowers treated with a pint of boiling water, and allowed to stand until cold, makes one of the best hair washes known. It has the singular power of preventing the hair from uncurling when exposed to a damp atmosphere. The herb is used in the preparation of *Eau de Cologne*.

Rosemary wine, taken in small quantities, acts as a quieting cordial to a heart of which the action is excitable or palpitating, and it relieves any accompanying dropsy by stimulating the kidneys. This wine may be made by chopping up sprigs of Rosemary, and pouring on them some sound white wine, which after two or three days, may be strained off and used. By stimulating the nervous system it proves useful against the headaches of weak circulation and of languid health. "If a garlande of the tree be put around the heade it is a remedy for the stuffing of the head that cometh from coldness."

The green-leaved variety of Rosemary is the sort to be used medicinally. There are also silver and gold-leaved diversities. Sprigs of the herb were formerly stuck into beef whilst roasting as an excellent relish. A writer of 1707 tells of "Rosemary-preserve to dress your beef."

The toilet of the Ancients was never considered complete without an infusion, or spirit of Rosemary; and in olden times Rosemary was entwined in the wreath worn by the bride at the altar, being first dipped in scented water. Anne of Cleves, one of Henry the Eighth's wives, wore such a wreath at her wedding; and when people could afford it, the Rosemary branch presented to each guest was richly gilded.

The custom which prevailed in olden times of carrying a sprig of Rosemary in the hand at a funeral, took its rise from the notion of an alexipharmick or preservative powder in this herb against pestilential disorders; and hence it was thought that the smelling thereof was a powerful defence against any morbid effluvia from the corpse.

For the same reason it was usual to burn Rosemary in the chambers of the sick, just as was formerly done with frankincense, which gave the Greeks occasion to call the Rosemary *Libanotis*. In the French language of flowers this herb represents the power of rekindling lost energy. "The flowers of Rosemary," says an old author, "made up into plates (lozenges), with sugar, and eaten, comfort the heart, and make it merry, quicken the spirits, and make them more lively." "There's Rosemary for you—that's for remembrance! Pray you, love, remember!" says Ophelia in *Hamlet*. The spirit of Rosemary is kept by all druggists, and may be safely taken in doses of from twenty to thirty drops with a spoonful or two of water. Rosemary tea will soon relieve hysterical depression. Some persons drink it as a restorative at breakfast. It will help to regulate the monthly flow of women. An infusion of the herb mixed with poplar bark, and used every night, will make the hair soft, glossy, and strong.

In Northern Ireland is found the Wild Rosemary, or Marsh Tea (*Ledum palustre*), which has admirable curative uses, and from which, therefore, though it is not a common plant in England, a medicinal tincture (H.) is made with spirit of wine.

The herb belongs to the Rock Rose tribe, and contains citric acid, leditannic acid, resin, wax, and a volatile principle called "ericinol."

This plant is of singular use as a remedy for chilblains, as well as to subdue the painful effects of a sting from a wasp or bee; also to relieve gouty pains, which attack severely, but do not cause swelling of the part, especially as regards the fingers and toes. Four or five drops of the tincture should be taken for a dose with a tablespoonful of cold water, three or four times in the day; and linen rags soaked in a lotion made with a teaspoonful of the tincture added to half a tumblerful of cold water, should be kept applied over the affected part.

It equally relieves whitlows; and will heal punctured wounds, if arnica, or the Marigold, or St. John's Wort is not indicated, or of use. When tested by provers in large doses, it has caused a widespread eruption of eczema, with itching and tingling of the whole skin, extending into the mouth and air passages, and occasioning a violent spasmodic cough. Hence, one may fairly assume (and this has been found to hold good), that a gouty, spasmodic cough of the bronchial tubes, attended with gouty eczema, and with pains in the smaller joints, will be generally cured by tincture or infusion of the Wild Rosemary in small doses of a diluted strength, given several times a day, the diet at the same time being properly regulated. Formerly this herb was used in Germany for making beer heady; but it is now forbidden by law.

RUE.

The wild Rue is found on the hills of Lancashire and Yorkshire, being more vehement in smell and in operation than the garden Rue. This latter, *Ruta graveolens*, (powerfully redolent), the common cultivated Rue of our kitchen gardens, is a shrub with a pungent aromatic odour, and a bitter, hot, penetrating taste, having leaves of a bluish-green colour, and remaining verdant all the year round. It is first mentioned as cultivated in England by Turner, in his *Herbal*, 1562, and has since become one of the best known and most widely grown Simples for medicinal and homely uses. The name *Ruta* is from the Greek *reuo*, to set free, because this herb is so efficacious in various diseases. The Greeks regarded Rue as an anti-magical herb, since it served to remedy the nervous indigestion and flatulence from which they suffered when eating before strangers: which infirmity they attributed to witchcraft. This herb was further termed of old "Serving men's joy," because of the multiplicity of common ailments which it was warranted to cure. It constituted a chief ingredient of the famous antidote of Mithridates to poisons, the formula of which was found by Pompey in the satchel of the conquered King. The leaves are so acrid, that if they be much handled they inflame the skin; and the wild plant possesses this acridity still more strongly.

Water serves to extract the virtues of the cultivated shrub better than spirit of wine is able to do. The juice of Rue is of great efficacy in some forms of epilepsy, operating for the most part insensibly, though sometimes causing vomiting or purging.

Piperno, a Neapolitan physician, in 1625, commended Rue as a specific against epilepsy and vertigo. For the former malady at one time some of this herb was suspended round the neck of the sufferer, whilst "forsaking the devil with all his works, and invoking the Lord Jesus." Goat's Rue, *Galega*, is likewise of service in epilepsy and convulsions.

If a leaf or two of Rue be chewed, a refreshing aromatic flavour will pervade the mouth, and any nervous headache, giddiness, hysterical spasm, or palpitation, will be quickly relieved. Two drachms of powdered Rue, if taken every day regularly as a dose for a long while together, will often do wonders. It was much used by the ancients, and Hippocrates commended it. The herb is strongly stimulating and anti-spasmodic; its most important constituent being the volatile oil, which contains caprinic, pelargonic, caprylic, and œnanthylic acids. The oxygenated portion is caprinic aldehyde. In too full doses the oil causes aching of the loins, frequent urination, dulness and weight of mind, flushes of heat, unsteadiness of gait, and increased frequency of the pulse, but with diminished force. Similar symptoms are produced during an attack of the modern epidemical influenza; as like-wise by oil of wormwood, and some other essential oils.

Externally, Rue is an active irritant to the skin, the bruised leaves blistering the hands, and causing a pustular eruption. Gerard says, "The wild Rue venometh the hands that touch it, and will also infect the face; therefore it is not to be admitted to meat, or medicine." It stimulates the monthly function in women, but must be used with caution.

The decoction and infusion are to be made from the fresh plant, or (when this plant cannot be got), the oil may be given in a dose of from one to five drops. Externally, compresses saturated with a strong decoction of the plant when applied to the chest, have been used beneficially for chronic bronchitis.

Rue is best adapted to those of phlegmatic habit, and of languid constitutional energies. It is often employed in the form of tea. The *Schola Salernitana* says about this plant:—

> "Ruta viris minuit venerem, mulieribus addit
> Ruta facit castum, dat lumen, et ingerit astum
> Coctaque ruta facit de pulicibus loca tuta."
>
> "Rue maketh chaste: and eke preserveth sight;
> Infuseth wit, and putteth fleas to flight."

The leaves promote the menses, being given in doses of from fifteen to twenty grains. "Pliny," says John Evelyn, "reports Rue to be of such effect for the preservation of sight that the painters of his time used to devour a great quantity of it; and the herb is still eaten by the Italians frequently mingled amongst their salads." With respect to its use in epilepsy, Julius Cæsar Baricellus said: "I gave to my own children two scruples of the juice of Rue, and a small matter of gold; and, by the blessing of God, they were freed from their fits." The essential oil of Rue may be used for the same purpose, and in like manner.

Formerly this plant was thought to bestow second sight; and so sacred a regard was at one time felt for it in our islands, that the missionaries sprinkled their holy water from brushes made of the Rue; for which cause it was named "Herb of Grace."

Gerard tells us: "The garden Rue, which is better than the wild Rue for physic's use, grows most profitably (as Dioscorides said) under a fig tree." Country people boil its leaves with treacle, thus making a conserve of them. These leaves are curative of croup in poultry.

In the early part of the present century it was customary for judges, sitting at Assize, to have sprigs of Rue placed on the bench of the dock, as defensive against the pestilential infection brought into court from gaol by the prisoners. The herb was supposed to afford powerful protection from contagion.

At the present time the medicinal tincture (H.) is used for the treatment of rheumatism when developed in the membranes which invest the bones.

If bruised and applied, the leaves will ease the severe pain of sciatica. The expressed juice taken in small quantities is a noted remedy for nervous nightmare. A quaint old rhyme says of the plant:—

"Nobilis est ruta quia lumina reddit acuta."

"Noble is Rue! it makes the sight of eyes both sharp and clear;
With help of Rue, oh! blear-eyed man! thou shalt see far and near."

This is essentially the case when the vision has become dim through over exertion of the eyes. It was with "Euphrasy and Rue" the visual nerve of Adam was purged by Milton's Angel.

As a preserver of chastity Ophelia was made by Shakespeare to give Rue to Hamlet's mother, the Queen of Denmark.

RUSHES.

THE true Rushes (*Juncaceæ*) include the Soft Rush (*effusus*); the Hard Rush (*glaucus*); and the Common Rush (*conglomeratus*). The Bulrush (Pool Rush) is a Sedge; the Club Rush is a Typha; and the flowering Rush, a Butomus. "Rish" was the old method of spelling the name.

A medicinal tincture is made (H.) from the fresh root of the *juncus effusus*. It will be found helpful against spinal irritability, with some crampy tightness felt in the arms and legs, together with headache and flatulent indigestion. Four or five drops should be given for a dose with a spoonful of water, three or four times in the day.

This, the Soft Rush, is commonly used for tying the bines of hops to the poles; and, as these bines grow larger in size, the rushes wither, setting the bines free in a timely fashion. To find a green-topped Seave, or Rush, and a four-leaved Clover, is, in rural estimation, equally lucky.

The generic title, *Juncus*, has been applied because Rushes are *in conjunction* when plaited together for making cordage.

The common Rush is found by roadsides in damp pastures, and is readily known by its long, slender, round, naked stem, containing pith, and showing about the middle of July a dense globular head of brown flowers. Rushes of this sort were employed by our remote ancestors for strewing, when fresh and green, about the floor of the hall after discontinuing its big fire at Eastertide. Shakespeare says in *Romeo and Juliet*:—

> "Wantons, light of heart,
> Tickle the senseless rushes with their heels."

In obedience to a bequest (1494), Rushes are still strewn about the pavement of Redcliff Church at Bristol every Whit-Sunday. The common phrase, "not worth a Rush," took its origin from this general practice. Distinguished guests were honoured in mediæval times with clean fresh Rushes; but those of inferior rank had either the Rushes left by their superiors, or none at all.

The sweet-scented "Flag," or Rush (*Acorus calamus*), was always used by preference when it could be procured. It is a native of this country, growing on watery banks, and very plentiful in the rivers of Norfolk, from whence the London market is supplied. The roots have a warm, bitter taste, and the essential oil is highly aromatic, this being used for preparing aromatic vinegar. In Norfolk the powdered dry rhizome is given for ague. With sugar it makes an agreeable cordial conserve. (*See Flag (Sweet), page* 201). For preserving the aromatic qualities within the dried rhizome, or root, it should be kept in stock unpeeled. This contains "oleum calami," and the bitter principle "acorin." Some of the root may be habitually chewed for the relief of chronic indigestion. The odorous delights of a pastoral time passed near these sweetly-fragrant plants have been happily alluded to in the well-known lines of idyllic verse :—

> "Green grow the Rushes, oh!
> Green grow the Rushes, oh!
> The sweetest hours that e'er I spent
> Were spent among the lasses, oh!"

> "Virent junci fluviales,
> Junci prope lymphas:
> Ah! quam ridet quœ me videt
> Hora inter Nymphas!"

The old saying, "As fit as Tib's Rush for Tom's forefinger," alludes to an ancient custom of making spurious marriages with a ring constructed from a Rush. Tom and Tib were vulgar epithets applied in Shakespeare's time to the rogue, and the wanton.

The Bulrush (*Scirpus lacustris*) is a tall, aquatic plant, which belongs to the Sedge tribe. It name was formerly spelt "Pole Rush," and was given because this grows in pools of water, and not like other Rushes, in mire. Bottoms of chairs are frequently made with its stems. Its seed is prepared medicinally, being astringent and somewhat sedative; "So soporiferous," says Gerard, "that care must be had in the administration thereof, lest in provoking sleep you induce a drowsiness, or dead sleep." Street hawkers, in Autumn, offer as Bulrushes the tall, round spikes of the Great Reed Mace, which is not a true Rush. Artists are responsible in the first instance for the mistake—notably Paul De la Roche, in his famous picture of "The Finding of Moses." The future great leader of the Israelites is there depicted in an ark amid a forest of Great Cat's-tail Reeds.

The flowering Rush, or water gladiole, which grows by the banks of rivers is called botanically "butomus," from the Greek, *bous*, an ox, and *temno*, to cut, because the sharp edges of the erect three-cornered leaf-blades wound the cattle which come in contact with them, or try to eat them. Its root is highly esteemed in Russia for the cure of hydrophobia, being regarded by the doctors as a specific for that disease. Its flowers are large, and of a splendid rose colour. The seeds promote the monthly flow in women, act on disordered kidneys, prove astringent against fluxes, and serve to woo sleep in nervous wakefulness. Gerard tells that "the seed of Rushes drieth the overmuch flowing of women's termes."

The Reed Mace, or Cat's-tail, is often incorrectly called Bulrush, though it is a typha (*tuphos*, marsh) plant.

The Bog Asphodel (*Narthecium ossifragum*) grows in bogs, and bears a spike of yellow, star-like flowers. Its second nominative was given to signify its causing the bones of cattle which feed thereon to become soft; but probably this morbid state is incurred rather through the exhalations arising from the bogs where the cattle are pastured. To the same plant has been given also the name "Mayden heere," because young damsels formerly used it for making their hair yellow.

The Great Cat's-tail (*Typha palustris*), or Great Reed Mace, a perennial reed common in Great Britain, affords by the tender white part of its stalks when peeled near the root, a crisp, cooling, pleasant article of food. This is eaten raw with avidity by the Cossacks. Aristophanes makes mention of the Mace in his comedy of frogs who were glad to have spent their day skipping about *inter Cyperum et Phleum*, among Galingale and Cat's-tail. Sacred pictures which represent our Saviour wearing the crown of thorns, place this reed in His hands as given Him in mockery for a kingly Mace. The same *Typha* has been further called "Dunse-down," from making persons "dunch," or deaf, if its soft spikes accidentally run into the ears. "*Ejus enim paniculæ flos si aures intraverit, exsurdat.*" It is reasonable to suppose that, on the principle of similars, a preparation of this plant, if applied topically within the ear, as well as taken medicinally, will be curative of a like deafness. Most probably the injury to the hearing caused by the spikes at first is toxic as well as of the nature of an injury. The Poet Laureate sings of "Sleepy breath made sweet with Galingale" (*Cyperus longus*). Other names again are, "Chimney-sweeper's brush"; "Blackheads" until ripe, then "Whiteheads"; and "Water torch," because its panicles, if soaked in oil, will burn like a torch.

SAFFRON (Meadow and Cultivated).

THE Meadow Saffron (*Colchicum autumnale*) is a common wild Crocus found in English meadows, especially about the Midland districts. The flower appears in the autumn before the leaves and fruit, which are not produced until the following spring. Its corollæ resemble those of the true Saffron, a native of the East, but long cultivated in Great Britain, where it is sometimes found apparently wild. They are plants of the Iris order.

From the Meadow Saffron is obtained a corm or bulb, dug up in the spring, of which the well-known tincture of colchicum, a specific for rheumatism, is made; and from the true Saffron flowers are taken the familiar orange red stigmata, which furnish the fragrant colouring matter used by confectioners in cakes, and by the apothecary for his syrup of Saffron, etc.

The flower of the Meadow Saffron rises bare from the earth, and is, therefore, called "Upstart" and "Naked Lady." This plant owes its botanical name *Colchicum*, to Colchis, in Natalia, which abounded in poisonous vegetables, and gave rise to the fiction about the enchantress Medea. She renewed the vitality of her aged father, Æneas, by drawing blood out of his veins and refilling them with the juices of certain herbs. The fabled origin of the Saffron plant ran thus. A certain young man named Crocus went to play at quoits in a field with Mercurie, when the quoit of his companion happened by misfortune to hit him on the head, whereby, before long, he died, to the great sorrow of his friends. Finally, in the place where he had bled, Saffron was found to be growing: whereupon, the people, seeing the colour of the chine as it stood, adjusted it to come of the blood of Crocus, and therefore they gave it his name. The medicinal properties of Colchicum have been known from a very early period. In the reign of James the First (1615), Sir Theodore Mayerne administered the bulb to his majesty together with the powder of unburied skulls. In France, it has always been a favourite specific for gout; and during the reign of Louis the Fifteenth, it became very fashionable under the name of *Eau Médicinale;* but the remedy is somewhat dangerous, and should never be incautiously used. Instances are on record where fatal results have followed too large a medicinal dose, even on the following day, after taking sixty drops of the wine of Colchicum overnight; and when given in much smaller doses it sometimes acts as a powerfully irritating purgative, or as an emetic. The medicine should not be employed except by a doctor; its habitual use is very harmful.

The acrimony of the bulb may be modified in a measure if it, or its seeds, are steeped in vinegar before being taken as a medicine.

The French designate the roots of the Meadow Saffron (*Colchicum*) as "*Tue-chien*"; "*morte aux chiens,*" "death to dogs."

Alexander of Tralles, a Greek physician of the sixth century, was the first to advise Colchicum (*Hermodactylon*) for gout, with the effect that patients, immediately after its exhibition, found themselves able to walk. "But," said he, and with shrewd truth, "it has this bad property, that it disposes those who take it curatively for gout or rheumatism, to be afterwards more frequently attacked with the disease than before."

Our druggists supply an officinal tincture of Colchicum (Meadow Saffron) made from the seeds, the dose of which is from ten to thirty drops, with a spoonful of water; also a wine infused from the bulb, of which the dose is the same as that of the tincture, twice or three times a day; and an acetous extract prepared from the thickened juice of the crushed bulbs, of which from half to two grains may be given in a pilule, or dissolved in water, twice or three times a day, until the active symptoms are subdued, and then less often for another day or two afterwards. The most important chemical constituent of the bulb, flowers, and seeds, is "Colchicin." Besides this there are contained starch, gum, sugar, tannin, and some fatty resinous matter. There is also a fixed oil in the seeds.

Crocus vernus, the True Saffron, grows wild about Halifax, and in the neighbourhood of Derby; but for commercial uses the supply of stigmata is had from Greece, and Asia Minor. This plant was cultivated in England as far back as during the reign of Edward the Third. It is said that a pilgrim then brought from the Levant to England the first root of Saffron, concealed in a hollow staff, doing the same thing at the peril of his life, and planting such root at Saffron Walden, in Essex, whence the place has derived its name.

The stigmata are picked out, then dried in a kiln, over a hair cloth, and pressed afterwards into cakes, of which the aromatic quality is very volatile. The plant was formerly cultivated at Saffron Walden, where it was presented in silver cups by the Corporation to some of our Sovereigns, who visited Walden for the ceremony. Five guineas were paid by the Corporation for the pound of Saffron which they purchased for Queen Elizabeth; and to constitute this quantity forty thousand flowers were required. The City Arms of Walden bears three Saffron plants, as given by a Charter of Edward the Sixth. Saffron Hill, in Holborn, London, belonged formerly to Ely House, and got its name from the crops of Saffron which were grown there: "*Occultā Spolia hi Croceo de colle ferebant*" (*Comic Latin Grammar*).

In our rural districts there is a popular custom of giving Saffron tea in measles, on the doctrine of colour analogy; to which notion may likewise be referred the practice of adding Saffron to the drinking water of canaries when they are moulting.

In England, it was fashionable during the seventh century to make use of starch stained yellow with Saffron; and in an old cookery book of that period, it is directed that "Saffron must be put into all Lenten soups, sauces, and dishes; also that without Saffron we cannot have well-cooked peas." Confectioners were wont to make their pastry attractive with Saffron. So the Clown says in Shakespeare's *Winter's Tale*, "I must have Saffron to colour the warden pies." We read of a Saffron-tub in the kitchen of Bishop Swinfield, 1296. During the fourteenth century Saffron was cultivated in the herbarium of the manor-house, and the castle. Throughout Devonshire this product is quoted to signify anything costly.

Henry the Eighth forbade persons to colour with Saffron the long locks of hair worn then, and called Glibbes. Lord Bacon said, "the English are rendered sprightly by a liberal use of Saffron in sweetmeats and broth": also, "Saffron conveys medicine to the heart, cures its palpitation, removes melancholy and uneasiness, revives the brain, renders the mind cheerful, and generates boldness." The restorative plant has been termed "*Cor hominis;*" "*Anima pulmonum*," "the Heart of Man"; and there is an old saying alluding to one of a merry temper, "*Dormivit in sacco Croci*," "he has slept in a sack of Saffron." It was called by the ancients "*Aurum philosophorum*," contracted to "*Aroph*." Also, *Sanguis Herculis*, and *Rex Vegetabilium*, "being given with good success to procure bodily lust." The English word Saffron comes from the Arabian—*Zahafram*—whilst the name Crocus of this golden plant is taken from the Greek *krokee*—a thread—signifying the dry thin stigmata of the flower. Old Fuller wrote "the Crocodile's tears are never true save when he is forced where Saffron groweth (whence he hath his name of *Croco-deilos*, or the Saffron-fearer), knowing himself to be all poison, and it all antidote." Frequently Marigold stigmata are cheaply used for adulterating the true Saffron.

Homer introduces Saffron as one of the flowers which formed the nuptial couch of Jupiter: and Solomon mentioned it as growing in his garden: "Spikenard and saffron: calamus, and cinnamon" (*Canticles* iv., 14). Pliny states that wine in which Saffron was macerated gave a fragrant odour to theatres about which it was sprinkled. The Cilician doctors advised Cleopatra to take Saffron for clearing her complexion.

The medicinal use of Saffron has always obtained amongst the Orientals. According to a treatise, *Crocologia* (1670), by Hartodt, it was then employed as a medicine, as a pigment, and for seasoning various kinds of food. The colouring matter of Saffron is a substance called polychroite, or crocin; and its slightly stimulating properties depend upon a volatile oil.

Boerhaave said that Saffron possesses the power of liquefying the blood; hence, "Women who use it too freely suffer from immoderate menses." A tincture is made (H.) from the Saffron of commerce, which is of essential use for controlling female hæmorrhages. Four or five drops of the tincture may be given with a spoonful of water every three or four hours for this purpose. The same tincture is good for impaired vision, when there is a sense of gauze before the eyes, which the person tries to wink, or wipe away. Smelling strongly and frequently at the Hay Saffron of commerce (obtained from Spain and France), will cause headache, stupor, and heavy sleep; whilst, during its internal use, the urine becomes of a deep yellow colour.

Of the syrup of Saffron, which is a slightly stimulating exhilarant, and which possesses a rich colour, from one to two teaspoonfuls may be given for a dose, with two tablespoonfuls of cold water. It serves to energise the organs within the middle trunk of both males and females; also to recruit an exhausted brain.

In Devonshire, Saffron used to be regarded as a most valuable remedy to restore consumptive patients, even when far advanced in the disease, and it was, therefore, esteemed of great worth :—

"Nec poteris croci dotes numerare, nec usus."

"Saffron is such a special remedy for those that have consumption of the lungs, and are—as we term it—at death's door, and almost past breathing, that it bringeth breath again, and prolongeth life for certain days, if ten, or twenty grains at most, be given in new, or sweet wine. It presently, and in a moment, removeth away difficulty of breathing, which most dangerously and suddenly happeneth."

In Westphalia, an apple mixed with Saffron, on the doctrine of signatures, is given on Easter Monday, against jaundice. Evelyn tells us: "The German housewives have a way of forming Saffron into balls, by mingling it with a little honey, which, when thoroughly dried, they reduce to powder, and sprinkle it over their sallets for a noble cordial." Those of Spain and Italy, we know, generally make use of this flower, mingling its golden tincture with almost everything they eat. But, an excessive use of Saffron proves harmful. It will produce an intense pain in the head, and imperil the reason. Half-a-scruple, *i.e.*, ten grains, should be the largest dose. In fuller doses this tincture will provoke a determination of blood to the head, with bleeding from the nose, and sometimes with a disposition to immoderate laughter. Small doses, therefore, of the diluted tincture, ought to relieve these symptoms when they occur as spontaneous illness. The inhabitants of Eastern countries regard Saffron as a fine restorative, and nuptial invitations are often powdered by them with this medicament.

In Ireland women dye their sheets with Saffron to preserve them from vermin, and to strengthen their own limbs.

> "Green herbs, red pepper, mussels, *Saffron*,
> Soles, onions, garlic, roach and dace;
> All these you eat at Ferre's tavern
> In that one dish of bouillabaisse."
>
> —*Thackeray*.

SAGE.

OUR garden Sage, a familiar occupant of the English herb bed, was formerly celebrated as a medicine of great virtue. This was the *Elelisphakos* of the Greeks, so called from its dry and withered looking leaves. It grows wild in the South of Europe, but is a cultivated Simple in England, France, and Germany. Like other labiate herbs it is aromatic and fragrant, because containing a volatile, camphoraceous, essential oil.

All parts of the plant have a strong-scented odour, and a warm, bitter, astringent taste. The Latin name, *Salvia*, has become corrupted through *Sauja*, *sauge*, to Sage, and is derived from *salvere*, "to be sound," in reference to the medicinally curative properties of the plant.

A well-known monkish line about it ran to this effect: *Cur moriatur homo cui Salvia crescit in horto?* "Why should a man die whilst Sage grows in his garden?" And even at this time, in many parts of England, the following piece of advice is carefully adopted every year:—

> "He that would live for aye
> Must eat Sage in May."

During the time of Charlemagne, the school of Salerno thought so highly of Sage that they originated the dictum quoted above of Saracenic old pharmacy, but they wisely added a second line:—

> "Contra vim mortis non est medicamen in hortis."

The essential oil of the herb may be more readily dissolved in a spirituous than in a watery vehicle. Of this, the active principle is "salviol," which confers the power of resisting putrefaction on animal substances; whilst the bitterness and condimentary pungency of the herb enable the stomach to digest rich, luscious meats and gravies, if it be eaten therewith.

Hence has arisen the custom of stuffing ducks for the table, and geese, with the conventional Sage and onions. Or there is no better way of taking Sage as a stomachic wholesome herb than by eating it with bread and butter. In Buckinghamshire a tradition maintains that the wife rules where Sage grows vigorously in the garden: and it is believed that this plant will thrive or wither, just as the owner's business prospers or fails. George Whitfield, when at Oxford (1733), took only Sage-tea, with sugar, and coarse bread.

Old sayings tell of the herb, as *Salvia salvatrix; naturæ conciliatrix;* and the line runs:—

> "Salvia cum rutâ faciunt tibi pocula tuta,"

recommending to plant Rue among the Sage so as to keep away noxious toads.

The Chinese are as fond of Sage as we are of their fragrant teas; and the Dutch once carried on a profitable trade with them, by exchanging a pound of Sage leaves for each three-pound parcel of tea.

It was formerly thought that Sage, if used in the making of cheese, improved its flavour.

> "Marbled with Sage the hardening cheese she pressed."
>
> —*Gay.*

"Sage," says Gerard, "is singular good for the head and brain; it quickeneth the senses and memory; strengtheneth the sinews; restoreth health to those that hath the palsy; and takes away shaky trembling of the members." Agrippa called it "the holy herb," because women with child, if they be likely to come before their time, "do eat thereof to their great good."

Pepys, in his well-known Diary says, "between Gosport and Southampton we observed a little churchyard where it is customary to sow all the graves with Sage." In *Franche Comte* the herb is supposed to mitigate grief, mental and bodily.

> "Salvia comfortat nervos, manuumque tremorem
> Tollit; et ejus ope febris acuta fugit."

> "Sage helps the nerves, and by its powerful might
> Palsy is cured, and fever put to flight."

But if Sage be smelt for some time it will cause a sort of intoxication, and giddiness. The leaves, when dried and smoked in a pipe as tobacco, will lighten the brain.

In Sussex, a peasant will munch Sage leaves on nine consecutive mornings, whilst fasting, to cure ague.

A strong infusion of the herb has been used with success to dry up the breast milk for weaning; and as a gargle Sage leaf tea, when sweetened with honey, serves admirably. This decoction, when made strong, is an excellent lotion for ulcers, and to heal raw abrasions of the skin. The herb may be applied externally in bags as a hot fomentation. Some persons value the Wormwood Sage more highly than either of the other varieties.

In the Sage flower the stamens swing round their loosely-connected anther cells against the back of any blundering bee who is in search of honey, just as in olden days the bag of sand caught the shoulders of a clumsy youth when tilting at the Quintin.

Wild Meadow Sage (*Salvia verbenaca*), or Meadow Clary, grows in our dry pastures, but somewhat rarely, though it is better known as a cultivated herb in our kitchen gardens. The leaves and flowers afford a volatile oil, which is fragrant and aromatic.

Some have attributed the name *Salvia sclarea*, Clary (Clear eye) to the fact of the seeds being so mucilaginous, that when the eye is invaded by any small foreign body, their decoction will remove the same by acting as an emulsion to lubricate it away. The leaves and flowers may be usefully given in an infusion for hysterical colic and similar troubles connected with nervous weakness. Also they make a pleasant fermented wine. The Wood Sage is the Wood Germander,

Teucrium scorodinia, a woodland plant with sage-like leaves, containing a volatile oil, some tannin, and a bitter principle. This plant has been used as a substitute for hops. It was called "hind heal" from curing the hind when sick, or wounded, and was probably the same herb as *Elaphoboscum*, the Dittany, taken by harts in Crete. A snuff has been made from its powder to cure nasal polypi: also the infusion (freshly prepared), should be given medicinally, two tablespoonfuls for a dose: or, of the powder, from thirty to forty grains. The name "Germander" is a corruption from Chamœdrys, *chamai*, ground, and *drus*, oak, because the leaves are like those of the oak.

SAINT JOHN'S WORT (*see page* 287).

SAVIN.

SAVIN, the Juniper Savin (*Sabina*), or Saffern, is a herb which grows freely in our bed of garden Simples, if properly cared for, and which possesses medicinal virtues of a potential nature. The shrub is a native of southern Europe, being a small evergreen plant, the twigs of which are densely covered with little leaves in four rows, having a strong, peculiar, unpleasant odour of turpentine, with a bitter, acrid, resinous taste. The young branchlets are collected for medicinal use. They contain tannin, resin, a special volatile oil, and extractive matters.

A medicinal tincture (H.) is made from the fresh leaves, and the points of the shoots of the cultivated Savin. But this is a powerful medicine, and must be used with caution. In small doses of two or three drops with a tablespoonful of cold water it is of singular efficacy for arresting an active florid flux from the womb at the monthly times of women when occurring too profusely, the remedy being given every two, three, or four hours. Or from one to four grains of powdered Savin may be taken instead of each dose of the tincture.

The stimulating virtues of Savin befit it for cleansing carbuncles, and for benefiting baldness. When mixed with honey it has removed freckles with success; the leaves, dried and powdered, serve, when applied, to dispel obstinate warty excrescences about the genitals.

Rubbed together with cerate, or lard, powdered Savin is used for maintaining the sores of blisters, and of issues, open when it is desired to keep up their derivative action.

The essential oil will stimulate the womb to functional activity when it is passively congested and torpid. As to its elementary composition this oil closely resembles the spirit of turpentine; and when given in small well diluted doses as a tincture (made of the oil mixed with spirit of wine), such medicine does good service in relieving rheumatic pains and swellings connected with impaired health of the womb. For these purposes the ordinary tincture (H.) of Savin should be mixed, one part thereof with nine parts of spirit of wine, and given in doses of from six to ten drops with a tablespoonful of water. Dr. Pereira says about the herb: "According to my own observation, Savin is the most certain and powerful stimulator of the monthly courses in the whole of our *Materia Medica*; and I never saw any ill effects result from its administration." The essential oil may be preferred in a dose of from one to four drops on sugar, or in milk, when this functional activity is sought.

Savin was known of old as the "Devil's Tree," and the "Magician's Cypress," because much affected by witches and sorcerers when working their spells.

SCURVY GRASS.

One of the most useful, but not best known, of the Cruciferous wild plants which are specifics against Scrofula is our English Scurvy Grass.

It grows by choice near the sea shore, or in mountainous places; and even when found many miles from the sea its taste is salt. It occurs along the muddy banks of the Avon; also in Wales, and in Cumberland, more commonly near the coast, and likewise on the mountains of Scotland; again it may be readily cultivated in the garden for medicinal uses. If eaten as a salad in its fresh state it is the most effectual of all the antiscorbutic plants.

The herb is produced with an angular smooth shining stem, twelve or fourteen inches high, having narrow green leaves, and terminating in thick clusters of white flowers. Its leaves are good and wholesome when eaten in spring with bread and butter. The juice, when diluted with water, makes a good mouth-wash for spongy gums.

The whole plant contains tannin, and a bitter principle, which is butyl-mustard oil, and on which the medicinal properties depend. This oil is of great volatility and penetrating power; one drop instilled on sugar, or dissolved in spirit, communicates to a quart of wine the taste and smell of Scurvy Grass.

The fresh plant taken as such, or the expressed fresh juice, confers the benefits of the herb in by far the most effectual way. A distilled water, and a conserve prepared with the leaves, were formerly dispensed by druggists; and the fresh juice mixed with that of Seville oranges went by the name of "spring drinks," or "juices."

The plant is found in large quantities at Lymington

(Hants), on low banks almost dipping into the sea. Its expressed juice was formerly taken in beer, or boiled in milk as a decoction, flavoured with pepper, aniseed, etc.

This Scurvy Grass has the botanical name *Cochlearia*, or, in English, Spoonwort, so named from its leaves resembling in shape the bowl of an old-fashioned spoon. It is supposed to be the famous *Herba Britannica* of the ancients. Our great navigators have borne unanimous testimony to its never-failing value in scurvy; and it has been justly noticed that the plant grows most plentifully in altitudes where scurvy is specially troublesome and frequent. The green herb bruised may be applied as a poultice.

For making a decoction of the plant as a blood purifier, and against scurvy, put two ounces of the whole plant and its roots into a quart jug, and fill up with boiling water, taking care to keep this well covered. When it is cold take a wineglassful thereof three, or four times in the day.

Another name for the plant is Scruby grass. The fresh herb has a strong pungent odour when bruised, and a warm bitter taste. Its beneficial uses in scurvy, are due to the potash salts which it contains. Externally, the juice will cleanse and heal foul ulcers, and ill-favoured eruptions.

SEA PLANTS and SEA WEEDS.

Of marine plants commonly found, the Samphire and the Sea Holly have certain domestic and medicinal uses which give them a position as Simples; and of the more ordinary Sea Weeds (cryptogamous, or flowerless plants) some few are edible, though sparingly nutritious, whilst curative and medicinal virtues are attributed to several others, as Irish Moss, Scotch Dulse, Sea Tang, and the

Bladderwrack. It may be stated broadly that the Sea Weeds employed as remedial Simples owe their powers to the bromine, iodine, and sulphate of soda which they contain. Pliny and Dioscorides in their days extolled the qualities of various Sea Weeds; and practitioners of medicine on our sea coasts are now unanimous in pronouncing Sea Weed liniments, and poultices, as of undoubted value in reducing glandular swellings, and in curing obstinate sprains; whilst they administer the Bladderwrack, etc., internally for alterative purposes with no little success. Bits of Sea Weed, called Ladies' trees, are still to be seen as chimney ornaments in many a Cornish cottage, being fixed on small stands, and supposed to protect the dwelling from fire, or other mishaps.

Samphire, of the true sort, is a herb difficult to be gathered, because it grows only out of the crevices of lofty perpendicular rocks which cannot be easily scaled. This genuine Samphire (*Crithmum maritimum*) is a small plant, bearing yellow flowers in circular umbels on the tops of the stalks, which flowers are followed by seeds like those of the Fennel, but larger.

The leaves are juicy, with a warm aromatic taste, and may be put into sauce; or they make a good appetising condimentary pickle, which is wholesome for scrofulous subjects. Persons living by the coast cook this plant as a pot herb. Formerly, it was regularly cried in the London streets, and was then called Crest Marine.

Shakespeare alludes in well-known lines to the hazardous proceedings of the Samphire gatherer's "dreadful trade":—

"How fearful
And dizzy 'tis to cast one's eyes so low!
The crows and choughs that wing the midway air
Show scarce so gross as beetles: half-way down
Hangs one that gathers Samphire: dreadful trade!
Methinks he seems no bigger than his head."—*King Lear*.

And Evelyn has praised the plant for excellence of flavour, as well as for aromatic virtues against the spleen. Pliny says Samphire is the very herb that the good country wife Hecate prepared for Theseus when going against the Bull of Marathon.

Its botanic name is from the Greek *crithe,* "barley," because the seeds are thought to resemble that grain. The title Samphire is derived from the French *Herbe de St. Pierre,* because the roots strike deep in the crevices of rocks. St. Peter's Wort has become corrupted to Sampetre, Sampier, and Samphire.

A spurious Samphire, the *Inula crithmoides,* or Golden Samphire, is often supplied in lieu of the real plant, though it has a different flavour, and few of the proper virtues. This grows more abundantly on low rocks, and on ground washed by salt water. Also a Salicornia, or jointed Glasswort, or Saltwort, or Crabgrass, is sold as Samphire for a pickle, in the Italian oil shops.

Gerard says of Samphire: "It is the pleasantest sauce, most familiar, and best agreeing with man's body." "Preferable," adds Evelyn, "for cleansing the passages, and sharpening appetite, to most of our hotter herbs, and salad ingredients."

The Sea Holly (*Eryngium maritimum*), or Sea Hulver, is a well-known prickly sea-green plant, growing in the sand on many parts of our coasts, or on stony ground, with stiff leaves, and roots which run to a great length among the sand, whilst charged with a sweetish juice.

A manufactory for making candied roots of the Sea Holly was established at Colchester, by Robert Burton, an apothecary, in the seventeenth century, as they were considered both antiscorbutic, and excellent for health.

Gerard says: "The roots, if eaten, are good for those that be liver sick; and they ease cramps, convulsions, and the falling sickness. If condited, or preserved with sugar, they are exceeding good to be given to old and aged people that are consumed and withered with age, and which want natural moisture." He goes on to give an elaborate receipt how to condite the roots of Sea Holly, or Eringos (which title is, according to Liddell and Scott, the diminutive of *eerungos*, "the beard of a goat." Or, Eryngo has been derived from the Greek *eruggarein*, to eructate, because the plant is, according to herbalists, a specific against belching). With healthy provers, who have taken the Sea Holly experimentally in *toxical* doses of varying strength the sexual energies and instincts became always depressed. This accounts for the fact that during the Elizabethan era the roots of the plant used *in moderation* were highly valued for renovating masculine vigour, such as Falstaff invoked, and which classic writers have extolled:—

> "Non male tum graiis florens eryngus n hortis
> Quæritur; hunc gremio portet si nupta virentem
> Nunquam inconcessos conjux meditabitur ignes."
>
> —*Rapinus.*

These Eryngo roots, prepared with sugar, were then called "Kissing Comfits." Lord Bacon when recommending the yolks of eggs for giving strength if taken with Malmsey, or sweet wine, says: "You shall doe well to put in some few slices of Eringium roots, and a little Ambergrice: for by this means, besides the immediate facultie of nourishment, such drinke will strengthen the back."

Plutarch writes: "They report of the Sea Holly, if one goat taketh it into her mouth, it causeth her first to stand still, and afterwards the whole flock, until such time as the shepherd takes it from her. Boerhaave thought the root "a principal aperient."

Irish Moss, or *Carraigeen*, is abundant on our rocky coasts, and is collected on the north western shores of Ireland, while some of it comes to us from Hamburg. Its chief constituent is a kind of mucilage, which dissolves to a stiff paste in boiling water, this containing some iodine, and much sulphur. But before being boiled in water or milk, the Moss should be soaked for an hour or more in cold water. Officinally, a decoction is ordered to be made with an ounce of the Moss to a pint of water: of which from one to four fluid ounces may be taken for a dose.

This Lichen contains starchy, heat-giving nourishment, about six parts of the same to one of flesh-forming food; therefore its jelly is found to be specially sustaining to persons suffering from pulmonary consumption, with an excessive waste of the bodily heat. At one time the Irish Moss fetched as high a price as half-a-crown for the pound. It bears the botanical name of *Chondrus crispus*, and varies much in size and colour. When growing in small pools, it is shallow, pale, and stunted; whilst when found at the bottom of a deep pool, or in the shadow of a great rock, it occurs in dense masses of rich ruddy purple, with reddish green thick fronds.

Iceland Moss contains the form of starch called "lichenin." It is a British lichen found especially in Wales and Scotland. Most probably the Icelanders were the first to learn its helpful properties. In two kinds of pulmonary consumption this lichen best promotes a cure—that with active bleeding from the lungs, and that with profuse purulent expectoration. The Icelanders boil the Moss in broth, or dry it in cakes used as bread. They likewise make gruel of it mixed with milk: but the first decoction of it in water, being purgative, is always thrown away. An ounce of the Iceland Moss boiled for a quarter-of-an-hour in a pint of milk, or water, will yield seven ounces of thick mucilage. This has been found particularly useful in dysentery. Also contained in the Moss are cetrarin, uncrystallizable sugar, gum, and green wax; with potash, and phosphate of lime. It affords help in diabetes, and for general atrophy; being given also in powder, or syrup, or mixed with chocolate. Francatelli directs for making *Iceland Moss Jelly*. Boil four ounces of the Moss in one quart of water: then add the juice of two lemons, and a bit of the rind, with four ounces of sugar (and perhaps a gill of sherry ?). Boil up and remove the scum from the surface. Strain the jelly through a muslin bag into a basin, and set it aside to become cold. It may be eaten thus, but it is more efficacious when taken warm. A Sea-Moss, the *Lichen marinum*, is "a singular remedy to strengthen the weakness of the back." It is called "Oister-green."

In New England the generic term "Moss" is a cant word signifying money: perhaps as a contraction of Mopuses, or as a play on the proverb, "a rolling stone gathers no moss."

The Dulse is used in Scotland and Ireland both as food and medicine. Botanically it bears the name of *Iridea edulis*, or *Rhodymenia palmata* (the sugar *Fucus* of Iceland).

There is a saying in Scotland: "He who eats of the Dulse of Guerdie, and drinks of the wells of Kindingie, will escape all maladies except black death." This marine weed contains within its cellular structure much iodine, which makes it a specific remedy for scrofulous glandular enlargements, or morbid deposits.

In Ireland the Dulse is first well washed in fresh water, and exposed in the air to dry, when it gives out a white powdery substance, which is sweet and palatable, covering the whole plant. The weed is presently packed in cases, and protected from the air, so that being thus preserved, it may either be eaten as it is, or boiled in milk, and mixed with flour of rye. The powdery substance is "mannite," which is abundant likewise on many of our Sea Weeds.

Cattle and sheep are very fond of Dulse, for which reason in Norway it is known as Soudsell, or Sheep's Weed. This *Iridea edulis* is pinched with hot irons by the fishermen in the south west of England, so as to make it taste like an oyster. In Scotland it is roasted in the frying-pan.

The Maritime Sea Tang (*Laminaria digitata*) was belauded in the *Proverbial Philosophy* of Martin Tupper:—

> "Health is in the freshness of its savour; and it cumbereth the beach with wealth;
> Comforting the tossings of pain with its violet tinctured essence."

Tang signifies Anglo-Saxon "thatch," from Sea Weed having been formerly used instead of straw to cover the roofs of houses. When bruised and applied by way of a poultice to scrofulous swellings and glandular tumours, the Sea Tang has been found very valuable. The famous John Hunter was accustomed to employ a poultice of sea water and oatmeal.

This weed is of common marine growth, consisting of a wide smooth brown frond, with a thick round stem, and broad brown ribbons like a flag at the end of it. It is familiarly known as Seagirdles, Tangle, Sea Staff, Sea Wand, and Cows' Tails. Fisher boys cut up the stems as handles for knives, or hooks, because, after the haft of the blade is inserted within the stem, this dries, and contracts on the iron staple, becoming densely hard and firm.

The absorbent stem power of the *Laminaria* for taking up iodine is very large; and this element is afterwards brought out by fire in the kelp kilns of Ireland and Scotland. Sea Tang acts most beneficially against the various forms of scrofulous disease; and signally relieves some rheumatic affections. It is also used largely in the making of glass.

Likewise for scrofula, seawater, being rich in chlorides and iodides, has proved both curative and preventive. Dr. Sena, of Valencia, gave bread made with seawater in the Misericordia Hospital for cases of scrofulous disease, and other states of defective nutrition, with singular success.

Another Laminaria (*Saccharina*), with a single olive yellow semi-transparent frond, yields an abundance of sweet "mannit" when boiled and evaporated.

The Bladderwrack (*Fucus vesiculosus*), Kelpware, or Our Lady's Wrack, is found on most of our sea coasts in heavy brown masses of coarse-looking Sea Weed, which cover, and shelter many small algæ. Kelp is an impure carbonate of soda containing sulphate, and chloride of sodium, with a little charcoal.

By its characteristic bladders, or vesicles studded about the blades of the branched narrowish fronds, this Sea Weed may be easily known.

These bladders are full of a glutinous substance, which makes the weed valuable both as a remedy for the glandular troubles of scrofula, and, when bottled in rum, as an embrocation, such as is specially useful for strengthening the limbs of rickety, or bandy-legged children. Against glandular swellings also the weed is taken internally as a medicine, when burnt to a black powder. An analysis of the Bladderwrack has shown it to contain an empyreumatic oil, sulphur, earthy salts, some iron, and iodine freely. Thus it is very rich in anti-scrofulous elements.

The fluid extract of this Sea Weed has the long standing reputation of safely diminishing an excess of personal fat. It is given for such a purpose three times a day, shortly after meals, in doses of from one to four teaspoonfuls. The remedy should be continued perseveringly, whilst cutting down the supplies of fat, starchy foods, sugar, and malt liquors. When thus taken (as likewise in the concentrated form of a pill, if preferred) the Bladderwrack will especially relieve rheumatic pains; and the sea pod liniment dispensed by many druggists at our chief marine health resorts, proves signally efficacious towards the same end. Furthermore, they prepare a sea-pod essence for applying on a wet compress beneath waterproof tissue to strumous tumours, goitre, and bronchocele; also for old strains and bruises.

This Sea Weed should not be obtained when too fully matured, as it quickly undergoes decomposition.

Wrack is Sea Weed thrown ashore, from *Vrage*, to reject. Wrack Grass (*Zostera Marina*), is a marine plant with long grass-like leaves.

There are four common *Fuci* on our coasts—the *Nodosus* (Knobbed Wrack), the *Vesiculosus* (Bladder Wrack), the *Serratus* (Saw-edged Sea Weed), and the *Caniculatus* (Channeled Sea Weed).

It is by reason of its contained bromine and iodine as safe medicinal elements, the *Fucus vesiculosus* acts in reducing fatness; these elements stimulating all the absorbent glands of the body to increased activity.

In common with the other *Fuci* it furnishes mannite, an odorous oil, a bitter principle, mucilage, and ash, this last constituent abounding in the bromine and iodine.

For internal use, a decoction may be made with from two to four drachms of the weed to a pint of water, boiled together for a few minutes; and for external application to enlarged or hardened glands, the bruised weed may be applied as a cold poultice.

This Bladder Wrack is reputed to be the *Anti-polyscarcique* nostrum of Count Mattæi.

Although diminishing fat it does no harm by inducing any atrophied wasting of the breast glands, or of the testicles.

The Bladderwrack yields a rich produce to the seaside agriculturist highly useful as manure for the potato field and for other crops: and it is gathered for this purpose all along the British coast. In Jersey and Guernsey it is called *vraic.* Among the Hebrides, cheeses, whilst drying, are covered with the ashes of this weed which abounds in salt. Patients who have previously suffered much from rheumatism about the body and limbs have found themselves entirely free from any such pains or trouble whilst taking the extract of *Fucus Vesiculosus* (Bladderwrack). This Sea Weed is in perfection only during early and middle summer. For fresh sprains and bruises a hot decoction of the Bladderwrack should be used at first as a fomentation; and, afterwards, a cold essence of the weed should be rubbed in, or applied on wet lint beneath light thin waterproof tissue, or oiled silk, as a compress: this to be changed as often as hot or dry.

Laver is the popular name given to some edible Sea Weeds—the *Porphyra lanciniata,* and the *Ulva latissima.* The same title was formerly bestowed by Pliny on an aquatic plant now unknown, and called also Sloke, or Sloken.

Porphyra, from a Greek word meaning "purple," is the true Laver, or Sloke. It is slimy, or semi-gelatinous of consistence when served at table, having been stewed for several hours until quite tender, and then being eaten with butter, vinegar, and pepper. At the London Reform Club Laver is provided every day in a silver saucepan at dinner, garnished with lemons, to flank the roast leg of mutton. Others prefer it cooked with leeks and onions, or pickled, and eaten with oil and lemon juice. The Englishman calls this Sea Weed, Laver; the Irishman, Sloke; the Scotchman, Slack; and the student, *Porphyra*. It varies in size and colour between tidemarks, being sometimes long and ribbon-like, of a violet or purple hue; sometimes long and broad, whilst changing to a reddish purple, or yellow.

It is very wholesome, and preventive of scurvy, being therefore valuable on sea voyages, as it will keep good for a long time in closed tin vessels.

The *Ulva latissima* is a deep-green Sea Weed, called by the fishermen Oyster Green, because employed to cover over oysters. This is likewise known as Laver, because sometimes substituted by epicures for the true Laver (*Porphyra*) when the latter cannot be got; but it is not by any means as good. The name *Ulva* is from *ul*, meaning "water."

Sea Spinach (*Salsolacea—Spirolobea*) is a Saltwort found growing on the shore in Hampshire and other parts of England, the best of all wild vegetables for the table, having succulent leaves shaped like worms, and being esteemed as an excellent antiscorbutic.

The Sea Beet—a Chenopod—which grows plentifully on our shores, gave origin to the cultivated Beetroot of our gardens. Its name was derived from a fancied resemblance borne by its seed vessels when swollen with seed to the Greek letter B (*beta*).

> "Nomine cum Graio cui litera proxima primœ
> Pangitur in cerâ docti mucrone magistri."
>
> "The Greeks gave its name to the Beet from their alphabet's second letter,
> As an Attic teacher wrote it on wax with a sharp stiletto."

By the Grecians the Beet was offered on silver to Apollo in his temple at Delphi. A pleasant wine may be made from its roots, and its juice when applied with a brush is an excellent cosmetic. The Mangel Wurzel, also a variety of Beet, means literally, "scarcity root."

Another Sea Weed, the Bladderlocks (*Alaria esculenta*), "henware," "honeyware," "murlins," is edible, the thick rib which runs through the frond being the part chosen. This abounds on the Northern coasts of England and Scotland, being of a clear olive yellow colour, with a stem as thick as a small goosequill, varying in length, with its fronds, from three to twenty feet. The fruit appears as if partially covered with a brown crust consisting of transparent spore cases set on a stalk in a cruciform manner.

Common Coraline (*Corallina Anglica*), a Sea Weed of a whitish colour, tinged with purple and green, and of a firm substance, is famous for curing worms.

The presence of gold in sea water, even as surrounding our own islands, has been sufficiently proved; though, as yet, its extraction is a costly and uncertain process. One analyst has estimated that the amount of gold contained in the oceans of the globe must be ten million tons, without counting the possible quantity locked up in floating icebergs about the Poles.

Professor Liveredge, of the Sydney University, examined sea water collected off the Australian coast, as also some from Northern shores, and obtained gold, from five-tenths to eight-tenths of a grain per ton of the sea water. It occurs as the chloride, and the bromide of gold; which salts, as recently shown by Dr. Compton Burnett, when administered in doses almost infinitesimally small, are of supreme value for the cure of epilepsy, secondary syphilis, sexual debility, and some disorders of the heart.

Dr. Russell wrote on the uses of sea water in diseases of the glands. He found the soapy mucus within the vesicles of the Bladderwrack an excellent resolvent, and most useful in dispersing scrofulous swellings. He advises rubbing the tumour with these vesicles bruised in the hand, and afterwards washing the part with sea water.

SELFHEAL.

SEVERAL Herbal Simples go by the name of Selfheal among our wild hedge plants, more especially the Sanicle, the common Prunella, and the Bugle.

The first of these is an umbelliferous herb, growing frequently in woods, having dull white flowers, in panicled heads, which are succeeded by roundish seeds covered with hooked prickles: the Wood Sanicle (*Europœa*).

It gets its name Sanicle, perhaps, from the Latin verb *sanare*, "to heal, or make sound;" or, possibly, as a corruption of St. Nicholas, called in German *St. Nickel*, who, in the *Tale of a Tub*, is said to have interceded with God in favour of two children whom an innkeeper had murdered and pickled in a pork tub; and he obtained their restoration to life.

Anyhow, the name Sanicle was supposed in the middle ages to mean "curative," whatever its origin:

thus, *Qui a la Bugle, et la Sanicle fait aux chirurgiens la nicle*—"He who uses Sanicle and Bugle need have no dealings with the doctor." Lyte and other herbalists say concerning the Sanicle: "It makes whole and sound all wounds and hurts, both inward and outward."

> "Celui qui Sanicle a
> De plaie affaire il n'a."
>
> "Who the Sanicle hath
> At the surgeon may laugh."

The name Prunella (which belongs more rightly to another herb) has been given to the Sanicle, perhaps, through its having been originally known as Brunella, Brownwort, both because of the brown colour of its spikes, and from its being supposed to cure the disease called in Germany *die braune*, a kind of quinsy; on the doctrine of signatures, because the corolla resembles a throat with swollen glands.

The Sanicle is popularly employed in Germany and France as a remedy for profuse bleeding from the lungs, bowels, womb, and urinary organs; also for the staying of dysenteric diarrhœa. The fresh juice of the herb may be given in tablespoonful doses.

As yet no analysis has been made of this plant; but evidence of tannin in its several parts is afforded by the effects produced when these are remedially applied.

The *Prunella vulgaris* is a distinct plant from the Self Heal, or Sanicle, and belongs to the labiate order of herbs. It grows commonly in waste places about England, and bears pink flowers, being sometimes called Slough heal. This is incorrect, as the surgical term "slough" was not used until long after the Prunella and the Sanicle became named Self-heal. Each of these was applied as a vulnerary, not to sloughing sores, but to fresh cut wounds.

The *Prunella vulgaris* has a flattened calyx, and whorls of purplish blue flowers, which are collected in a head. It is also known as Carpenter's Herb, perhaps, from its corolla, when seen in profile, being shaped like a bill hook; and therefore, on the doctrine of signatures, it was supposed to heal wounds inflicted by edge tools; whence it was likewise termed Hook-heal and Sicklewort, and in Yorkshire, Black man.

By virtue of its properties as a vulnerary it has also been called *Consolida;* but the daisy is the true *Consolida minor.*

"The decoction of Prunell," says Gerard, "made with wine and water, doth join together and make whole and sound all wounds, both inward and outward, even as Bugle doth. To be short, it serveth for the same that the Bugle serveth; and in the world there are not two better wound herbs, as hath been often proved."

The Bugle, or middle Comfrey, is also a Sanicle, because of its excellence for healing wounds, in common with the Prunella and the true Sanicle. It grows in almost every wood, and copse, and moist shadowy place, being constantly reckoned among the Consounds.

This herb (*Ajuga reptans*) is of the labiate order, bearing dark blue or purple flowers, whorled, and crowded into a spike. Its decoction, "when drunk, healeth and maketh sound all wounds of the body." "It is so singular good for all sorts of hurts that none who know its usefulness will be ever without it. If the virtues of it make you fall in love with it (as they will if you be wise), keep a syrup of it to take inwardly, and an ointment and plaister of it to use outwardly, always by you."

The chemical principles of the Prunella and the Bugle

resemble those of other Labiate herbs, comprising a volatile oil, some bitter principle, tannin, sugar, and cellulose. The Ladies' Mantle, Alchemilla—a common inconspicuous weed, found everywhere—is called Great Sanicle, also Parsley-breakstone, or Piercestone, because supposed to be of great use against stone in the bladder. It contains tannin abundantly, and is said to promote quiet sleep if placed under the pillow at night. "*Endymionis somnum dormire.*"

SHEPHERD'S PURSE.

THE small Shepherd's Purse (*Bursa Capsella Pastoris*) is one of the most common of wayside English weeds. The name *Capsella* signifies a little box, in allusion to the seed pods. It is a Cruciferous plant, made familiar by the diminutive pouches, or flattened pods at the end of its branching stems. This herb is of natural growth in most parts of the world, but varies in luxuriance according to soil and situation, whilst thickly strewn over the whole surface of the earth, facing alike the heat of the tropics, and the rigours of the arctic regions; even, if trodden underfoot, it rises again and again with ever enduring vitality, as if designed to fulfil some special purpose in the far-seeing economy of nature. It lacks the winged valves of the *Thlaspi*.

Our old herbalists called it St. James's Wort, as a gift from that Saint to the people for the cure of various diseases, St. Anthony's Fire, and several skin eruptions. In France, too, the plant goes by the title of *Fleur de Saint Jacques*. It flowers from early in Spring until Autumn, and has, particularly in Summer, an acrid bitter taste. Other names for the herb are, "Case weed," "Pick pocket," and "Mother's heart," as called so by children. If a pod is picked they raise the cry, "You've plucked out your mother's heart." Small birds are fond of the seeds.

Bombelon, a French chemist, has reported most favourably about this herb as of prompt use to arrest bleedings and floodings, when given in the form of a fluid extract, one or two teaspoonfuls for a dose. He explains that our hedge-row Simple contains a tannate, an alkaloid "bursine," (which resembles sulphocyansinapine), and bursinic acid, this last constituent being the active medicinal principle. English chemists now prepare and dispense the fluid extract of the herb. This is given for dropsy in the U. S. America as a diuretic; from half to one teaspoonful in water for a dose.

Dr. Von Ehrenwall relates a recent case of female flooding, which had defied all the ordinary remedies, and for which, at the suggestion of a neighbour, he tried an infusion of the Shepherd's Purse weed, with the result that the bleeding stopped after the first teacupful of the infusion had been taken a few minutes. Since then he has used the plant in various forms of hæmorrhage with such success that he considers it the most reliable of our medicines for staying fluxes of blood. "Shepherd's Purse stayeth bleeding in any part of the body, whether the juice thereof be drunk, or whether it be used poultice-like, or in bath, or any way else."

Besides the ordinary constituents of herbs, it is found to contain six per cent. of soft resin, together with a sulphuretted volatile oil, which is identical with that of Mustard, as obtained likewise from the bitter Candytuft, *Iberis amara.*

Its medicinal infusion should be made with an ounce of the plant to twelve ounces of water, reduced by boiling to half-a-pint; then a wineglassful may be given for a dose.

The herb and its seeds were employed in former times to promote the regular monthly flow in women.

It bears, further, the name of Poor Man's Permacetty (or Spermaceti), "the sovereignst remedy for bruises;"—"perhaps," says Dr. Prior, "as a joke on the Latin name *Bursa pastoris*, or 'Purse,' because to the poor man this is always his best remedy." And in some parts of England the Shepherd's Purse is known as Clapper Pouch, in allusion to the licensed begging of lepers at our crossways in olden times with a bell and a clapper. They would call the attention of passers-by with the bell, or with the clapper, and would receive their alms in a cup, or a basin, at the end of a long pole. The clapper was an instrument made of two or three boards, by rattling which the wretched lepers incited people to relieve them. Thus they obtained the name of Rattle Pouches, which appellation has been extended to this small plant, in allusion to the little purses which it hangs out by the wayside. Because of these miniature pockets the herb is also named Toy Wort; and Pick Purse, through being supposed to steal the goodness of the land from the farmer. In Queen Elizabeth's time leper hospitals were common throughout England; and many of the sufferers were banished to the Lizard, in Cornwall.

The Shepherd's Purse is now announced as the chief remedy of the seven "marvellous medicines" prepared by Count Mattæi, of Bologna, which are believed by his disciples to be curative of diseases otherwise intractable, such as cancer, internal aneurism, and destructive leprosy.

Count Mattæi professed to extract certain vegetable

electricities found stored up in this, and some other plants, and to utilize them for curative purposes with almost miraculous success. His other herbs, as revealed by a colleague, Count Manzetti, are the Knotgrass, the Water Betony, the Cabbage, the Stonecrop, the Houseleek, the Feverfew, and the Watercress. Lady Paget, when interviewing Count Mattæi, gathered that Shepherd's Purse is the herb which furnishes the so-called "blue electricity," of extraordinary efficacy in controlling hæmorrhages.

Small birds are fond of the seeds: and the young radical leaves are sold in Philadelphia as greens in the Spring.

SILVERWEED.

Two *Potentillas* occur among our common native plants, and possess certain curative virtues (as popularly supposed), the Silverweed and the Cinquefoil. They belong to the Rose tribe, and grow abundantly on our roadsides, being useful as mild astringents.

The *Potentilla anserina* (Silverweed) is found, as its adjective suggests, where geese are put to feed.

Country folk often call it Cramp Weed: but it is more generally known as Goose Tansy, or Goose Gray, because it is a spurious Tansy, fit only for a goose; or, perhaps, because eaten by geese. Other names for the herb are Silvery Cinquefoil, and Moorgrass. It occurs especially on clay soils, being recognised by its pinnate white silvery leaves, and its conspicuous golden flowers.

In Yorkshire the roots are known as "moors," which boys dig up and eat in the winter; whilst swine will also devour them greedily. They have then a sweet taste like parsnips. In Scotland, also, they are eaten roasted, or boiled; and sometimes, in hard seasons, when other provisions were scanty, these roots have been known to support the inhabitants of certain islands for months together.

Both the roots and the leaves are mildly astringent; so that their infusion helps to stay diarrhœa, and the fluxes of women; making also with honey a useful gargle. The leaf is of an exquisitely beautiful shape, and may be seen carved on the head of many an old stall in Church, or Cathedral. By reason of its five leaflets, this gives to the plant the title "five leaf," or five fingered grass, *Pentedaktulon*. *Potentilla* comes from the Latin *potens*, as alluding to the medicinal virtues of the species.

In former days the Cinquefoil was much affected as a heraldic device through the number of the leaflets answering to the five senses of man; whilst the right to bear Cinquefoil was considered an honourable distinction to him who had worthily mastered his senses, and conquered his passions.

Silverweed tea is excellent to relieve cramps of the belly; and compresses, wrung out of a hot decoction of the herb, may at the same time be helpfully applied over the seat of the cramps. A potent Anglo-Saxon charm against crampy bellyache was to wear a gold ring with a Dolphin engraved on it, and bearing in Greek the mystic words:—"Theos keleuei mee keneoon ponois," "*God forbids the pains of colic.*" This acted doubtless by mental suggestion, as in the cure of warts. The knee-cap bone, or patella, of a sheep, known locally as the "cramp-bone," is worn in Northamptonshire for a like purpose; also the application of a gold wedding ring (first wetted with saliva, an ingredient in the holy salve of the Saxons), to a stye threatened in an eyelid is often found to disperse the swelling; but in this case it may be, that a sulphocyanide of gold is formed with the spittle, which promotes the cure by absorption.

A strong infusion, if used as a lotion, will check the bleeding of piles, the ordinary infusion being meantime taken as a medicine.

The good people of Leicestershire were accustomed in bygone days to prevent pitting by small-pox with the use of Silverweed fomentations. A distilled water of the herb takes away freckles, spots, pimples in the face, and sunburnings; whilst all parts of the plant are found to contain tannin.

The Creeping Cinquefoil (*Potentilla reptans*) grows also abundantly on meadow banks, having astringent roots, which have been used medicinally since the times of Hippocrates and Dioscorides.

They were found to cure intermittent fevers, such as used to prevail in marshy or ill-drained lands much more commonly than now in Great Britain; though country folk still use the infusion or decoction for the same purpose in some districts; also for jaundice.

Likewise, because of the tannin contained in the outer bark of the roots, their decoction is useful against diarrhœa; and their infusion as a gargle for relaxed sore throats. But, except in mild cases, other more positively astringent herbs are to be preferred. The roots afford a useful red dye.

SKULLCAP.

A useful medicinal tincture (H.) is made from the Skullcap (*Scutellaria*), which is a Labiate plant of frequent growth on the banks of our rivers and ponds, having bright blue flowers, with a tube longer than the calyx. This is the greater variety (*Galericulata*). There is a lesser variety (*Scutellaria minor*), which is infrequent, and grows in bogs about the West of England, with flowers of a dull purple colour. Each kind gets its name from the Latin *scutella*, "a little cap," which the calyx resembles, and is therefore called Hood Wort, or Helmet flower. The upper lip of the calyx bulges outward about its middle, and finally closes down like a lid over the fruit. When the seed is ripe it opens again.

Provers of the tincture (H.) in toxic doses experienced giddiness, stupor, and confusion of mind, twitchings of the limbs, intermission of the pulse, and other symptoms indicative of the epileptiform "petit mal"; for which morbid affection, and the disposition thereto, the said tincture, of a diluted strength, in small doses, has been successfully given.

The greater Skullcap contains, in common with most other plants of the same order, a volatile oil, tannin, fat, some bitter principle, sugar, and cellulose.

If a decoction of the plant is made with two ounces of the herb to eight ounces of water, and is taken for some weeks continuously in recent epilepsy, or when the disease has only functional causes, it will often prove very beneficial. Likewise, this decoction, in common with an extract of the herb, has been given curatively for intermittent fever and ague, as well as for some depressed, and disordered states of the nervous system.

A dried extract of the lesser Skullcap (*Lateriflora*) is made by chemists, and given in doses of from one to three grains as a pill to relieve severe hiccough, and as a nervine stimulant; also for the sleeplessness of an exhausted brain.

SLOE.

THE parent tree which produces the Sloe is the Blackthorn, our hardy, thorny hedgerow shrub (*Prunus spinosa*), Greek *Prounee*, common everywhere, and starting into blossom of a pinky white about the middle of March before a leaf appears, each branchlet ending in a long thorn projecting beyond the flowers at right angles to the stem. From the conspicuous blackness of its rind at the time of flowering, the tree is named Blackthorn, and the spell of harsh unkindly cold weather which prevails about then goes by the name of "blackthorn winter."

The term Sloe, or Sla, means not the fruit but the hard trunk, being connected with a verb signifying to slay, or strike, probably because the wood of this tree was used as a flail, and nowadays makes a bludgeon.

In the Autumn every branch becomes clustered with the oval blue-black fruit presently covered with a fine purple bloom; and until mellowed by the early frosts, this fruit is very harsh and sour.

The leaves, when they unfold late in the spring, are small and narrow. If dried, they make a very fair substitute for tea, and when high duties were placed on imported tea, it was usual to find the sloe trees stripped of their marketable foliage.

Furthermore, the dark ruby juice of Sloes enters largely into the manufacture of British port wine, to which it communicates a beautiful deep red colour, and a pleasant sub-acid roughness. Letters marked upon linen fabric with this juice, when used fresh, will not wash out.

If obtained by expression from the unripe fruit, it is very useful as an astringent medicine, and is a popular remedy for stopping a flow of blood from the nose. It may be gently boiled to a thick consistence, and will then keep throughout the year without losing its virtues. Winter-picks is a provincial name for the Sloe fruit, and winter-pick wine takes the place of port in the rustic cellar. The French call them Prunelles.

Sloe-blossoms make a safe, harmless, laxative medicine. To use these, "Boil them up, and drink a cup of the tea daily for three or four days; it will act gently, painlessly, but thoroughly." The syrup is especially useful for children.

Country people bury the Sloes in jars to preserve them for winter use; and the bush which bears this fruit is sometimes called, provincially, Scroggs.

Sloes may be gathered when ripe on a dry day, picked clean, and put into jars or bottles, without any boiling or other process, and then covered with loaf sugar; a tablespoonful of brandy should presently be added, and the jar sealed. By Christmas, the syrup formed from the juice, the sugar, and the spirit, will have covered and saturated the fruit, and then a couple of tablespoonfuls will not only make an agreeable dessert liqueur, but will act as an astringent cordial of a very pleasant sort.

In Somersetshire the Sloe is named Snag (as corrupted from "Slag," *i. e.*, Sloe). The juice is viscid, and when thickened to dryness, is the German Gum Acacia.

Those provers who have taken experimentally a tincture made from the wood and bark and leaves of the Blackthorn, all had to complain of sharp pains in the right eyeball; and accordingly the diluted tincture is found, when administered in small quantities, to give signal relief for ciliary neuralgia, arising from a functional disorder of the structures within the eyeball. Dr. Hughes says: "It not only relieves such pains, but also checks the inflammation, and clears the vision." The medicinal tincture is made (H.) with proof spirit of wine from the flower buds collected in early spring before they expand. The Sloe has been employed as a styptic ever since the time of Dioscorides. "From the effects," says Withering, "which I have repeatedly observed to follow a wound from the thorns, I find reason for believing that there is something poisonous in their nature, particularly in the autumn."

Next to the Sloe in order of development comes the Bullace (*Prunus insititia*), a shrub with fewer thorns, and bearing its flowers after the leaves have begun to unfold.

The fruit is five times as big as the Sloe, but likewise of a delicate bluish colour. It is named from the Latin plural *bullas*, meaning the round bosses which the Romans put on their bridles. Lydgate (1440) used the phrase, "As bright as Bullaces," in one of his poems. In Lincolnshire the blossom is known as "Bully bloom," and the fruit are "Bullies." After harvest the women and children go out gathering them for Bullace-wine. Boys in France call Sloes "*Sibarelles*," because it is impossible to whistle immediately after eating them. Some writers say the signification of "Sloe" is "that which sets the teeth on edge."

Finally comes the true Wild Plum (*Prunus domestica*), which is far less common than the two preceding sorts. Its flowers are large, and in small clusters, whilst the leaves unfold with the blossom. The fruit is a small brownish plum, intensely sharp and acrid to the taste, and the tree is thorny. Only in this latter respect does it differ from an inferior kind of garden plum of which the cultivation has been neglected.

The cultivated Plum has been developed from the Wild Plum, and has been made to exhibit some fifty varieties of form and character. The fruit of Damascus was formerly much valued, being now known as Damascenes, (damsons), Damasin, or Damask prune.

All the Wild Plums develop thorns; but the cultivated kinds have entirely cast them off. The Plum, as a fruit, was known to the Romans in Cato's time, but not the tree.

"Little Jack Horner," says the familiar nursery rhyme, "sat in a corner, eating a Christmas pie; he put in his thumb, and he pulled out a plum, and said 'What a good boy am I.'"

> "Inquit, et unum extraheus prunum,
> Horner, quam fueris nobile pueris
> Exemplar imitabile"!

When ripe, cultivated Plums are cooling and slightly laxative, especially the French fruit, which is dried and bottled for dessert. They are useful for costive habits, and may be made into an electuary; but, when unripe, Plums provoke choleraic diarrhœa. The garden fruit contains less sugar than cherries, but a large amount of gelatinising pectose. Dr. Johnson was specially fond of veal pie with plums and sugar. He taunted Boswell about the need of gardeners to produce in Scotland what grows wild in England. "Pray, Sir," said he, "are you ever able to bring the Sloe to perfection there?" On Change a hundred thousand pounds are whimsically known as "a plum," and a million of money is "a marigold." Lately a Chicago physician whilst officiating at a Reformatory found that the boys behaved themselves much better when taking prunes in their diet than at any other time. These act, he supposes, on certain organs which are the seats, and centres of the passions.

From France comes the Greengage, named in that country (out of compliment to the Queen of Francis the First) *La Reine Claude.* It was brought to England from the Monastery of La Grande Chartreuse, about the middle of the eighteenth century, by the Rev. John Gage, brother to the owner of Hengrave Hall, near Coldham, Suffolk; and taking his name this fruit soon became diffused throughout England.

French Prunes are conveyed to England in their dried state from Marseilles. With their pulp, figs, tamarinds, and senna, the officinal "lenitive electuary" is made; and apothecaries prepare a medicinal tincture from the fresh flower-buds of the Blackthorn.

Culpeper says: "All Plumbs are under Venus, and are like women—some better, some worse."

In Sussex and some other counties, a superstitious fear attaches itself to the Blackthorn in bloom, because of the apparent union of life and death when the tree is clothed in early Spring with white flowers, but is destitute of leaves; so that to carry, or wear a piece of Blackthorn in blossom, is thought to signify bringing a death token.

SOAPWORT.

The Soapwort (*Saponaria officinalis*) grows commonly in England near villages, on roadsides, and by the margins of woods, in moist situations. It belongs to the *Caryophyllaceæ*, or Clove and Pink tribe of plants; and a double flowered variety of it is met with in gardens. This is Miss Mitford's "Spicer" in *Our Village*. It is sometimes named "Bouncing Bet," and "Fuller's herb."

The root has a sweetish bitter taste, but no odour. It contains resin and mucilage, in addition to saponin, which is its leading principle, and by virtue of which decoctions of the root produce a soapy froth. Saponin is likewise found in the nuts of the Horse-chestnut tree, and in the Scarlet Pimpernel.

A similar soapy quality is also observed in the leaves, so much so that they have been used by mendicant monks as a substitute for soap in washing their clothes. This "saponin" has considerable medicinal efficacy, being especially useful for the cure of inveterate syphilis without giving mercury. Several writers of note aver that such cases have been cured by a decoction of the plant; though perhaps the conclusion has been arrived at through the resemblance between the roots of Soapwort and those of Sarsaparilla.

Gerard says: "Ludovicus Septalius, when treating of decoctions in use against the French poxes, mentions the singular effect of the Soapwort against that filthy disease"; but, he adds, "it is somewhat of an ungrateful taste, and therefore must be reserved for the poorer sort of patients." He employed it *sæpe et sæpius.*

The *Pharmacopœia Chirurgica* of 1794, teaches: "A decoction of this plant has been found useful for scrofulous, impetiginous, and syphilitic affections. Boil down half a pound of the bruised fresh herb in a gallon of distilled water to two quarts, and give from one to three pints in the twenty-four hours."

Formerly the herb was called Bruisewort, and was thought of service for contusions. It will remove stains, or grease almost as well as soap, but contains no starch.

Saponin, when smelt, excites long-continued sneezing; if injected or administered, it reduces the frequency and force of the heart's pulsations, paralyzing the cardiac nerves, and acting speedily on the vaso-motor centres, so as to arrest the movements of the heart; on which principle, when given in a diluted form, and in doses short of all toxic effects, it has proved of signal use in low typhoid inflammation of the lungs, where restorative stimulation of the heart is to be aimed at.

Also, likewise for passive suppression of the female monthly flow, it will act beneficially as a stimulant of the womb to incite its periodical function.

In a patient who took a poisonous quantity of Saponin at Saint Petersburg all the muscular contractile sensitiveness was completely abolished; whilst, nevertheless, all the bodily functions were normally performed. *Per contra*, this effect should be a curative guide in the use of Soapwort as a Simple.

Saponin is found again in the root and unripe seeds of the Corn Cockle, and in all parts of the Nottingham Catch-fly except the seeds; also in the wild Lychnis, and some others of the Pink tribe.

SOLOMON'S SEAL.

THE Solomon's Seal (*Convallaria polygonatum*) is a handsome woodland plant by no means uncommon throughout England, particularly in Berkshire, Bucks, Hants, Kent, and Suffolk.

It grows to the height of about two feet, bearing along its curved drooping branches handsome bells of pure white, which hang down all along the lower side of the gracefully weeping flower stalks.

The oval leaves are ribbed, and grow alternately from the stem, for which reason the plant is called Ladder-to-heaven; or, "more probably," says Dr. Prior, "from a confusion of *Seal de notre Dame* (our Lady's Seal), with *Echelle de notre Dame* (our Lady's Ladder). The round depressions resembling seal marks, which are found on the root, or the characters which appear when it is cut transversely, gave rise to the notion that Solomon, "who knew the diversities of plants, and the virtues of roots," had set his seal upon this in testimony of its value to man as a medicinal root. The rhizome and herb contain convallarin, asparagin, gum, sugar, starch, and pectin.

In Galen's time the distilled water was used by ladies as a cosmetic for removing pimples and freckles from the skin, "leaving the place fresh, fair, and lovely." During the reign of Elizabeth it had great medical celebrity, so that, as we learn from a contemporary writer, "The roots of Solomon's Seal, stamped whilst fresh and green, and applied, taketh away, in one night, or two at the most, any bruise, black or blue spots gotten by falls, or woman's wilfulness in stumbling upon their hasty husband's fists, or such like," and "that which might be trewly written of this herb as touching the knitting of bones, would seem to some well nigh incredible; yea, although they be but slenderly, and unhandsomely wrapped-up; but common experience teacheth that in the worlde there is not to be found another herbe comparable for the purpose aforesaid. It was given to the patients in ale to drink—as well unto themselves as to their cattle—and applied outwardly in the manner of a pultis."

The name Lady's Seal was conferred on this plant by old writers, as also St. Mary's Seal, *Sigillum sanctæ Mariæ*.

The Arabs understand by Solomon's Seal the figure of a six-pointed star, formed by two equilateral triangles intersecting each other, as frequently mentioned in Oriental tales. Gerard maintains that the name, *Sigillum Solomonis*, was given to the root "partly because it bears marks something like the stamp of a seal, but still more because of the virtue the root hath in sealing or healing up green wounds, broken bones, and such like, being stamp't and laid thereon."

The bottle of brass told of in the *Arabian Nights* as fished up was closed with a stopper of lead bearing the

"Seal of our Lord Suleyman." This was a wonderful talisman which was said to have come down from heaven with the great name of God engraved upon it, being composed of brass for the good genii, and iron for the evil jinn.

The names *Convallaria polygonatum* signify "growth in a valley," and "many jointed." Other titles of the plant are Many Knees, Jacob's Ladder, Lily of the Mountain, White wort, and Seal wort.

The Turks eat the young shoots of this plant just as we eat Asparagus.

SORREL.

(*See* "Dock," *page* 157.)

SOUTHERNWOOD.

SOUTHERNWOOD, or Southern Wormwood, though it does not flower in this country, is well known as grown in every cottage garden for its aromatic fragrance. It is the *Artemisia Abrotanum*, a Composite plant of the Wormwood tribe, commonly known as "Old Man." Pliny explains that this title is borne because of the plant being a sexual restorative to those in advanced years, as explained by Macer :—

> "Hœc etiam venerem pulvino subdita tantum
> Incitat."

Pliny says further that this herb is potent against syphilis, and *veneficia quibus coitus inhibeatur*. Its odour is lemon-like, and depends on a volatile essential oil which consists chiefly of absinthol, and is common to the other Wormwoods. "Abrotanum" is a Greek term. Another appellation of this plant is "Lad's love," and "Boy's love," from the making of an ointment with its ashes, to be used by youngsters for promoting the growth of the beard. "Cinis Abrotani barbam segnius tardiusque enascentem cum aliquo dictorum oleorum elicit." The plant is found in Spain and Italy as an indigenous herb. Its leaves and tops have a strong aromatic odour, and a penetrating warm, bitterish taste which is rather nauseous. An infusion, or tea, of the herb is agreeable : but a decoction is distasteful, having lost much of the aroma. The plant was formerly in great repute as a cordial against hysterics, and to strengthen the stomach of a weakly person. It will expel both round worms and thread worms, whilst its presence is hostile to moths; and hence has been got one of its French names, "Garde robe." Externally it will promote the growth of the hair. In Lincolnshire it is known as "Motherwood."

SOWBREAD, or CYCLAMEN.

(*See page* 450, "Primrose.")

SPEEDWELL.

THIS little plant, with its exquisite flowers of celestial blue, grows most familiarly in our hedgerows throughout the Spring, and early Summer. Its brilliant, gemlike blossoms show a border of pale purple, or delicate violet, marked with deeper veins or streaks. But the lovely circlet of petals is most fragile, and falls off at a touch; whence are derived the names Speedwell, Farewell, Good-bye, and Forget-me-not.

Speedwell is a Veronica (*fero*, "I bring," *nikee*, "victory"), which tribe was believed to belong especially to birds. So the plant bears the name "Birds' Eyes," as well as "Blue Eyes," "Strike Fires," and "Mammy Die" (because of the belief that if the herb were brought into a family the mother would die within the year). Turner calls the plant "Fluellin," or "Lluellin," a name "the shentleman of Wales have given it because it saved her nose, which a disease had almost gotten from her." Further, it is the Paul's Betony, called after Paulus Œgineta. The plant belongs to the Scrofula-curing order.

It is related that a shepherd observed how a stag, whose hind-quarters were covered with a scabby eruption brought about through the bite of a wolf, cured itself by rolling on plants of the Speedwell, and by eating its leaves. Thereupon he commended the plant to his king, and thus promoted his majesty's restoration to health.

In Germany it bears the title *Grundheele*, from having cured a king of France who suffered from a leprosy for eight years, which disease is named *grund* in German. At one time the herb was held in high esteem as a specific for gout in this country, but it became adulterated, and its fame suffered a downfall.

The only sensible quality of the Speedwell is the powerful astringency of its leaves, and this property serves to protect it from herbivorous foes.

It has been long held famous among countryfolk as an excellent plant for coughs, asthma, and pulmonary consumption. The leaves are bitter, with a rough taste; and a decoction of the whole plant stimulates the kidneys. The infusion promotes perspiration, and reduces feverishness. The juice may be boiled into a syrup with honey, for asthma and catarrhs.

When applied outwardly, it is said to cure the itch; and by some it has been asserted that a continued use of the infusion will overcome sterility, if taken daily as a tea. The French still distinguish the plant as the

Thé d'Europe; and a century ago it was used commonly in Germany in substitution for tea. As a medicine, by reason of its astringency, it became called *Polychresta herba veronica.*

"My freckles with the Speedwell's juices washed," says Alfred Austin, our Poet Laureate.

The Germans also name this plant *Ehren-preis*, or Prize of Honour, which fact favours the supposition of its being the true "Forget-me-not," or *souveigne vous de moy*, as legendary on knightly collars of yore to commemorate a famous joust fought in 1465 between the most accomplished champions of England and France.

The present Forget-me-not is a *Myosotis*, or Mouse Ear, or Scorpion Grass.

In Somersetshire, the pretty little Germander Speedwell is known as Cat's Eye: and because seeming to reflect by its azure colour the beautiful blue firmament above, this pure-tinted blossom has got its name of *veron eikon*, the "true image" (*Veronica*); just as the napkin with which a compassionate maiden wiped the face of Christ on the morning of His crucifixion, held imprinted for ever on its fabric a miraculous portrait, which led to her being afterwards canonised on this account as Saint Veronica.

The Emperor Charles the Fifth of Spain is said to have derived much relief to his gout from the use of this herb. It contains tannin, and a particular bitter principle.

SPINACH.

SPINACH (*Lapathum hortense*) is a Persian plant which has been cultivated in our gardens for about two hundred years; and considerably longer on the Continent. Some say the Spinach was originally brought from Spain. It was produced by monks in France at the middle of the 14th century.

This is a light vegetable, easily digested, and rather laxative, besides having some wonderful properties ascribed to its use. Its sub-order, the Saltworts (*Salsolaceæ*), are found growing in marshes by the seashore, and as weeds by waste places, serving some of them to expel worms.

"Spinach," says John Evelyn, "if crude, the oft'ner kept out of sallets the better; but being boiled to a pulp, and without other water than its own moisture, is a most excellent condiment with butter, vinegar, or lemon, for almost all sorts of boiled flesh, and may accompany a sick man's diet. 'Tis laxative and emollient, and therefore profitable for the aged." Spinach is richer in iron than the yolk of the egg, which contains more than beef. Its juice produced in cooking the leaves without adding any water is a wholesome drink, and improves the complexion.

It was with a delicate offering of "gammon and spinach" in his hands, Mr. Anthony Roley, of nursery fame, went so sadly a wooing:—

> "Ranula furtivos statuebat quœrere amores:
> Me miserum! tristi Rolius ore gemit.
> Ranula furtivos statuebat quœrere amores,
> Mater sive daret, sive negaret iter."

A wild species of Spinach, the "Good King Henry," grows in England, and is popular as a pot herb in Lincolnshire.

SPINDLE TREE (Celastraceæ).

During the autumn, in our woody hedgerows a shrub becomes very conspicuous by bearing numerous rose-coloured floral capsules, strikingly brilliant, each with a scarlet and orange-coloured centre. This is the Spindle Tree (*Euonymus*), so called because it furnishes wood for spindles, or skewers, whence it is also named Prickwood, Skewerwood, and Gadrise, or Gad Rouge. The word "gad" is used in our western counties for a stick pointed at both ends to fasten down thatch. The Spindle Tree has a green bark, and glossy leaves, producing only small greenish flowers: whilst the pendulous ornaments so brilliantly borne in autumn are four-lobed capsules of a pale red hue, which open out and disclose ruddy orange-coloured seeds wrapped in a scarlet arillus. It is further known as the Louseberry Tree, from the fruit being applied to destroy lice in children's heads, whilst its powdered bark will kill nits, and serve to remove scurf. Other popular titles owned by this shrub are "gatter," "gatten," and "gatteridge." The ripe fruit, from which a medicinal tincture is prepared, furnishes euonymin, a golden resin, which is purgative and emetic. This acts specially on the liver, and promotes a free flow of bile. The plant also yields asparagin, and euonic acid. An ointment is made with the fruits: and the powdered resin is given in doses of from half-a-grain to two grains.

In the United States of America, this tree is the Wahoo, or Burning Bush. The green leaves of one species are eaten by the Arabs to induce watchfulness. In allusion to the actively irritating properties of the shrub, its name, *Euonymus*, is associated with that of Euonyme, the Mother of the Furies. The bark is mildly aperient and causes no nausea, whilst at the same time stimulating the liver somewhat freely. To make its decoction add an ounce to a pint of water, and boil together slowly. A small wineglassful may be given, when cool, for a dose two or three times in the day. Of the medicinal tincture made from the bark with spirit of wine, a dose of from five to ten drops may be taken with water in the same way. French doctors call the shrub Fusain, or *bonnet de prètre* (birretta). They give the fruit, three or four for a dose, as a purgative in rural districts : and employ the decoction, whilst adding some vinegar, as a lotion against mange in horses and cattle. Also, they make from the wood when slightly charred a delicate crayon for artists.

SPURGE.

CONSPICUOUS in Summer by their golden green leaves, and their striking epergnes of bright emerald blossoms, the Wood Spurge, and the Petty Spurge, adorn our woodlands and gardens commonly and very remarkably. Together with many other allied plants, foreign and indigenous, they yield from their severed stems a milky juice of medicinal properties. The name *Euphorbiœ* has been given to this order from Euphorbus, the favourite physician of Juba, King of Mauritania. All the Spurges possess the same poisonous principle, which may, however, be readily dissipated by heat; and then, in many instances, the root becomes a nourishing and palatable food. For example, the Manioc, a South American Spurge, furnishes a juice which has been known to kill in a few minutes. Nevertheless, its root baked, after first draining away the juice, makes a wholesome bread: and by washing the fresh pulp a starch is produced which we know as Tapioca for our table. This is so sustaining that half-a-pound a day is said to be sufficient of itself to support a healthy man. The Indian rubber and Castor oil plants belong also to this order of Euphorbiœ.

The Wood Spurge, seen so frequently during our country rambles, suggests by its spreading aspect a clever juggler balancing on his upturned chin a widely-branched series of delicate green saucers on fragile stems, which ramify below from a single rod. Each saucer is the bearer again of sub-divided pedicels which stretch out to support other brightly verdant little leafy dishes; so that the whole system of well poised flowering perianths forms a specially handsome candelabrum of emerald (cup-like) bloom. The botanical title Spurge is derived from *expurgare*, to act as a purgative, because of the acrid juice possessing this property. Gerard says "the juice of the Wood Spurge, if given as physic, must be ministered with discretion, and prepared with correctories by some honest apothecary." Furthermore, this juice, "if mixed with honey causeth hair to fall from that part which is anointed therewith, if it be done in the sun." Therefore, what better place may there be than a wooded English meadow on a sunny day for a clean and convenient natural shave by those of the fair sex who, unhappily, own hirsute facial appendages of which they would gladly be rid? *Euphorbia Peplus*, the Petty Spurge, is equally common, and often called "wart weed." It signifies, "Welcome to our house," and turns its flowers towards the sun. The Irish Spurge (*Hiberna*), is so powerful that a small bundle of its bruised plant will kill the fish for several miles down a river. Yet another Spurge (*Lathyris*), a twin brother, bears caper-like seeds which are sometimes dishonestly pickled and sold as a (dangerous) substitute for the toothsome flowerbuds taken in sauce with our boiled mutton. The whole tribe of Spurges contains two hundred genera, and forms, what we call now-a-days, "a large order." The roots of several common kinds are used in making quack medicines, which are unsafe, and violent in action. Because of its milk-white sap the Wood Spurge bears the name in Somersetshire of Virgin Mary's Nipple: and yet in other parts, for the like reason, this plant is known as Devil's Milk. Chemically, most of the Spurges contain caoutchouc, resin, gallic acid, and their particular acrid principle which has not been fully defined. In France the rustics sometimes purge themselves with a dose of from six to twelve grains of the dried Wood Spurge: and its juice is used in this country as an application to destroy warts; also, to be rubbed in behind the ear for ear-ache, or face-ache. The famous surgeon, Cheselden, employed a noted plaster made with the resin of Spurge for relieving disease of the hip joint by counterstimulation. But, to sum up, I would say with wise Gerard, "these herbes by mine advice should not be received into the body, considering there be so many other good and wholesome potions to be made with other herbes that may be taken without peril." Nevertheless, a tincture prepared (H.) from the Wood Spurge, with spirit of wine, may be given admirably in much diluted doses for curing the same severe symptoms which the plant produces when taken to a toxical degree. Offensive diarrhœa, with prolapse of the lowest bowel, will be certainly remedied by four or five drops of this tincture, first decimal strength, with water, every two or three hours: especially if, at the same time, there be a burning and stinging soreness of the throat. Said young Rosamond Berew (1460), in *Malvern Chase*, concerning "a tall gaunt figure," noted for her knowledge of herbs, sometimes called the Witch, but worshipped by the hinds and their children:—"There is Mary, of Eldersfield; I expect she has been on Berthill after Nettles to make a capon sit, or to gather Spurges for ointments."

STITCHWORT.

THE Stitchworts, greater and less (*Stellaria holostea*), grow very abundantly as herbal weeds in all our dry hedges and woods, having tough stems which run closely together, and small white star-like (*stellaria*) blossoms.

These plants are of the same order (Chickweed) as the Alsine and the small Chickweed. Their second name, *Holostea*, signifies "all bones," because the whole plant is very brittle from the flinty elements which its structures contain.

As its title declares, the great Stitchwort has a widespread reputation for curing the stitch, or sharp muscular pain, which often attacks one or other side of the body about the lower ribs.

In the days of the old Saxon leechdoms it was customary against a stitch to make the sign of the cross, and to sing three times over the part :—

> "Longinus miles lanceâ pinxit dominum :
> Restet sanguis, et recedat dolor !"
>
> "The spear of Longinus, the soldier, pierced our Saviour's side :
> May the blood, therefore, quicken : and the pain no longer abide !"

Or some similar form of charm.

Gerard said of folk, in his day : "They are wont to drink it in wine (with the powder of acorns) against the pain in the side, stitches, and such like." But according to Dr. Prior, the herb is named rather because curing the sting (in German *stich*) of venomous reptiles. In country places the Stitchwort is known as Adder's meat, and the Satin Flower : also Miller's Star, Shirtbutton, and Milk Maid, in Yorkshire : the early English name was Bird's Tongue.

About Plymouth, it is dedicated to the Pixies; whilst the lesser variety is called White Sunday, because of its delicate white blossoms, with golden-dusted stamens. These were associated with the new converts baptised in white garments on Low Sunday—the first Sunday after Easter—named, therefore, White Sunday.

But in some parts of Wales the Stitchwort bears the names of Devil's-eyes and Devil's-corn. Boys in Devonshire nickname the herb Snapjack, Snapcrackers, and Snappers.

Parkinson tells us that in former days it was much commended by some to clear the eyes of dimness by dropping the fresh juice into them. Again, Galen said: "The seed is sharp and biting to him that tastes it."

As a modern curative Simple, the Stitchworts, greater and less, stand related to silica, a powerfully remedial preparation of highly pulverised flint. This is because of the exquisitely subdivided flint found abundantly dispersed throughout the structures of Stitchwort plants; which curative principle is eminently useful in chronic diseases, such as cancer, rickets, and scrofula. It exercises a deep and slow action, such as is remedially brought to bear by the Bethesda waters of America, and the powdered oyster shells of Sir Spencer Wells.

The fresh infusion should be steadily taken, a teacupful three times daily, for weeks or months together. It may be made with a pint of boiling water to an ounce of the fresh herb. Likewise, the fresh plant should be boiled and eaten as "greens," so as to secure medicinally the insoluble parts of the silica. This further serves against albumen, and sugar in the urine.

STONE CROP (*See House Leek, page 273*).

STRAWBERRY.

PROPERLY, our familiar Strawberry plant is a native of cold climates, and so hardy that it bears fruit freely in Lapland. When mixed with reindeer cream, and dried in the form of a sausage, this constitutes Kappatialmas, the plum pudding of the Polar regions.

"Strawberry" is from the Anglo-Saxon *Strowberige*, of which the first syllable refers to anything *strewn*.

The wild woodland Strawberry (*Fragaria vesca*) is the progenitor of our highly cultivated and delicious fruit. This little hedgerow and sylvan plant has a root which is very astringent, so that when held in the mouth it will stay any flow of blood from the nostrils. Its berries are more acid than the garden Strawberry, and make an excellent cleanser of the teeth, the acid juice dissolving incrustations of tartar without injuring the enamel.

A medicinal tincture is ordered (H.) from the berries of this Woodland Strawberry, which is of excellent service for nettle rash, or allied erysipelas: also for a suffocative swelling of the swallowing throat. "*Ipsa tuis manibus sylvestri nata sub umbrâ: mollia fraga leges*," says Ovid. An infusion of the leaves is of excellent service in dysentery.

It is incorrect to call the fruit a berry, because the edible, succulent pulp is really a juicy cushion over which numerous small seeds are plentifully dotted; whilst the name Strawberry is a corruption of Stray-berry, in allusion to the trailing runners, which stray in all directions from the parent stock.

Being of very ancient date, the Strawberry is found widely diffused throughout most parts of the world.

Among the Greeks its name *Komaros*, "a mouthful," indicated the compact size of the fruit. By the Latins it was termed *Fragaria*, because of its delicate perfume.

Virgil ranked it with sweet-smelling flowers; Ovid gave it a tender epithet; Pliny mentions the Strawberry as one of the native fruits of Italy; Linnæus declared he kept himself free from gout by eating plentifully of the fruit; and Hoffman says he has known consumption cured by the same means.

From Shakespeare we learn that in his day the fruit was grown in Holborn, now the centre of London. Gloster, when contemplating the death of Hastings, wishes to get the Bishop of Ely temporarily out of the way, and thus addresses him:—

> "My Lord of Ely—when I was last in Holborn
> I saw good Strawberries in your garden there;
> I do beseech you send for some of them."

In Elizabeth's time doctors made a tea from the leaves to act on the kidneys, and used the roots as astringent.

All former Herbalists agreed in pronouncing Strawberries wholesome and beneficial beyond every other English fruit. Their smell is refreshing to the spirits; they abate fever, promote urine, and are gently laxative. The leaves may be used in gargles for quinsies and sore mouths, but, "if any one suffering from a wound in the head should partake of this fruit, it would certainly prove fatal," in accordance with a widespread superstition.

So wholesome are Strawberries, that if laid in a heap and left by themselves to decompose, they will decay without undergoing any acetous fermentation; nor can their kindly temperature be soured even by exposure to the acids of the stomach. They are constituted entirely of soluble matter, and leave no residuum to hinder digestion. It is probably for this reason, and because the fruit does not contain any actual nutriment as food, that a custom has arisen of combining rich clotted cream with it at table, whilst at the same time the sharp juices are thus agreeably modified.

"Mella que erunt epulis, et lacte fluentia fraga":—

"Then sit on a cushion, and sew up a seam;
And thou shalt have Strawberries, sugar, and cream."

Cardinal Wolsey regaled off this delicate confection with the Lords of the Star Chamber; and Charles Lamb is reported to have said, "Doubtless, God Almighty could have made a better berry, but He never did."

Parkinson advised that water distilled from Strawberries is good for perturbation of the spirits, and maketh the heart merry.

The fruit especially suits persons of a bilious temperament, being "a surprising remedy for the jaundice of children, and particularly helping the liver of pot companions, wetters, and drammers." "Some also do use thereof to make a water for hot inflammations in the eyes, and to take away any film that beginneth to grow over them. Into a closed glass vessel they put so many strawberries as they think meet for their purpose, and let this be set in a bed of hot horse manure for twelve or fourteen days, being afterwards distilled carefully, and the water kept for use."

The chemical constituents of the Strawberry are—a peculiar volatile aroma, sugar, mucilage, pectin, citric and malic acids in equal parts, woody fibre, and water.

The fruit is mucilaginous, somewhat tart and saccharine. It stimulates perspiration, and imparts a violet scent to the urine. When fermented for the purpose it yields an ardent spirit. If beaten into a pulp when ripe, and with water poured thereupon, it makes a capital cooling drink which is purifying, and somewhat laxative.

Strawberries are especially suitable in inflammatory and putrid fevers, and for catarrhal sore throats. French herbalists direct that when fresh, and recently crushed, the fruit shall be applied on the face at night for heat spots and freckles by the sun. From the juice, with lemon, sugar, and water, they concoct a most agreeable drink, *Bavaroise à la grecque;* also they employ the roots and leaves against passive hemorrhages, and in chronic diarrhœa.

In Germany, stewed strawberries, and strawberry jam are taken at dinner with roasted meats, or with chicken. This jam promotes a free flow of urine.

It is to be noticed that though most commonly wholesome and refreshing, yet with some persons, particularly those of a strumous bodily habit, Strawberries will often disagree. The late Dr. Armstrong held a very strong opinion that the seed grains which lie sprinkled all over the outer surface of each pulpy berry are prone to excite much intestinal irritation, and he advised his patients to suck their Strawberries through muslin, in order to prevent these diminutive seeds from being swallowed.

German legends dedicate Strawberries to the Virgin, with whom they are reputed to have been a favourite fruit. She went a berrying with the children on St. John's morning; and therefore no mother who has lost a young child, will taste the delicacy then. The Strawberries symbolise little children who have died when young, and the mothers suppose they ascend to heaven concealed in the fragrant pulp.

From the French, *fraise*, signifying the Strawberry

leaves borne on the family shield, is derived in Scotland the name of the Frazers. And eight of these (so called) leaves wrought in ornamental gold form a part of the coronet which our English dukes claim as one of their proud insignia, conferred by Henry the Fourth. Being desirous of adding fresh splendour to the Coronation of a Lancastrian Prince he introduced these leaves into the regal Crown. An earl's coronet has eight leaves: that of a marquis four.

SUCCORY.

THE Wild Succory (*Cichorium intybus*) is a common roadside English plant, white or blue, belonging to the Composite order, and called also Turnsole, because it always turns its flowers towards the sun.

It blows with a blue blossom somewhat paler than the Cornflower, but "bearing a golden heart."

Its fresh root is bitter, and a milky juice flows from the rind, which is somewhat aperient and slightly sedative, so that this specially suits persons troubled with bilious torpor, and jaundice combined with melancholy. An infusion of the herb is useful for skin eruptions connected with gout. If the root and leaves are taken freely, they will produce a gentle diarrhœa, their virtue lying chiefly in the milky juice; and on good authority the plant has been pronounced useful against pulmonary consumption. In Germany it is called Wegwort, or "waiting on the way." The Syrup of Succory is an excellent laxative for children.

The Succory or Cichorium was known to the Romans, and was eaten by them as a vegetable, or in salads. Horace writes (*Ode* 31):

> "Me pascunt olivæ,
> Me chicorea, levesque malvæ."

And Virgil, in his first *Georgic*, speaks of *Amaris intuba fibris*. When cultivated it becomes large, and constitutes Chicory, of which the taproot is used extensively in France for blending with coffee, being closely allied to the Endive and the Dandelion.

This is the *Chicorée frisée* when bleached, or the *Barbe de Capucin*. The cortical part of the root yields a milky saponaceous juice which is very bitter and slightly sedative. Some writers suppose the Succory to be the Horehound of the Bible. In the German story, *The Watcher of the Road*, a lovely princess, abandoned for a rival, pines away, and asking only to die where she can be constantly on the watch, becomes transformed into the wayside Succory.

This Succory plant bears also the name of *Rostrum porcinum*. Its leaves, when bruised, make a good poultice for inflamed eyes, being outwardly applied to the grieved place. Also the leaves when boiled in pottage or broths for sick and feeble persons that have hot, weak, and feeble stomachs, do strengthen the same.

It is said that the roots, if put into heaps and dried, are liable to spontaneous combustion. The taproot of the cultivated plant is roasted in France, and mixed with coffee, to which, when infused, it gives a bitterish taste and a dark colour.

The chemical constituents of Succory and Chicory are—in addition to those ordinarily appertaining to vegetables—inulin, and a special bitter principle not named.

Chicory, when taken too habitually or too freely, causes venous passive congestion in the digestive organs within the abdomen, and a fulness of blood in the head. Both it and Succory, if used in excess as a medicine, will bring about amaurosis, or loss of visual power in the retina of the eyes. Therefore, when given in a much diluted form they are remedial for these affections.

The only benefit of quality which Chicory gives to coffee is by increase of colour and body, with some bitterness, but not by possessing any aroma, or fragrant oil, or stimulating virtue. French writers say it is *contra-stimulante,* and serving to correct the excitation caused by the active principles of coffee, and therefore it suits sanguineo-bilious subjects who suffer from habitual tonic constipation. But it is ill adapted for persons whose vital energy soon flags ; and for lymphatic, or bloodless people its use should be altogether forbidden.

The flowers of Succory used to rank among the four cordial flowers, and a water was distilled from them to allay inflammation of the eyes. The seeds contain abundantly a demulcent oil, whilst the petals furnish a glucoside which is colourless unless treated with alkalies, when it becomes of a golden yellow.

SUNDEW.

THE Sundew (*Ros solis*, or *Drosera rotundifolia*) is a little plant always eagerly recognised in marshy and heathy grounds by ardent young botanists. In the sun its leaves seem tipped with dew (*drosos*). It grows plentifully in Hampshire and the New Forest, bearing a cluster of hairy leaves in a stellate form, at the top of a slender stem. These leaves either from lack of other sustenance in so barren a soil, or more probably as an advance in plant evolution to a higher grade of development, excrete a sticky moisture or dew, which entangles unwary flies settling on the plant, and which serves to digest these victims therewith. Each of the long red hairs on the leaves is viscid, and possesses a small secreting gland at its top.

Some writers say the word Sundew means "sin" ever, moist (dew). The plant is also called Redrot, and Moor Grass, because the soil in which it grows is unwholesome for sheep.

It goes further by the additional names of Youthwort, and Lustwort—*quia acrimonia sua sopitum venerts desiderium excitat* (Dodœus). The fresh juice of the herb contains malic acid in a free state, various salts, and a red colouring matter; also glucose, and a peculiar crystallisable acid. Cattle of the female gender are said to have their copulative instincts excited by eating even a small quantity of the plant. Throughout Europe it has long been esteemed a remedy of repute for chronic bronchitis and asthma; and more recently, in the hands of homœopathic practitioners, it has acquired a fame for specifically curing whooping cough in its spasmodic stages, after the first feverishness of this malady has become subdued. It signally lessens the frequency and force of the spasmodic attacks, besides diminishing the sickness.

Provers who have pushed on themselves the administration of the Sundew in toxical quantities, developed hoarseness, with expectoration of yellow mucus from the throat and upper lungs, as well as a hacking cough, and loss of flesh, this combination of symptoms closely resembling the form of tubercular consumption which begins in the throat, and extends mischievously to the lungs. Regarded from such point the Sundew may be justly pronounced a homœopathic antidote to consumptive disease of the nature here indicated, when attacking spontaneously from constitutional causes.

Moreover, country folk notice that sheep who eat the Sundew in their pasturage have often a violent cough, and waste away. Dr. Curie, of Paris, fed cats with this plant, and they died subsequently with all the symptoms of lung consumption, their chest organs being afterwards found studded with tubercular deposit though cats are not ordinarily liable to tubercle.

So the Sundew may fairly be accepted as a medicinal Simple for laryngeal and pulmonary consumption in its early stages, as well as for whooping-cough, after the manner already explained. A tincture is made (H.) from the entire fresh plant, with spirit of wine, of which a couple of drops may be given in water several times a day, to a child of from four to eight years old, for confirmed whooping-cough; and if this dose seems to aggravate the paroxysms, or to provoke sickness, it must be reduced in strength, and dilution.

Also from four to ten drops of the tincture may be administered with a tablespoonful of cold water, two or three times a day, for several consecutive weeks, to a consumptive adult, in the early stages of this disease.

Dr. Hughes (Brighton) has employed a diluted tincture of the Sundew (one part of this tincture admixed with nine parts of spirit of wine) in doses of from three to five drops with water, to a child of from three to eight years of age, for spasmodic whooping-cough, several times in the day, with marked success; whilst a larger dose or the stronger tincture served only to increase the cough in violence and frequency. The same results may perhaps follow too strong or full a dose to a consumptive patient, so that it must be regulated by the effects produced. Externally, the juice of the fresh Sundew has been used for destroying warts.

SUNFLOWER.

THE Sunflower (*Helianthus annuus*), which is so popular and brilliant an ornament of cottage gardens throughout England in summer and autumn, is an importation of long standing, and has been called the Marigold of Peru.

Its general nature and appearance are so well known as scarcely to need any description. The plant is of the Composite order, indigenous to tropical America, but flourishing well in this country, whilst bearing the name of *Heli-anthus* (Sunflower), and smelling of turpentine when the disc of the flower is broken across.

The growing herb is highly useful for drying damp soils, because of its remarkable power of absorbing water; for which reason several acres of Sunflowers are now planted in the Thames Valley. Swampy districts in Holland have been made habitable by an extensive culture of the Sunflower, the malarial miasmata being absorbed and nullified, whilst pure oxygen is emitted abundantly.

An old rhyme declares, for some unknown reason:—

> "The full Sunflower blew
> And became a starre of Bartholomew."

The name Sunflower has been given as most persons think because the flowers follow the sun by day turning always towards its shining face. But Gerard says, about this alleged fact, he never could observe it to happen; though he spared no pains to observe the matter; he rather thought the flower to have got its title because resembling the radiant beams of the sun. Likewise, some have called it Corona Solis, and Sol Indianus, the Indian Sunne-floure: by others it is termed Chrysanthemum Peruvianum. In Peru this flower was much reverenced because of its resemblance to the radiant sun, which luminary was worshipped there. In their Temples of the Sun the priestesses were crowned with Sunflowers, and wore them in their bosoms, and carried them in their hands. The early Spanish invaders found in these temples numerous representations of the Sunflower wrought in pure virgin gold, the workmanship of which was so exquisite that it far out-valued the precious metal whereof they were made. Some country folk call it "Lady eleven o'clock."

If the buds of the Sunflower before expanding be boiled, and eaten with butter, vinegar and pepper, after the manner of serving the Jerusalem Artichoke, they are exceeding pleasant meat, surpassing the artichoke moreover in provoking the *desiderium veneris.*

The Chinese make their finest yellow dye from the Sunflower, which they worship because resembling the sun.

All parts of the plant contain much carbonate of potash; and the fruit, or seed, furnishes a fixed oil in abundance. The kernels of the seeds contain helianthic acid, and the pith of the plant will yield nine per cent. of carbonate of potash. The oil of the Sunflower may be used as olive oil, and the cake after expressing away this oil makes a good food for cattle. A medicinal tincture (H.) is prepared from the seed with rectified spirit of wine; also from the fresh juice with diluted spirit. Each of these serves admirably against intermittent fever and ague, instead of quinine. The Sunflower is adored by the Chinese as the most useful of all vegetables. From its seeds the best oil is extracted, and an excellent soap is made. This oil burns longer than any other vegetable oil, and Sunflower cake is more fattening to cattle than linseed cake.

The flowers furnish capital food for bees, and the leaves are of use for blending with tobacco. The stalk yields a fine fibre employed in weaving Chinese silk, and Evelyn tells of "The large Sunflower, ere it comes to expand and show its golden face, being dressed as an artichoke, and eaten as a dainty."

The plant is closely allied in its species to the Globe Artichoke, and the Jerusalem Artichoke (*girasole*), so named from turning *vers le soleil*, or *au soleil*, this being corrupted to "Jerusalem," and its soup by further perversion to "Palestine" soup. The original Moorish name was Archichocke, or Earththorn.

The Globe Artichoke (*Cinara maxima anglicana*) of our kitchen gardens, when boiled and brought to table, has a middle pulp which is eaten as well as the soft delicate pulp at the base of each prickly floret. "This middle pulp," says Gerard, "when boiled with the broth of fat flesh, and with pepper added, makes a dainty dish being pleasant to the taste, and accounted good to procure bodily desire. (It stayeth the involuntary course of the natural seed)." Evelyn tells us: "This noble thistle brought from Italy was at first so rare in England that they were commonly sold for crowns apiece." Pliny says: "Carthage spent three thousand pounds sterling a year in them." The plant is named Cinara, from *cinis*, "ashes," because land should be manured with these. It contains phosphoric acid, and is, therefore, stimulating.

The leaves of the Globe Artichoke afford somewhat freely on expression a juice which is bitter, and acts as a brisk diuretic in many dropsies. Such a constituent in the plant was known to the Arabians for curdling milk.

The Jerusalem Artichoke (*Helianthus tuberosus*) is of the Sunflower genus, having been brought at first from Brazil, and being now commonly cultivated in England for its edible tubers. These are red outside, and white within; they contain sugar, and albumen, with an aromatic volatile principle, and water. The tuber is the *Topinambour*, and *Pois de terre* of the French; having been brought to Europe in 1617. It furnishes more sugar and less starch than the Potato.

In 1620 the Jerusalem Artichoke was quite common as a vegetable in London: though, says Parkinson, when first introduced, it was "a dainty for a queen." Formerly, it was baked in pies with beef marrow, dates, ginger, raisins, and sack. The juice pressed out before the plant blossoms was used by the ancients for restoring the hair of the head, even when the person was quite bald.

The Sunflower has been from time immemorial a popular remedy for malarial fevers in Russia, Turkey, and Persia, being employed as a tincture made by steeping the stems and leaves in brandy. It is considered even preferable to quinine, sometimes succeeding when this has failed, and being free from any of the inconveniences which often arise from giving large doses of the drug: whilst the pleasant taste of the plant is of no small advantage in the case of children.

Cases in which both quinine and arsenic proved useless have been completely cured by the tincture of Sunflower in a week or ten days.

Golden Sunflowers are introduced at Rheims into the stained glass of an Apse window in the church of St. Remi, with the Virgin and St. John on either side of the Cross, the head of each being encircled with an aüreole havng a Sunflower inserted in its outer circle. The flowers are turned towards the Saviour on the Cross as towards their true Sun.

TAMARIND.

THE Tamarind pod, though of foreign growth, has been much valued by our immediate ancestors as a household medicinal Simple; and a well stocked jar of its useful curative pulp was always found in the store cupboard of a prudent housewife. But of late years this serviceable fruit has fallen into the background of remedial resources, from which it may be now brought forward again with advantage. The natives of India have a prejudice against sleeping under the Tamarind; and the acid damp from the trees is known to affect the cloth of tents pitched under them for any length of time. So strong is this prejudice of the natives against the Tamarind tree that it is difficult to prevent them from destroying it, as they believe it hurtful to vegetation. The parent tree, Tamar Hindee, "Indian date," is of East, or West Indian growth; but the sweet pulpy jam containing shining stony seeds, and connected together by tough stringy fibres, may be readily obtained at the present time from the leading druggists, or the general provision merchant. It fulfils medicinal purposes which entitle it to high esteem as a Simple for use in the sick-room. Large quantities of this luscious date are brought to our shores from the Levant and Persia, but before importation the shell of the pod is removed; and the pulp ought not to exhibit any presence of copper, as shown on a clean steel knife-blade held within the same, though the fruit by nature possesses traces of gold in its composition. Chemically, this pulp contains citric, tartaric, and malic acids, as compounds of potassium ; with gum, pectin and starch. Boiled syrup has been poured over it as a preliminary. The fruit is sharply acid, and may be made into an excellent cooling drink by infusion with boiling water, being allowed to become cold, and then strained off as an agreeable tea, which proves highly grateful to a fevered patient.

The Arabians first taught the use of Tamarinds, which contain an unusual proportion of acids to the sweet constituents. They are anti-putrescent, and exert a laxative action corrective of bilious sluggishness. A capital whey may be made by boiling two ounces of the fruit with two pints of milk, and then straining. Gerard tells that "travellers carry with them the pulp mixed with sugar throughout the desert places of Africa."

Tamarinds are an efficient laxative if enough (from one to two ounces) can be taken at a time: but this quantity is inconvenient, and apt to clog by its excess of sweetness. Therefore a compressed form of the pulp is now in the market, known as Tamar Indien lozenges, coated with chocolate. These are combined, however, with a purgative of greater activity, most probably jalap.

The fruit of the Tamarind is certainly antibilious, and by the virtue of its potash salts it tends to heal any sore places within the mouth. In India it is added as an ingredient to punch ; but the tree is superstitiously regarded as the messenger of the God of death.

When acids are indicated, to counteract septic fever, and to cool the blood, whilst in natural harmony with the digestive functions, the Tamarind will be found exceptionally helpful ; and towards obviating constipation a dessertspoonful, or more, of the pulp may be taken with benefit as a compôte at table, together with boiled rice, or sago. The name Tamarind is derived from *tamar*, the date palm ; and *indus*, of Indian origin. Formerly this fruit was known as Oxyphœnica (sour date). Officinally apothecaries mix the pulp with senna as an aperient confection. It is further used in flavouring curries on account of its acid.

TANSY.

THE Tansy (*Tanacetum vulgare*—"buttons,"—bed of Tansy), a Composite plant very familiar in our hedgerows and waste places, being conspicuous by its heads of brilliant yellow flowers, is often naturalized in our gardens for ornamental cultivation. Its leaves smell like camphor, and possess a bitter aromatic taste ; whilst young they were commonly used in times past, and are still employed, when shredded, for flavouring cakes, puddings, and omelets. The roots when preserved with honey, or sugar, are reputed to be of special service against the gout, if a reasonable quantity thereof be eaten fasting every day for a certain space. The fruit is destructive to round worms

The seed also of the Tansy is a singular and appropriate medicine against worms : for "in whatsoever sort taken it killeth and driveth them forth." In Sussex a peasant will put Tansy leaves in his shoes to cure ague ; and the plant has a rural celebrity for correcting female irregularities of the functional health. The name Tansy is probably derived from the Greek word *athanasia* which signifies immortality, either, as, says Dodœus, *quia non cito flos inflorescit*, "because it lasts so long in flower," or, *quia ejus succus, vel oleum extractum cadavera a putredine conservat* (as Ambrosius writes), "because it is so capital for preserving dead bodies from corruption." It was said to have been given to Ganymede to make him immortal. The whole herb contains resin, mucilage, sugar, a fixed oil, tannin, a colouring matter, malic or tanacetic acid, and water. When the camphoraceous bitter oil is taken in any excess it induces venous congestion of the abdominal organs, and increases the flow of urine.

If given in moderate doses the plant and its essential oil are stomachic and cordial, whether the leaves, flowers, or seeds be administered, serving to allay spasm, and helping to promote the monthly flow of women; the seeds being also of particular use against worms, and relieving the flatulent colic of hysteria. This herb will drive away bugs from a bed in which it is placed. Meat rubbed with the bitter Tansy will be protected from the visits of carrion flies.

Ten drops of the essential oil will produce much flushing of the head and face, with giddiness, and with heat of stomach; whilst half a drachm of the oil has been followed by a serious result. But from one to four drops may be safely given for a dose according to the symptoms it is desired to relieve. Cases of epilepsy (not inherited) have been successfully treated with the liquid extract of Tansy in doses of a drop with water four times in the day. The essential oil will toxically produce epileptic seizures.

The plant has been used externally with benefit for some eruptive diseases of the skin; and a hot infusion of it to sprained, or rheumatic parts will give relief from pain by way of a fomentation. In Scotland the dried flowers are given for gout, from half to one teaspoonful for a dose two or three times in the day; or an infusion is drank prepared from the flowers and seeds. This has kept inveterate gout at bay for years.

A medicinal tincture is made (H.) from the fresh plant with spirit of wine. From eight to ten drops of the same may be given with a tablespoonful of cold water to an adult twice or three times in the day.

Formerly this was one of the native plants dedicated to the Virgin Mary; and the "good wives" used to take a syrup of Tansy for preventing miscarriage. "The Laplanders," says Linnœus, "use Tansy in their baths to facilitate parturition."

At Easter also it was the custom, even by the Archbishops, the Bishops, and the clergy of some churches, to play at handball (so say the old chroniclers), with men of their congregations, whilst a Tansy cake was the reward of the victors, this being a confection with which the bitter herb Tansy was mixed. Some such a corrective was supposed to be of benefit after having eaten much fish during Lent.

The Tansy cake was made from the young leaves of the plant mixed with eggs, and was thought to purify the humours of the body. "This Balsamic plant" said Boerhaave, "will supply the place of nutmegs and cinnamon." In Lyte's time the Tansy was sold in the shops under the name of Athanasia.

TARRAGON.

THE kitchen herb Tarragon (*Artemisia dracunculus*) is cultivated in England, and more commonly in France, for uses in salads, and other condimentary purposes.

It is the "little Dragon Mugwort: in French, *Herbe au Dragon*"; to which, as to other Dragon herbs, was ascribed the faculty of curing the bites and stings of venomous beasts, and of mad dogs. The plant does not fructify in France.

It is of the Composite order, and closely related to

our common Wormwood, and Southern-wood, but its leaves are not divided. This herb is a native of Siberia, but has been long grown largely by French gardeners, and has since become widespread in this country as a popular fruit, also for making a vinegar, and for adding to salads. The word Tarragon is by corruption "a little dragon." French cooks commonly mix their table mustard with the vinegar of the herb.

Many strange tales have been told about the origin of the plant, one of which, scarce worth the noting, runs that the seed of flax put into a radish root, or a sea onion, and being thus set doth bring forth this herb Tarragon (so says Gerard).

In Continental cookery the use of Tarragon is advised to temper the coldness of other herbs in salads, like as a Rocket doth. "Neither," say the authorities, "do we know what other use this herb hath."

The volatile essential oil of Tarragon is chemically identical with that of Anise, and it is found to be sexually stimulating. Probably by virtue of its finely elaborated camphor it exercises its specific effects, the fact being established that too much camphor acts in the opposite direction.

John Evelyn says of the plant "'Tis highly cordial and friendly to the head, heart, and liver."

THISTLES.

THISTLES are comprised in a large mixed genus of our English weeds, and wild plants, several of them possessing attributed medicinal virtues. Some of these are Thistles proper, as the *Carduus*, the *Cnicus*, and the *Carlina*: others are Teasels, Eryngiums, and Globe Thistles, etc. Consideration should be given here to the *Carduus marianus*, or Lady's Thistle, the common

Carline Thistle, the *Carduus benedictus* (Blessed Thistle), the wild Teasel (*Dipsacus*), and the Fuller's Teasel, as Herbal Simples; whilst others of minor curative usefulness are to be incidentally mentioned.

As a class Thistles have been held sacred to Thor, because, say the old authors, receiving their bright colours from the lightning, and because protecting those who cultivate them from its destructive effects.

In Devon and Cornwall Thistles are commonly known as Dazzels, or Dashel flowers. As a rule they flourish best in hot dry climates.

The *Carduus marianus* (Lady's Thistle), Milk Thistle, or Holy Thistle, grows abundantly in waste places, and near gardens throughout the British Isles, but it is not a native plant. The term *Carduus*, or Cardinal, refers to its spring leaves, and the adjectives "Marianus," "Milk," and "Holy," have been assigned through a tradition that some drops of the Virgin Mary's milk fell on the herb, and became exhibited in the white veins of its leaves. By some persons this Thistle is taken as the emblem of Scotland.

Dioscorides told of the Milk Thistle, "the seeds being drunk are a remedy for infants that have their sinews drawn together." He further said: "The root if borne about one doth expel melancholy, and remove all diseases connected therewith." Modern writers do laugh at this: "Let them laugh that win! My opinion is that this is the best remedy that grows against all melancholy diseases."

The fruit of the *Carduus marianus* contains an oily bitter seed: the tender leaves in spring may be eaten as a salad; and the young peeled stalks, after being soaked, are excellent boiled, or baked in pies. The heads of this Thistle before the flowers open may be cooked like artichokes. The seeds were formerly thought to cure hydrophobia. They act as a demulcent in catarrh and pleurisy, being also a favourite food of Goldfinches. A decoction of the seeds when applied externally is said to have proved beneficial in cases of cancer.

Thistle down was at one time gathered by poor persons and sold for stuffing pillows. It is very prolific in germination, and an old saying runs on this score :—

> "Cut your Thistles before St. John,
> Or you'll have two instead of one."

This Milk Thistle (*Carduus marianus*) is said to be the empirical nostrum, *anti-glaireux*, of Count Mattæi.

"Disarmed of its prickles," writes John Evelyn, "and boiled, it is worth esteem, and thought to be a great breeder of milk, and proper diet for women who are nurses."

In Germany it is very popular for curing jaundice and kindred biliary derangements. When taken by healthy provers in varying quantities to test its toxic effects the plant has caused distension of the whole abdomen, especially on the right side, with tenderness on pressure over the liver, and with a deficiency of bile in hard knotty stools, the colouring matter of the fæces being found by chemical tests present in the urine: so that a preparation of this Thistle modified in strength, and considerably diluted in its doses proves truly homœopathic to simple obstructive jaundice through inaction of the liver, and readily cures the disorder. A tincture is prepared (H.) for medicinal use from equal parts of the root, and the seeds (with the hull on) together with spirit of wine.

The *Carduus benedictus* (Blessed Thistle) was first

cultivated by Gerard in 1597, and has since become a common medicinal Simple. It was at one time considered to be almost a panacea, and capable of curing even the plague by its antiseptic virtues.

This Thistle was a herb of Mars, and, as Gerard says: "It helpeth giddiness of the head: also it is an excellent remedy against the yellow jaundice. It strengthens the memory, cures deafness, and helps the bitings of mad dogs and venomous beasts." It contains a bitter principle "cnicin," resembling the similar tonic constituent of the Dandelion, this being likewise useful for stimulating a sluggish liver to more healthy action.

The infusion should be made with cold water: when kept it forms a salt on its surface like nitre. The herb does not yield its virtues to spirit of wine as a tincture. Its taste is intensely bitter.

The Carline Thistle (*Carlina vulgaris*) was formerly used in magical incantations. It possesses medicinal qualities very like those of Elecampane, being diaphoretic, and in larger doses purgative. The herb contains some resin, and a volatile essential oil of a camphoraceous nature, like that of Elecampane, and useful for similar purposes, as cordial and antiseptic. This Thistle grows on dry heaths especially near the sea, and is easily distinguished from other Thistles by the straw-coloured glossy radiate long inner scales of its outer floral cup. They rise up over the florets in wet weather. The whole plant is very durable, like that of the "everlasting flowers:" Cudweed (*Antennaria*).

The name Carlina was given because the Thistle was used by Charles the Great as a remedy against the plague. It was revealed to him when praying for some means to stay this pestilence which was destroying his army. In his sleep there appeared to him an angel who shot an arrow from a cross bow, telling him to mark the plant upon which it fell : for that with such plant he might cure his soldiers of the dire epidemic : which event really happened, the herb thus indicated being the said thistle. In Anglo-Saxon it was the ever-throat, or boar-throat.

On the Continent a large white blossom of this species is nailed upon cottage doors by way of a barometer to indicate the weather if remaining open or closing.

The wild Teasel (*Dipsacus sylvestris*) grows commonly in waste places, having tall stems or stalks, at the bottom of which are leaves (like bracts) united at their sides so as to form a cup, open upwards, around the base of the stalk, and hence the term "*Dipsacus*," thirsty. This cup serves to retain rain water, which is thought to acquire curative properties, being used, for one purpose, to remove warts. The cup is called Venus' basin, and its contents, says Ray, are of service *ad verrucas abigendas*; also it is named Barber's Brush, and Church Broom.

The Fuller's Teasel, or Thistle (*Dipsacus fullonum*) is so termed from its use in combing and dressing cloth, —*teasan*, to tease,—three Teaselheads being the arms of the Cloth Weavers' Company. This is found in the neighbourhood of the cloth districts, but is not considered to be a British plant. It is probably a cultivated variety of the wild Teasel, but differs by having the bristles of its receptacles hooked.

The Sow Thistle (*Sonchus oleraceus*), named *sonchus* because of its soft spikes instead of prickles, grows commonly as a weed in gardens, and having milky stalks which are reputed good for wheezy and short-winded folk, whilst the milk may be used as a wash for the face. It is named also "turn sole" because always facing the sun, and Hare's Thistle (the hare's panacea, says an old writer, is the Sow Thistle), or Hare's Lettuce because "when fainting with the heat she recruits her strength with the herb; or if a hare eat of this herb in the summer when he is mad he shall become whole." Another similar title of the herb is Hare's palace, since the creature was thought to get shelter and courage from it. Some suppose that the botanical term *Sonchus* signifies *apo tou soon ekein*, from its yielding a salubrious juice.

The Sow thistle has been named also Milkweed. According to tradition it sometimes conceals marvels, or treasures; and in Italian stories the words, "Open Sow Thistle" are used as of like significance with the magical invocation "Open sesame." Another name is "Du Tistel" or Sprout Thistle, because the plant may be used for its edible sprouts, which Evelyn says, were eaten by Galen as a lettuce. And Matthiolus told of the Tuscans in his day "*Soncho nostri utuntur hyeme in acetariis.*"

The Melancholy Thistle (*Carduus heterophyllus*) has been held curative of melancholy. It grows most frequently in Scotland and the North of England, and is a non-prickly plant.

THYME.

THE Wild English Thyme (*Thymus serpyllum*) belongs to the Labiate plants, and takes its second title from a Greek verb signifying "to creep," which has reference to the procumbent habit of the plant. It bears the appellation "Brotherwort."

Typically the *Thymus serpyllum* flourishes abundantly on hills, heaths, and grassy places, having woody stems, small fringed leaves, and heads of purple flowers which diffuse a sweet perfume into the surrounding air, especially in hot weather. Shakespeare's well known line alludes to this pleasant fact: "I know a bank where the wild Thyme grows."

The name Thyme is derived from the Greek *thumos*, as identical with the Latin *fumus*, smoke, having reference to the ancient use of Thyme in sacrifices, because of its fragrant odour: or, it may be, as signifying courage (*thumos*), which its cordial qualities inspire.

With the Greeks Thyme was an emblem of bravery, and activity; also the ladies of chivalrous days embroidered on the scarves which they presented to their knights the device of a bee hovering about a spray of Thyme, as teaching the union of the amiable and the active.

Horace has said concerning Wild Thyme:—

"Impune tutum per nemus arbutos
Quærunt latentes, et thyma deviæ
Olentis uxores mariti."

Wild Thyme is subject to variations in the size and colour of its flowers, as well as in the habits of the varieties.

This wild Thyme bears also the appellation, "Mother of Thyme," which should be "Mother Thyme," in allusion to its medicinal influence on the womb, an organ which the older writers always termed the "Mother." Isidore tells that the wild Thyme was called in Latin, *Matris animula, quod menstrua movet.* Platearius says of it: *Serpyllum matricem comfortat et mundificat. Mulieres Saliternitanæ hoc fomento multum utuntur.*

Dr. Neovius writes enthusiastically in a Finnish Journal on the virtues of common Thyme in combating whooping cough. He has found that if given *fresh*, from an ounce and a half to six ounces a day, mixed with a little syrup, regularly for some weeks, it is practically a specific. If taken from the first, the symptoms vanish in two or three days, and in a fortnight the disease is expelled. The simplicity, harmlessness, and cheapness of this remedy are great supporters of its claims.

Other titles of the herb are Pulial mountain, and creeping Thyme. It is anti-spasmodic, and good for nervous or hysterical headaches, for flatulence, and the headache which follows inebriation. The infusion may be profitably applied for healing skin eruptions of various characters.

Virgil mentions (in *Eclogue* xi., lines 10, 11) the restorative value of Thyme against fatigue :—

> "Thestylis et rapido fessis messoribus œstu
> Allia, Serpyllumque herbas contundit olentes."

Or,

> "Thestlis for mowers tired with parching heat
> Garlic and Thyme, strong smelling herbs, doth beat."

Tournefort writes: "A conserve made from the flowers and leaves of wild Thyme (*Serpyllum*) relieves those troubled with the falling sickness, whilst the distilled oil promotes the monthly flow in women."

The delicious flavour of the noted honey of Hymettus was said to be derived from the wild Thyme there visited by the bees. Likewise the flesh of sheep fed on pasturage where the wild Thyme grows freely has been said to gain a delicate flavour and taste from this source: but herein a mistake is committed, because sheep are really averse to such pasturage, and refuse it if they can get other food.

An infusion of the leaves of Thyme, whether wild, or cultivated, makes an excellent aromatic tea, the odour of which is sweet and fragrant, whilst the taste of the plant is bitter and camphoraceous. There is in some districts an old superstition that to bring wild Thyme into the house conveys severe illness, or death to some member of the family.

In Grecian days the Attic elegance of style was said to show an odour of Thyme. Shenstone's schoolmistress had a garden :—

> "Where herbs for use and physic not a few
> Of grey renown within those borders grew,
> The tufted Basil, —*pun provoking* Thyme,
> The lordly Gill that never dares to climb."

Bacon in his *Essay on Gardens* recommends to set whole alleys of Thyme for the pleasure of its perfume when treading on the plant. And Dioscorides said Thyme used in food helps dimness of sight.

Gerard adds: "Wild Thyme boiled in wine and drunk is good against the wamblings and gripings of the belly": whilst Culpeper describes it as "a strengthener of the lungs, as notable a one as grows." "The Thyme of Candy, Musk Thyme, or Garden Thyme is good against the sciatica, and to be given to those that have the falling sickness, to smell to."

The volatile essential oil of Wild Thyme (as well as of Garden Thyme) consists of two hydrocarbons, with thymol as the fatty base, this thymol being readily soluble in fats and oils when heated, and taking high modern rank as an antiseptic. It will arrest gastric fermentation when given judiciously as a medicine, though an overdose will bring on somnolence, with a ringing in the ears. Officinally Thymol, the stearoptene obtained from the volatile oil of *Thymus vulgaris*, is directed to be given in a dose of from half to two grains.

Thymol is valued by some authorities more highly even than carbolic acid for destroying the germs of disease, or for disinfecting them. It is of equal service with tar for treating such skin affections as psoriasis, and eczema. When inhaled thymol is most useful against septic sore throat, especially during scarlet fever. At the hospital for throat diseases the following formula is ordered: Thymol twenty grains to rectified spirit of wine three drachms, and carbonate of magnesia ten grains, with water to three ounces; a teaspoonful to be used in a pint of water at 150° Fahrenheit for each inhalation.

Against ringworm an ointment made with one drachm of thymol to an ounce of soft paraffin is found to be a sure specific.

The spirit of thymol should consist of one part of thymol to ten parts of spirit of wine; and this is a convenient form for use to medicate the wool of antiseptic respirators. As a purifying and cleansing lotion for wounds and sores, thymol should be mixed in the proportion of five grains thereof to an ounce of spirit of wine, an ounce of glycerine, and six ounces of water.

The common Garden Thyme is an imported sort from the South of Europe. Its odour and taste depend on an essential oil known commercially as oil of origanum.

Another variety of the Wild Thyme is Lemon Thyme (*Thymus citriodorus*), distinguished by its parti-coloured leaves, and by its lilac flowers. Small beds of this Thyme, together with mint, are cultivated at Penzance, in which to rear millepedes, or hoglice, administered as pills for several forms of scrofulous disease. The woodlouse, sowpig, or hoglouse abounds with a nitrous salt which has long found favour for curing scrofulous disease, and inveterate struma, as also against some kinds of stone in the bladder.

The Hoglouse, or Millepede was the primitive medicinal pill. It is found in dry gardens under stones, etc., and rolls itself up into a ball when touched. These are also called Chiselbobs, and Cudworms. From three to twelve were formerly given in Rhenish wine for a hundred days together to cure all kinds of cancers; or they were sometimes worn round the neck in a small bag (which was absurd !). In the Eastern counties they are known as "Old Sows," or "St. Anthony's Hogs." Their Latin name is *Porcellus Scaber*. The Welsh call this small creature the "withered old woman of the wood," "the little pig of the wood," and "the little grey hog," also "Grammar Sows." Their word "gurach" like "grammar" means a dried up old dame.

Cat Thyme (*Teucrium marum verum*) was imported from Spain, and is cultivated in our gardens as a cordial aromatic herb, useful in nervous disorders. Its flowers are crimson, and its bark is astringent. The dried leaves may be given in powder or used in snuff. A tincture (H.) is made from the whole herb which is effectual against small thread worms. Provers of the herb in material toxic quantities have experienced troublesome itching and irritation of the fundament. For similar conditions, and to expel thread worms, two or three drops of the tincture diluted to its first decimal strength should be given with a spoonful of water three or four times in the day to a child of from four to six years.

TOADFLAX.

THE Toadflax, or Flaxweed (*Linaria vulgaris*) belongs to the scrofula-curing order of plants, getting its name from *linum*, flax, and being termed "toad" by a mistaken translation of its Latin title *Bubonio*, this having been wrongly read *bufonio*,—belonging to a toad,—or because having a flower (as the Snapdragon) like a toad's mouth: whereas "bubonio" means "useful for the groins."

It is an upright herbaceous plant most common in hedges, having leaves like grass of a dull sea green aspect, and bearing dense clusters of yellow flowers shaped like those of the garden Snapdragon, with spurs at their base. It continues in flower until the late autumn. The Russians cultivate the Snapdragon for the oil yielded by its seeds.

The Toadflax has a faint disagreeable smell, and a bitter saline taste. It acts medicinally as a powerful purge, and promoter of urine, and therefore it is employed for carrying off the water of dropsies, being in this respect a well known rural Simple. Waller says: "Country people boil the whole plant in ale, and drink the decoction; but the expressed juice of the fresh plant acts still more powerfully."

In many districts the herb is familiarly known as "butter and eggs;" and in Germany though dedicated to the Virgin it is called "devil's band."

Again in Devonshire it goes by the names of "Rambling," or "Wandering Sailor," "Pedler's Basket," "Mother of Millions" (the ivy-leaved sort), "Lion's Mouth" and "Flaxweed."

When used externally an infusion of the herb acts as an anodyne to subdue irritation of the skin, and it may be taken as a medicine to modify skin diseases. The fresh juice is attractive to flies, but at the same time it serves to poison them: so if it be mixed with milk, and placed where flies resort they will drink it and perish at the first sip.

As promoting a free flow of urine, the herb has been named "Urinalis," or sometimes "Ramsted." The flowers contain a yellow colouring matter, mucilage, and sugar. In Germany they are given with the rest of the plant for dropsy, jaundice, piles, and some diseases of the skin. Gerard says: "The decoction openeth the stoppings of the liver, and spleen: and is singular good against the jaundice which is of long continuance." He advises an ointment made from the plant stampt with lard for certain skin eruptions, and a decoction made with four drachms of the herb in eight ounces of boiling water. The bruised leaves are useful externally for curing blotches on the face, and for piles.

An old distich says of the Toadflax as compared with the Larkspur :—

"Esula lactescit: sine lacte Linaria crescit;"

or,

"Larkspur with milk doth flow:
Toadflax without milk doth grow,"

(alluding to the dry nature of the toadflax). To which the Hereditary Marshal of Hesse added the following line :—

"Escula nil nobis, sed dat linaria *taurum*,"

implying that the herb was of old valued for its good effects when applied externally to piles as an ointment, a fomentation, or a poultice, each being made from the leaves and the flowers. The originator of this ointment was a Dr. Wolph, physician to the Landgrave of Hesse, who only divulged its formula on the prince promising to give him *a fat ox* annually for the discovery.

TOMATO (or LOVE APPLE).

THOUGH only of recent introduction as a common vegetable in this country, and though grown chiefly under glass for the table in England, yet the Tomato is so abundantly imported, and so extensively used by all classes now-a-days throughout the British Isles that it may fairly take consideration for whatever claims it can advance as a curative Simple. Imported early in the present century from South America it remained for a while an exclusive luxury produced for the rich like pine apples and melons. But gradually since then the Tomato has steadily acquired an increasing popularity, and now large crops of the profitable fruit are brought from Bordeaux and the Channel Islands, to meet the demands of our English markets. Much of the favour which has become attached to this ruddy, polished, attractive-looking fruit is due to a widespread impression that it is good for the liver, and a preventive of biliousness. Nevertheless, rumours have also gone abroad that habitual Tomato-eaters are especially liable to cancerous disease in this, or that organ.

Belonging to the Solanums the Tomato (*Lycopersicum*) is a plant of Mexican origin. Its brilliant fruit was first known as *Mala æthiopica*, or the Apples of the Moors, and bearing the Italian designation *Pomi dei Mori*. This name was presently corrupted in the French to *Pommes d'amour*; and thence in English to the epithet Love Apples, a perversion which shows by what curious methods primary names may become incongruously changed. They are also called Gold Apples from their bright yellow colour before getting ripe. The term *Lycopersicum* signifies a "wolf's peach," because some parts of the plant are thought to excite animal passions.

The best fruit is supposed to grow within sight, or smell of the sea. It needs plenty of sunlight and heat. The quicker it is produced the fewer will be the seeds discoverable in its pulp.

Green when young, Tomatoes acquire a bright yellow hue before reaching maturity, and when ripe they are smooth, shining, furrowed, and of a handsome red.

Chemically this Love Apple contains citric and malic acids: and it further possesses oxalic acid, or oxalate of potash, in common with the Sorrel of our fields, and the Rhubarb of our kitchen gardens. On which account each of this vegetable triad is ill suited for gouty constitutions disposed to the formation of irritating oxalate of lime in the blood. With such persons a single indulgence in Tomatoes, particularly when eaten raw, may provoke a sharp attack of gout.

Otherwise there are special reasons for supposing the Tomato to be a wholesome fruit of remarkable purifying value.

Dr. King Chambers classifies it among remedies against scurvy, telling us that Tomatoes mixed with brown bread make a capital sauce for costive persons. And the fruit owns a singular property in connection with diseases of plants, suggesting its probable worth as protective against bacterial germs, and microbes of disease in our bodies when it is taken as food, or medicinally. If a Tomato shrub be uprooted at the end of the summer, and allowed to wither on the bough of a fruit tree, or if it be burnt beneath the fruit tree, it will not only kill any blight which may be present, but will also preserve the tree against any future invasion by blight. The hostility thus evinced by the plant to low organisms is due to the presence of sulphur, which the Tomato shrub largely contains, and which is rendered up in an active state by decay, or by burning. Now remembering that digestion likewise splits up the Tomato into its chemical constituents, and releases its sulphur within us, we may fairly assume that persons who eat Tomatoes habitually are likely to have a particular immunity from bacterial and putrefactive diseases.

Wherefore it is altogether improbable that Tomatoes will engender cancer, which is essentially a disease of vitiated blood, and of degenerate cell tissue. Possibly the old exploded doctrine of signatures may have suggested, or started this accusation against the maligned, though unguarded Tomato: for it cannot be denied the guileless fruit bears a nodulated tumour-like appearance, whilst showing, when cut, an aspect of red raw morbid fleshy structure strangely resembling cancerous disease.

Vegetarians who eat Tomatoes constantly and freely claim that cancer is a disease almost unknown among their ranks; but an Italian doctor writing from Rome gives it as the experience of himself and his medical brethren that cancer is as common in Italy and Sicily among vegetarians as with mixed eaters. Most of our American cousins, who are the enterprising fathers of this medicinal fruit, persuade themselves that they are never in perfect health except during the Tomato season. And with us the ruddy Solanum has obtained a wide popularity not simply at table as a tasty cooling sallet, or an appetising stew, but essentially as a supposed antibilious purifier of the blood. When uncooked it contains a notable quantity of Solanin, and it would be dangerous to let animals drink water in which the plant had been boiled. The Staff of the Cancer Hospital at Brompton have emphatically declared "they see no ground whatever for supposing that the eating of Tomatoes predisposes to cancer."

Nevertheless some country people in the remote American States attribute cancer to an excessively free use of the wild uncultivated tomato as food.

The first mention of this fruit by the London Horticultural Society occurred in 1818.

Chemically in addition to the acids already named the Tomato contains a volatile oil, a brown resinous extractive matter very fragrant, a vegeto-mineral matter, muco-saccharin, some salts, and in all probability an alkaloid. The whole plant smells unpleasantly, and its juices when subjected to heat by the action of fire emit a vapour so powerful as to provoke vertigo and vomiting.

The specific principles furnished by the Tomato will, when concentrated, produce, if taken medicinally, effects very similar to those brought about by taking mercurial salts, viz., an ulcerative state of the mouth, with a profuse flow of saliva, and with excessive stimulation of the liver: peevishness also on the following day, with a depressing backache in men, suggesting paralysis, and with a profuse fluor albus in women. When given in moderation as food, or as physic, the fruit will remedy this chain of symptoms.

By reason of its efficacy in promoting an increased flow of bile if judiciously taken, the Tomato bears the name in America of Vegetable Mercury, and it has almost superseded calomel there as a biliary medicinal provocative. Dr. Bennett declares the Tomato to be the most useful and the least harmful of all known medicines for correcting derangements of the liver. He prepares a chemical extract of the fruit and plant which will, he feels assured, depose calomel for the future.

Across the Atlantic an officinal tincture is made from the Tomato for curative purposes by treating the apples, and the bruised fresh plant with alcohol, and letting this stand for eight days before it is filtered and strained. A teaspoonful of the tincture is a sufficient dose with one or two tablespoonfuls of cold water, three times in the day.

The fluid extract made from the plant is curative of any ulcerative soreness within the mouth, such as nurses' sore mouth, or canker. It should be given internally, and applied locally to the sore parts.

Spaniards and Italians eat Tomatoes with pepper and oil. We take them as a salad, or stewed with butter, after slicing and stuffing them with bread crumb, and a spice of garlic.

The green Tomato makes a good pickle, and in its unripe state is esteemed an excellent sauce with rich roast pork, or goose. The fruit when cooked no longer exercises active medicinal effects, as its volatile principles have now become dispelled through heat.

By the late Mr. Shirley Hibberd, who was a good naturalist, it was asserted with seeming veracity that the cannibal inhabitants of the Fiji Islands hold in high repute a native Tomato which is named by them the *Solanum anthropophagorum*, and which they eat, *par excellence*, with "Cold Missionary." Nearer home a worthy dame has been known with pious aspirations to enquire at the stationer's for "Foxe's book of To-Martyrs."

"Chops and Tomato sauce" were ordered from Mrs. Bardell, in Pickwick's famous letter. "Gentlemen!" says Serjeant Buzfuz, in his address to the jury, "What does this mean?" But he missed a point in not going on to add—"I need not tell you, gentlemen, the popular name for the Tomato is *love apple!* "Is it not manifest, therefore, what the base deceiver intended?"

"A cucumber in early spring
 Might please a sated Cæsar,
Rapture asparagus can bring,
 And dearer still green peas are:
Oh! far and wide, where mushrooms hide,
 I'll search, as wide and far too
For watercress; but all their pride
 Must stoop to thee,—Tomato!"

TORMENTIL.

THE Tormentil *(Potentilla Tormentilla)* belongs to the tribe of wild Roses, and is a common plant on our heaths, banks, and dry pastures. It is closely allied to the *Potentilla,* but bears only four petals on its flowers, which are of bright yellow. The woody roots are medicinally useful because of their astringent properties. Sometimes the stem is trailing, making this the *Tormentilla Reptans,* but more commonly it ascends. The name comes from *tormina,* which signifies such griping of the intestines as the herb will serve to relieve, as likewise the twinges of toothache. The root is employed both for tanning leather, and for dyeing it by the thickened red juice. Furthermore through its astringency this root is admirable for arresting bleedings. Vesalius considered it to be as useful against syphilis as Guiacum, and Sarsaparilla. A decoction of Tormentil makes a capital gargle, and will heal ulcers of the mouth if used as a wash. If a piece of lint soaked therein be kept applied to warts, they will wither and disappear. Chemically the herb contains "*Tormentilla Red,*" identical with that of the Horse Chestnut, also tannic, and kinoric acids. The decoction should be made with four drams to half-a-pint of water boiled together for ten minutes, adding half a dram of Cinnamon stick at the end of boiling; one or two tablespoonfuls will be the dose, or of the powdered root (dried) the dose will be from five to thirty grains.

"*In fluxu sanguinis, fluore albo, et mictu involuntario Tormentilla valet.*" Dr. Thornton (1810) tells of a labouring botanist who learnt the powers of this root, and by its decoction, sweetened with honey, cured intractable agues, severe diarrhœas, and scorbutic ulcers (which had been turned out of hospitals as inveterate), also many fluxes. Lord William Russell heard about this, and allowed the poor man a piece of his park in which to cultivate the herb. "*Non est vegetabile quod in fluxionibus alvi efficacius est.*" The root is so rich in tannin that it may be used instead of oak bark.

TURNIP.

THE Turnip (*Brassica Rapa*) belongs to the Cruciferous Cabbage tribe, being often found growing in waste places, though not truly wild. In this state it is worth nothing to man or beast; but, by cultivation, it becomes a most valuable food for cattle in the winter, and a good vegetable for our domestic uses. It exercises some aperient action, and the liquid in which turnips are boiled will increase the flow of urine. It is called also "bagie," and was the "gongyle" of the Greeks, so named from the roundness of the root.

When mashed, and mixed with bread and milk, the Turnip makes an excellent cleansing and stimulating poultice for indolent abscesses or sores.

The Scotch eat small, yellow-rooted Turnips as we do radishes. "Tastes and Turnips proverbially differ."

At Plymouth, and some other places, when a girl rejects a suitor, she is said to "give him turnips," probably with reference to his sickly pallor of disappointment.

The seventeenth of June—as the day of St. Botolph, the old turnip man,—is distinguished by various uses of a Turnip, because in the Saga, which figuratively represents the seasons, the seeds were sown on that day.

It is told that the King of Bithynia in some expedition against the Scythians during the winter, and when at a great distance from the sea, had a violent longing for a small fish known as *aphy*—a pilchard, or anchovy. His cook cut a Turnip to a perfect imitation of its shape, which, when fried in oil, well salted, and powdered with the seeds of a dozen black poppies, so deceived the king that he praised the root at table as an excellent fish.

Being likely to provoke flatulent distension of the bowels, Turnips are not a proper vegetable for hysterical persons, or for pregnant women. The rind is acrimonious, but the tops, when young and tender, may be boiled for the table as a succulent source of potash, and other mineral salts in the Spring.

The fermented juice of Turnips will yield an ardent spirit. When properly cooked they serve to sweeten the blood. An essential volatile oil contained in the root, chiefly in the rind, disagrees, by provoking flatulent distension. This root is sometimes cut up and partly substituted for the peel and pulp of oranges in marmalade.

If Turnips are properly grown in dry, lean, sandy earth, a wholesome, agreeable sort of bread can be made from them, "of which we have eaten at the greatest persons' tables, and which is hardly to be distinguished from the best of wheat." Some persons roast Turnips in paper under the embers, and serve them with butter and sugar. The juice made into syrup is an old domestic remedy for coughs and hoarseness.

A nice wholesome dish of Piedmontese Turnips is thus prepared: Half boil your Turnip, and cut it in slices like half-crowns; butter a pie dish, and put in the slices, moisten them with a little milk and weak broth, sprinkle over lightly with bread crumbs, adding pepper and salt; then bake in the oven until the Turnips become of a light golden colour.

The Turnip, a navew, or variety of Rape (*navus*), should never be sown in a rich soil, wherein it would become degenerate and lose its shape as well as its dry agreeable relish. Horace advised field-grown Turnips as preferable at a banquet to those of garden culture. They may be safely eaten when raw, having been at one time much consumed in Russia by the upper classes.

Turnips have been introduced into armorial bearings to represent a person of liberal disposition who relieves the poor.

Dr. Johnson's famous illustration of false logic ran thus :—

"If a man fresh Turnips cries :
But cries not when his father dies,
Is this a proof the man would rather
Possess fresh Turnips than a father ?"

TURPENTINE.

FROM our English Pines, if their stems be wounded, the oleo-resin known as Turpentine, can be procured. This is so truly a vegetable product, and so readily available for medical uses in every household, being withal so valuable for its remedial and curative virtues that no apology is needed for giving it notice as a Herbal Simple. The said oleo-resin which exudes on incising the bark furnishes our oil, or so-called spirit of Turpentine. But larger quantities, and of a richer resin, can be had from abroad than it is practicable for England to provide, so that our Turpentine of commerce is mainly got from American and French sources.

The oleo-resin consists of a resinous base and a volatile essential oil, which is usually termed the spirit.

The *Pinus Picra*, or Silver Fir-tree, yields common

Turpentine; and to sleep on a pillow made from its yellow shavings is a capital American device for relieving asthma. Fir cones are called "buntins," and "oysters."

"Tears," or resin drops, which trickle out on the stems of the Pine, if taken, five or six of these tears in a day, will benefit chronic bronchitis, and will prove useful to lessen the cough of consumption.

When swallowed in a full dose, Turpentine gives a sensation of warmth, and excites the secretion of urine, to which it imparts a violet hue. It also promotes perspiration, and stimulates the bronchial mucous membrane. From eight to twenty drops may be given as a dose to produce these effects; but an immoderate dose will purge, or intoxicate, and stupefy, causing strangury, and congestion of the kidneys.

For bleeding from the lungs, five drops may be given, and repeated at intervals of not less than half-an-hour, whilst needed. The dose may be taken in milk, or on sugar, or bread.

With the object of meeting for a curative purpose such symptoms occurring as disease which large doses of this particular drug will produce, as if by poisoning, in a healthy person, quite small doses of Turpentine oil will promptly relieve simple congestion of the kidneys, when occurring as illness, it may be from exposure to cold, and accompanied by some feverishness, with frequent urination, as well as a dragging of the loins. On which principle three or four drops of a diluted tincture of Turpentine (made with one part of Turpentine to nine parts of spirit of wine), given in a spoonful of milk every four hours, will speedily dispel the congestion, thus acting as an infallible specific, and a similar dose of the same tincture will quickly subdue rheumatic inflammation of the eyes.

A pleasant form in which to administer Turpentine, whether for chronic bronchitis or for kidney congestion from cold, is a confection. This may be made by rubbing up one part of oil of turpentine, with one part of liquorice powder, and with two parts of clarified honey. Combine the first two together, then add the honey. If the Turpentine separates, pour it off, and add it again with plenty of rubbing until it unites. From half to one teaspoonful of this confection, when mixed with two tablespoonfuls of peppermint-water, will be found palatable, and may be repeated two or three times in the day.

What is called Terebene, a most useful medicine for winter cough, is produced by the action of sulphuric acid on Turpentine. From five to ten drops may be taken on sugar three or four times in the day, and its vapour acts by inhalation as a very useful antiseptic sedative in consumptive disease of the lungs.

Externally, Turpentine is stimulating and counter-irritating, and derivative. When applied to the skin, unless properly diluted, Turpentine will cause redness and smarting to a painful degree, with an outbreak of small blisters. As an embrocation, the oil of turpentine mixed with spirit of wine and camphor, together with soap liniment, proves very efficacious for the relief of sciatica, and for the chronic rheumatism of joints. Also, when compounded with wax and resin, it makes an excellent healing ointment for indolent, and unhealthy sores.

In Dublin, Turpentine is commingled with peppermint water, and used as an external stimulant for chronic bronchitis.

The famous liniment of St. John Long consisted of oil of turpentine one part, acetic acid one part, and liniment of camphor one part. This was of admirable service for rubbing along the spine to relieve the irritability of the spinal nerves, and it has proved effectual to modify or prevent epileptic attacks, by being thus applied. In cases of colic attending obstinate constipation, with strengthless distension of the bowels, Turpentine mixed with starch or thin gruel, an ounce to the pint, and administered as a clyster, makes one of the most reliable and safe evacuants. Also as a remedy for round worms, six or eight drops (more or less according to age) may be safely and effectively given to a child on one or more nights in milk.

Pills made from Chian Turpentine, which is got from Cyprus, were extolled by Dr. Clay of Manchester, in 1880, as a cure for cancer of the womb, and for some other forms of cancerous disease. From five to ten grains were to be given in a pill, or mixed with mucilage as an emulsion, so that in all daily, after food, and in divided doses, one hundred and eighty grains of this Turpentine were swallowed; and the quantity was gradually increased until five hundred grains a day were taken. In many cases this method of treatment proved undoubtedly useful.

A small quantity of powdered sulphur was also incorporated by Dr. Clay in his Chian pills. About the fourth day the pain was relieved, and the cancerous growth would melt away in a period of from four to thirteen weeks. The arrest of bleeding and the continued freedom from glandular infection after a prolonged use of this Chian Turpentine were highly important points in the improvement produced.

From the *Pinus Sylvestris* an oil is distilled by steam, and of this from ten drops to a teaspoonful may be given for a dose, in milk, for chronic rheumatism or chronic bronchitis

It is most useful in the treatment of diphtheria to burn in the room, near the patient, a mixture of turpentine and tar in a pan or deep dish. The fumes serve to dissolve the false membrane, and have helped to effect a cure in desperate cases.

This tree had the Anglo-Saxon name Pimm, from pen, or pin, a sharp rock,—"*ab acumine foliorum,*" or perhaps as a contraction of *picinus*—pitchy. It furnishes from its leaves an extract, and the volatile oil. Wool is saturated with the latter, and dried, being then made into blankets, jackets, spencers, and stockings, for the use of rheumatic sufferers. There are establishments in Germany where the Pine Cure is pursued by the above means, together with medicated baths. Pine cones were regarded of old by the Assyrians as sacred symbols, and were employed as such in the decoration of their temples. From the tops of the Norway Spruce fir a favourite invigorating drink is brewed which is known in the north as spruce beer. This has an excellent reputation for curing scurvy, chronic rheumatism, and cutaneous maladies. Laplanders make a bread from the inner bark of the Pine.

Tar (*pix liquida*) is furnished abundantly by the *Pinus Sylvestris*, or Scotch Fir, and is extracted by heat. The tree is cut into pieces, which are enclosed in a large oven constructed for the purpose: fire is applied, and the liquid tar runs out through an opening at the bottom. It is properly an empyreumatic oil of turpentine, and has been much used in medicine both externally and internally. Tar water was extolled in 1744, by Bishop Berkley, almost as a panacea. He gave it for scurvy, skin eruptions, ulcers, asthma, and rheumatism. It evidently promotes the secretions, especially the urine.

Tar yields pyroligneous acid, oil of tar, and pitch: as well as guiacol and creasote.

Syrup of tar is an officinal medicine in the United States of America for chronic bronchitis, and winter cough. By this the expectoration is made easier, and the sleep at night improved. From one to two teaspoonfuls are given as a dose, with or without water. Also tar pills are prepared of pitch and liquorice powder in equal parts, five grains in the whole pill. Two or three of these may be taken twice or three times in the day.

Tar ointment is highly efficacious against some forms of skin disease; but in eczema and allied maladies of the skin, no preparation of tar should be employed as long as the skin is actively inflamed, or any exudation of moisture is secreted by it.

Dr. Cullen met with a singular practice respecting Tar. A leg of mutton was put to roast, being basted during the whole process with tar instead of butter. Whilst roasting, a sharp skewer was frequently thrust into the substance of the meat to let the juices escape, and with the mixture of tar and gravy found in the dripping pan, the body of the patient was anointed all over for three or four nights consecutively, throughout all this time the same body linen being worn. The plan proved quite successful in curing obstinate lepra.

A famous liquor called "mum" was concocted by the House of Brunswick, some of which was sent to General Monk. It was chiefly brewed from the rind and tops of firs, and was esteemed very powerful against the formation of stone, and to cure all scorbutick distempers. Various herbs, as best approved by the maker, were infused with the mum in concocting it, such as betony, birch, burnet, brooklime, elder-flowers, horse-radish, marjoram, thyme, water-cress, pennyroyal, etc., together with several eggs, "the shells not cracked or broken"! The Germans, especially in Saxony, have so great a veneration for mum that they fancy their bodies can never decay as long as they are lined, and embalmed with so powerful a preserver. The Swedes call the fir "the scorbutick tree" to this day.

Tar is soluble in its own bulk of spirit of wine, rectified, but separates when water is added. Inhaled, its vapour is very useful in chronic bronchitis.

Tar water should be made by stirring a pint of tar with half a gallon of water for fifteen minutes, and then decanting it. From half-a-pint to a pint may be taken daily, and it may be used as a wash. Or from twenty to sixty drops of tar are to be swallowed for a dose several times in the day, whether for chronic catarrhal affections, or for irritable urinary passages. Tar ointment is prepared with five parts of tar to two pounds of yellow wax. It is an excellent application for scald head in a child.

Juniper tar oil is known as "oil of Cade," and Birch tar is got from the Butcher's Broom. A recognised plaster and an ointment are made with Burgundy pitch (from the *Picus Picea*) and yellow wax.

Probably the modern employment of carbolic acid, and its various combinations—all derived from tar—for neutralising the septic elements of disease, and for acting as germicides, was unknowingly forestalled by the sagacious Right Reverend Lord Bishop of Cloyne, in his *Philosophical Reflections and Inquiries concerning the virtues of Tar Water*, two centuries ago, when the cup which "cheers but not inebriates" was first told of by him, long before Cowper. Bishop Berkley said, "I do, verily, think there is not any other medicine whatsoever so effectual to restore a crazy constitution and to cheer a dreary mind: or so likely to subvert that gloomy empire of the spleen which tyranniseth over the better sort."

In *Great Expectations*, by Charles Dickens, the wife of Joe Gargery is described as possessed of great faith in the curative virtues of Tar water.

VALERIAN.

THE great Wild Valerian, or Heal-all (from *valere*, to be well), grows abundantly throughout this country in moist woods, and on the banks of streams. It is a Benedicta, or blessed herb, being dedicated to the Virgin Mary, as preservative against poisons; and it bears the name of Capon's tail, from its spreading flowers.

When found among bushes, in high pastures, and on dry heaths, it is smaller, with the leaves narrower, but the roots more aromatic, and less nauseous.

The Valerian family of plants is remarkable for producing aromatic and scented genera, which are known as "Nards" (the Spikenard of Scripture), and which are much favoured in Asiatic harems under several varieties, according to the situation of growth. Judas valued the box of ointment made from the Spikenard (*Valeriana Jatamansi*), with which Mary anointed the feet of our Saviour at two hundred denarii (£6: 9s : 2d.).

We have also the small Marsh Valerian, which is wild, and the cultivated Red Valerian, of our cottage gardens.

The roots of our Wild Valerian exercise a strange fascination over cats, causing an ecstasy of delight in these animals, who become almost intoxicated when brought into contact with the Simple. And rats strangely exhibit the same fondness for these roots which they grub up. It has been suggested that the Pied Piper of Hamelin may have carried one of such roots in his wallet.

They have been given from an early period with much success for hysterical affections, and for epileptic attacks induced by strong emotional excitement, as anger or fear: likewise, they serve as a safe and effectual remedy against habitual constipation when active purgatives have failed to overcome this difficulty.

The plant is largely cultivated for the apothecary's uses about the villages near Chesterfield, in Derbyshire. It is named Setwall in the North of England; and, says Gerard, "No broths, pottage, or physicall meats be worth anything if Setwall (a corruption from Zedoar), be not there":—

> "They that will have their heale,
> Must put *Setwall* in their keale."

The Greeks employed one kind of Valerian named *Phu* for hanging on doors and windows as a protective charm. But some suppose this to have been a title of aversion, like our English "faugh" against any thing which stinks. Dr. Uvedale introduced the Valerian into his garden, at Eltham Palace, before 1722; and Uvedale House still exists in Church Street, at Chelsea. The herb is sometimes called Cut-heal, not because, as Gerard thought, it is "useful for slight cuts and wounds," but from its attributed efficacy in disorders of the womb (kutte cowth). Joined with Manna, Valerian has proved most useful in epilepsy; and when combined with Guiacum it has resolved scrofulous tumours. In Germany imps are thought to be afraid of it.

At Plymouth, the broad-leaved Red Valerian goes by the name of Drunken Sailor, and Bovisand Soldier, the larger sort being distinguished as Bouncing Bess, whilst the smaller, paler kind is known as Delicate Bess throughout the West of Devon.

An officinal tincture is made from the rhizome of Valerian with spirit of wine, of which from one to two teaspoonfuls may be given for a dose, with a little water. Also a tincture (ammoniated) is prepared with aromatic spirit of ammonia on the rhizome, and this is considerably stronger; from twenty to forty drops is a sufficient dose with a spoonful or two of water.

The essential oil of Valerian lessens the sensibility of the spinal cord after primary stimulation of its nervous substance. A drop of this oil in a spoonful of milk will be a proper dose: especially in some forms of constipation.

Used externally, by friction, the volatile oil of Valerian has proved beneficial as a liniment for paralyzed limbs. The powdered root mixed in snuff is of efficacy for weak eyes.

The cultivated plant is less rich in the volatile oil than the wild herb. On exposure to the air Valerian oil becomes oxidised, and forms valerianic acid, which together with an alcohol, "borneol," constitutes the active medicinal part of the plant.

The root also contains malic, acetic, and formic acids, with a resin, tannin, starch, and mucilage. It is by first arousing and then blunting the reflex nervous activities of the spinal cord, that the oil of Valerian overcomes chronic constipation.

Preparations of Valerian act admirably for the relief of nervous headache associated with flatulence, and in a person of sensitive temperament. They likewise do good for infantine colic, and they diminish the urea when the urine contains it in excess.

The Greek Valerian is another British species, found growing occasionally in the North of England and in Scotland, being known as the blue Jacob's Ladder. It is also named "Make bate," because said to set a married couple quarrelling if put in their bed. This must be a play on its botanical name *Polemonium*, from the Greek *polemos*, war. It is called Jacob's Ladder from its successive pairs of leaflets.

VERBENA.

THE Verbena, or Common Vervain, is a very familiar herb on waste ground throughout England, limited to no soil, and growing at the entrance into towns and villages, always within a quarter of a mile of a house, and hence called formerly the Simpler's joy. Of old, much credit for curative virtues attached itself to this plant, though it is without odour, and has no taste other than that of slight astringency. But a reputation clings to the Vervain because it used to be held sacred, as "Holy Herb," and was employed in sacrificial rites, being worn also around the neck as an amulet. It was called "Tears of Isis," "Tears of Juno," "Persephonion," and "Demetria." The juice was given as a remedy for the plague. Vervain grew on Calvary: and Gerard says "the devil did reveal it as a secret, and divine medicine."

It is a slender plant with but few leaves, and spikes of small lilac flowers, when wild; but its cultivated varieties, developed by the gardener, are showy plants, remarkable for their brilliant colours.

The name Frogfoot has been applied to the Vervain because its leaf somewhat resembles in outline the foot of that creature. Old writers called the plant *Verbinaca* and *Peristerium* :—

"Frossis fot men call it,
For his levys are like the frossy's fet."

The practice of wearing it round the neck became changed from a religious observance to a medicinal proceeding, for which reason it was ordered that the plant should be *bruised* before being appended to the person ; and thus it gained a name for curing inveterate headaches. Presently also it was applied to other parts as a cataplasm.

Nevertheless, the Vervain has fallen of late years into disfavour as a British Herbal Simple, though a pamphlet has recently appeared, written by a Mr. Morley, who strongly advises the revived use of the herb for benefiting scrofulous disease. Therein it is ordered that the root of Vervain shall be tied with a yard of white satin ribband round the neck of the patient until he recovers. Also an infusion and an ointment are to be prepared from the leaves of the plant.

The expressed juice of Verbena will act as a febrifuge ; and the infusion by its astringency makes a good lotion for weak and inflamed eyes, also for indolent ulcers, and as a gargle for a relaxed sore throat. The Druids gathered it with as much reverence as they paid to the Mistletoe. It was dedicated to Isis, the goddess of birth, and formed a famous ingredient in love philtres.

Pliny saith : "They report that if the dining chamber be sprinkled with water in which the herb Verbena has been steeped, the guests will be the merrier."

Geoffrey St. Hilaire and Pasteur praise the Vervain highly as beneficial against ailments of the hair, the fresh juice being especially used.

Other names of the plant are Juno's tears, Mercury's moist blood, Pigeons' grass, and Columbine—the two latter being assigned because pigeons show a partiality for the herb.

Verbena plants were named *Sagmina*, of old, because

cut up by the Prætor in the Capitol. When borne by an Ambassador Verbena rendered his person inviolable. All herbs used in sacred rites were probably known as Verbena. They were reported as of singular force against the tertian and quartan agues; "but one must observe Mother Bombic's rules—to take just so many knots, or sprigs, and no more, lest it fall out that it do you no good, if you catch no harm by it."

VINE.

THE fruit of the Vine (*Vitis vinifera*) has already been treated of here under the heading "Grapes," as employed medicinally whether for the purgation of the bilious—being then taken crude, and scarcely ripe,—or for imparting fat and bodily warmth in wasting disease by eating the luscious and richly-saccharine berries.

It should be added that the fumes exhaled from the wine-presses whilst the juice is fermenting, prove highly beneficial as a restorative for weakly and delicate young persons (an example which might be followed perhaps at our home breweries).

Consumptive patients are sent with this view to the Gironde, where the vapour from the wine vats is more stimulating and curative than in Burgundy. Young girls who suffer from atrophy are first made to stand for some hours daily in the sheds when the wine pressing is going forward. After a while, as they become less weak, they are directed to jump into the wine press, where, with the vintagers and labourers they skip about and inhale the fumes of the fermenting juice, until they sometimes become intoxicated, and even senseless. This effect passes off after one or two trials, and the girls return to their labour with renewed strength and heightened colour, hopeful, joyous, and robust. The vats of the famous *Chateau d'yquem* are the most celebrated of all for the wondrous cures they have effected even in cases considered past human aid.

VIOLET.

THE Wild Violet or Pansy (*Viola tricolor*) is found commonly throughout Great Britain on banks and in hilly pastures, from whence it has come to be cultivated in our gardens.

Viola, a corruption of "Ion," is a name extended by old writers to several other different plants. But the true indigenous representative of the Violet tribe is our Wild Pansy, or Paunce, or Pance, or Heart's ease; called also "John of my Pink," "Gentleman John," "Meet her i' th' entry; kiss her i' th' buttery" (the longest plant name in the English language), and "Love in idleness."

> "A little Western flower,
> Before milk-white, now purple with love's wound,
> And maidens call it—'Love in idleness.'"

From its coquettishly half hiding its face, as well as from some fancied picture in the throat of the corolla it has received various other amatory designations, such as "cuddle me to you," "tittle my fancy," "jump up and kiss me," and "garden gate": also it is called "Flamy," because its colours are seen in the flame of burning wood, and Flame Flower.

The term "heart's ease" has signified a cordial which is comforting to the heart. But the fact is that Pansies, "pretty little Puritans," produce anything but heart's ease if eaten, and their roots provoke sickness so speedily that these are sometimes employed as an emetic.

Dr. Johnson derived the word Pansy from Panacea,

as curing all diseases; but this was a mistake. The true derivation is from the French *pensée*, "thoughts," as Shakespeare knew, when making Ophelia say: "There is pansies—that's for thoughts."

From its three colours it has been called the herb Trinity. A medicinal tincture is made (H.) from the *Viola tricolor* with spirit of wine, using the entire plant. Hahnemann found that the Pansy violet, when taken by provers, served to induce cutaneous eruptions, or to aggravate them, and he reasoned out the curative action of the plant in small diluted doses for the cure of these symptoms, when occurring as disease.

"For milk crust and scald head," says Dr. Hughes (Brighton)—the plague of children, "I have rarely needed any other medicine than this *Viola tricolor*; and I have more than once given it in recent impetigo (pustular eczema) for adults, with very satisfactory effects." For the first of these maladies the tincture should be given in doses of from three to six drops, to a child of from two to six or eight years, three times a day in water.

Again, "for curing scalled (from *scall*, a shell) head in children, a small handful of the fresh plant, or half a drachm of the dried herb, boiled for two hours in milk, is to be taken each night and morning; also a bread poultice made with this decoction should be applied to the affected part.

"During the first eight days the eruption increases, and the urine, when the medicine succeeds, has a nauseous odour like that of the cat, which presently passes off; then, as the use of the plant is continued, the scabs disappear, and the skin recovers its natural clean condition."

The root of the *Viola tricolor* has similar properties

to that of Ipecacuanha, and is often used beneficially as a substitute by country doctors. An infusion thereof is admirable for the dysentery of young children. It loves a mixture of chalk in the soil where it grows.

The Pansy contains an active chemical principle, "violin," resin, mucilage, sugar, and the other ordinary constituents of plants. When bruised the plant, and especially its root, smells like peach kernels, or prussic acid. It acts as a slight laxative: and "the distilled water of the flowers" says Gerard—"cureth the French disease."

The Germans style the Pansy *Stief-mutter*, because figuratively the mother-in-law appears in the flower predominant in purple velvet, and her own two daughters gay in purple and yellow, whilst the two poor little Cinderellas, more soberly and scantily attired, are squeezed in between. Again, another fable says, with respect to the five petals and the five sepals of the Pansy, two of which petals are plain in colour, whilst each has a single sepal, the three other petals being gay of hue, one of these (the largest of all) having two sepals; that the Pansy represents a family of husband, wife, and four daughters, two of the latter being step-children of the wife.

The plain petals are the step-children, with only one chair; the two small gay petals are the daughters, with a chair each; and the large gay petal is the wife, with two chairs. To find the father, one must strip away the petals until the stamens and pistils are bare. These then bear a fanciful resemblance to an old man with a flannel wrapper about his neck, having his shoulders upraised, and his feet in a bath tub. The French also call the Pansy "The Step-mother."

The chemical principle, "violin," contained in the

flowering Wild Pansy resembles emetin in action. If the dried plant is given medicinally, from ten to sixty grains may be taken as a dose, in infusion.

The Sweet Violet (*Viola odorata*) is well known for its delicious fragrance of perfume when growing in our woods, pastures, and hedge banks. The odour of its petals is lost in drying, but a pleasant syrup is made from the flowers which is a suitable laxative for children.

A conserve, called "violet sugar," prepared from the flowers, has proved of excellent use in consumption. This conserve was made in the time of Charles the Second, being named "Violet plate." Also, the Sweet Violet is thought to possess admirable virtues as a cosmetic. Lightfoot gives a translation from a Highland recipe in Gaelic, for its use in this capacity, rendered thus: "Anoint thy face with goat's milk in which violets have been infused, and there is not a young prince upon earth who will not be charmed with thy beauty."

There is a legend that Mahomet once compared the excellence of Violet perfume above all other sweet odours to himself above all the rest of creation: it refreshes in summer by its coolness, and revives in winter by its warmth.

The Syrup of Sweet Violets should be made as follows: To one pound of sweet violet flowers freshly picked, add two-and-a-half pints of boiling water: infuse these for twenty-four hours in a glazed china vessel, then pour off the liquid, and strain it gently through muslin; afterwards add double its weight of the finest loaf sugar, and make it into a syrup, but without letting it boil.

Violets are cultivated largely at Stratford-on-Avon for the purpose of making the syrup, which when mixed with almond oil, is a capital laxative for children, and will help to soothe irritative coughs, or to relieve a sore throat.

The flowers have been commended for the cure of epilepsy and nervous disorders ; they are laxative when eaten in a salad. The seeds are diuretic, and will correct gravel. The Sweet Violet contains the chemical principle " violin " in all its parts. A medicinal tincture (H.) is made from the entire fresh plant with proof spirit. It acts usefully for a spasmodic cough, with hard breathing; also for rheumatism of the wrists especially the right one.

This Violet is highly esteemed likewise in Syria, chiefly because of its being chosen for making the violet sugar used in sherbet. That which is drunk by the Grand Signior himself is compounded of sweet violets, and sugar.

From the flower may be pleasantly contrived a pretty miniature bird, by carefully removing the calyx and corolla, leaving only the stamens and pistil attached to the receptacle ; then the stigma forms the head and neck, whilst the anthers make a golden breast, and their tongues appear like a pair of green wings.

Mademoiselle Clarion, a noted French actress, had a nosegay of violets sent her every morning of the season for thirty years ; and to enhance the value of the gift, she stripped off the petals every evening, being passionately devoted to the flower, and took them in an infusion as tea.

Pliny recommended a garland of sweet violets as a cure for headache. The Romans made wine of the flowers ; and Napoleon the Great claimed the Violet as *par excellence* his own, for which reason he was often styled, *Le pere la violette.* This floral association took date from the time of his exile to Elba. The Emperor's return was alluded to among his adherents by a pass word, "*Aimez vous la Violette? Eh, bien! reparaitra au printemps.*"

The scentless Dog Violet (*Viola canina*) is likewise mildly laxative, and possesses the virtues of the *Viola odorata* in a lesser degree.

The Water Violet is "feather foil" (*Hottonia palustris*).

VIPER'S BUGLOSS.

THE Simpler's passing consideration should be given to this tall handsome English herb which grows frequently in gravel pits, and on walls. It belongs to the Borage tribe (see page 60), and, in common with the Lungwort (*Pulmonaria*), the Comfrey, and the ordinary Bugloss, abounds in a soft mucilaginous saline juice. This is demulcent to the chest, or to the urinary passages, being also slightly laxative. Bees favour the said plants, which are rich in honey. Each herb goes by the rustic name of "Abraham, Isaac, and Jacob," because bearing spires of tricoloured flowers, blue, purple, and red. The Viper's Bugloss is called botanically *Echium*, having been formerly considered antidotal to the bite of (*Echis*) a viper: and its seed was thought to resemble the reptile's head: wherefore such a curative virtue became attributed to it after the doctrine of signatures. "*In Echio, herba contra viperarum morsus celeberrima, natura semen viperinis capitibus simile procreavit.*" Similarly the Lungwort (or Jerusalem Cowslip), because of its spotted leaves, was held to be a remedy for diseased lungs. This rarely grows wild, but it is of frequent cultivation in cottage gardens, bearing also the rustic name, "Soldiers and Sailors," "To-day and to-morrow," and "Virgin Mary." From either of these herbs a fomentation of the flowers, or a decoction of the whole bruised plant, may be employed with benefit locally to sore or raw surfaces:

whilst an infusion made with three drams of the dried herb to a pint of boiling water will be good in feverish pulmonary catarrh. By our ancestors viper broth was thought to be highly invigorating : and vipers cooked like eels were given to patients suffering from ulcers. The Sardinians still take them in soup. Marvellous powers were supposed to be acquired by the Druids through their possession of a viper's egg, laid in the air, and caught before reaching the earth. All herbs of the Borage order are indifferently "of force and virtue to drive away sorrow and pensiveness of the mind : also to comfort and strengthen the heart." With respect to the Comfrey (see page 120), quite recently the President of the Irish College of Surgeons has reported the gradual disappearance of a growth ("malignant, sarcomatous, twice recurrent, and of a bad type"), since steadily applying poultices of this root to the tumour. "I know nothing," says Professor Thomson, "of the effects of Comfrey root : but the fact that this growth has simply disappeared is one of the greatest surprises and puzzles I have met with."

WALLFLOWER.

THE Wallflower, or Handflower (*Cheiranthus cheiri*), or Wall-gilliflower, has been cultivated in this country almost from time immemorial, for its fragrance and bright colouring. It is found wild in France, Switzerland, and Spain, as the Keiri or Wallstock. Formerly this flower was carried in the hand at classic festivals Herrick, in 1647, gave a more romantic origin to the name Wallflower :—

> "Why this flower is now called so
> List, sweet maids, and you shall know :
> Understand this wilding was
> Once a bright and bonny la

Who a sprightly springal loved,
And to have it fully proved
Up she got upon a wall
Tempting to slide down withal:
But the silken twist untied,
So she fell: and, bruised, she died.
Love, in pity of the deed,
And such luckless eager speed,
Turned her to this plant we call
Now the 'Floweret of the Wall.'"

It is the only British species belonging to the Cruciferous order of plants, and flourishes best on the walls of old buildings, flowering nearly all the summer, though scantily supplied with moisture. We may presume it was one of the earliest cultivated flowers in English gardens, as it is discovered on the most ancient houses.

Turner, an early writer on Plants, calls it Wall-gelouer, or "Hartisease;" and by Spencer it was termed Cherisaunce, as meaning a cordial to the heart, this being really the herb to which the name Heart's-ease was originally given. By rustics it is known also as the "Beeflower."

But the common Stock likewise bore the appellation, "Gilliflower": and the probability is, there was in old days, as Cotgrave suggests, a popular medicine or food "for the passions of the heart," called "gariofile," from the cloves which it contained, the Latin for a clove being *caryophyllum.* Hence it came about that the Wallflower, the Pansy, and the Stock, by virtue of their cordial qualities, were alike called Gilliflowers, or Heart's-ease.

There are two varieties of the cultivated Wallflower, the Yellow and the Red; those of a deep colour growing on old rockeries and similar places, are often termed

Bloody Warriors, and Bleeding Heart. The double Wallflower has been produced for more than two centuries. If the flowers are steeped in oil for some weeks, they contribute thereto a stimulating warming property useful for friction to limbs which are rheumatic, or neuralgic. Gerard suggests that the "oyle of Wallflowers is good for use to annoint a paralyticke." An infusion of the flowers, made with boiling water, will relieve the headache of debility, and is cordial in nervous disorders, by taking a small wine-glassful immediately, and repeating it every half-hour whilst required. The aromatic volatile principles of the flowers are *caryophyllin* and *eugenol.* "This Wallflower," adds Gerard, "and the Stock Gilliflower are used by certain empiricks and quack salvers about love and lust, —matters which for modesty I omit."

WALNUT.

THE Walnut tree is known of aspect to most persons throughout Great Britain as of stately handsome culture, having many spreading branches covered with a silvery grey bark, which is smooth when young, though thick and cracked when old.

The flowers occur in long, hanging, inconspicuous spikes or catkins, of a brownish green colour.

This tree is a native of Asia Minor, but is largely grown in England. The Greeks called it "Karuon," and the Latins "Nux." Its botanical title is *Juglans regia*, a corruption of *glans*, the acorn, *jovis*, of Jupiter, or the "royal nut of Jupiter," food fit for the Gods! Its fruit is also named Ban nut, or Ball nut, and Welsh nut, or Walnut—the word Wal, or Welsh, being Teutonic for "stranger." "As for the timber," said Fuller, "it may be termed the English Shittim Wood."

The London Society of Apothecaries has directed that the unripe fruit of the Walnut should be used pharmaceutically on account of its worm-destroying virtues. It is remarkable that no insects will prey on the leaves of this tree. In good seasons the produce of nuts is weighty enough to pay the rent of the land occupied by the trees.

The vinegar of the pickled fruit makes a very useful gargle for sore throats, even when slightly ulcerated: and the green husks, or early buds of the blossom, being dried to powder, serve in some places for pepper.

The kernel of the nut (or the part of the inside taken at dessert) affords an oil which does not congeal by cold, and which painters find very useful on such account. This oil has proved useful when applied externally for troublesome skin diseases of the leprous type. Indeed, the Walnut has been justly termed vegetable arsenic, because of its curative virtues in eczema, and other obstinately diseased conditions of the skin.

The tincture when made (H.) from the rind of the green fruit and the fresh leaves, with spirit of wine, and given in material doses, will determine in a sound person a burning itching eruption of the skin, of an eczematous character, lasting a long time, and leaving the parts which have been affected afterwards blue and swollen. Reasoning from which it has been found that the tincture, in a reduced form, and of a diminished strength, proves admirably curative of eczema, impetigo, and ecthyma.

The unripe fruit is laxative, and of beneficial use in thrush, and in ulcerative sore throat. The leaves are said to be anti-syphilitic: likewise the green husk, and unripe shell. Obstinate ulcers may be cured with sugar well moistened in a strong decoction of the leaves.

Well kept, kiln-dried Walnuts, of some age, are better digested than newer fruit; in contrast to old gherkins, about which it has been humorously said, "avoid stale Q-cumbers: they will W-up." In many parts of Germany the peasants literally subsist on Walnuts for several months together; and a young farmer before he marries has to own a certain number of flourishing Walnut trees.

The bark or yellow skin which clothes the inner nut is a notable remedy for colic, being given when dried and powdered, in a dose of thirty or forty grains mixed with some carminative water; and the same powder will help to expel worms.

According to the Salernitan maxim, if the fruit of the Walnut be eaten after fish, the digestion of the latter is promoted :—

> Post pisces nux sit : post carnes caseus esto.

Or,

> "Take Welsh nuts after fish : take cheese after flesh meat."

But with some persons coughing is excited by eating Walnuts.

The roots, leaves, and rind yield a brown dye which is supposed to contain iodine, and which gipsies employ for staining their skins. It also serves to turn the hair black. "A custom prevails (says a Latin sentence) among certain country folk to thrash the nuts out of their husks while still on the trees, so that they may grow more abundantly the following year. In allusion to which practice the lines run thus :—

> "Nux, asinus, mulier, simili sunt lege ligata;
> Hæc tria nil fructûs faciunt si verbera cessant."

> "A woman, a donkey, a walnut tree—
> The more you beat them, the better they be."

It is a fact, that by acting in this way, the barren ends of the branches are knocked off, and fresh fruit-bearing twigs spring out at each side in their stead.

Walnut cake, after expressing out the oil from the kernels, is a good food for cattle, these kernels being the crumpled cotyledons or seed leaves. They contain oil, mucilage, albumen, mineral matter, cellulose, and water.

The rook has a most abiding affection for Walnuts. As soon as there is any fruit on the trees worth eating, this bird finds it out, and brings it to the ground, choosing only those nuts which are soft enough for him to penetrate.

Ovid has left a charming little poem, *Nucis Elegia*—the plaint of the Walnut tree—because beaten with sticks and pelted with stones, in return for the generosity with which it bestows on mankind its fair produce.

A valuable medicinal spirit is distilled by druggists from the fruit of the Walnut. It is an admirable remedy for spasmodic indigestion, and to relieve the morning sickness of pregnancy. A teaspoonful of the spirit (*Spiritus nucis juglandis*) may be given with half a wine-glassful of water every hour or two, for most forms of sickness, and the dose may be increased if necessary.

"Nucin," or "juglon," is the active chemical principle of the several parts of the tree and its fruit.

The leaves, when slightly rubbed, emit a rich aromatic odour, which renders them proof against the attacks of insects. Qualities of this odoriferous sort commended the tree to King Solomon, whose "garden of nuts" was clearly one of Walnuts, according to the Hebrew word *eghoz*. The longevity of the tree is very great. There is at Balaclava, in the Crimea, a Walnut tree believed to be a thousand years old.

The shade of the Walnut tree was held by the Romans to be baneful, but the nuts were thought propitious, and favourable to marriage as a symbol of fecundity. The ceremony of throwing nuts, for which boys scrambled at a wedding, was of Athenian origin :—

> "Let the air with Hymen ring
> Hymen ! Io ! Hymen sing !
> Soon the nuts will now be flung:
> Soon the wanton verses sung."
>
> —*Catullus.*

In Italy this is known as the "Witches tree." It is hostile to the oak.

The leaves of the American Black Walnut tree, which grows naturally in Virginia, are of the highest curative value for scrofulous diseases and for strumous eruptions. Chronic, indolent sores have been healed by these after every other remedy has failed. The parts should be washed several times a day with a strong decoction of the leaves, and an infusion of the same should be taken internally ; also of the extract made from the leaves, four grains in a pill each night and morning. For such purposes the leaves of our English Walnut are almost equally efficacious. To make an infusion one ounce should be used to twelve ounces of boiling water. For a syrup mix eight grains of the extract with an ounce of simple syrup : and give one teaspoonful of this twice a day with water. Also apply to any sore some of the powdered leaves on lint soaked in the decoction. For scrofulous joints, or glands, this treatment is invaluable. A green English Walnut, boiled in syrup and preserved in the same, is an excellent homely remedy for constipation. It will be noticed that the fruit becomes black by boiling. The Chinese put the raw kernels into their tea to give it a flavour.

By the Romans Walnuts were scattered among the people when a marriage was celebrated, as an intimation that the wedded couple henceforth abandoned the frivolities of youth.

The "titmouse" walnut produces very delicate fruit, rich in oil, and with thin shells, so that the little creatures can pierce the husks and shells while the fruit is still on the bough.

Nuts of various kinds, being charged with carbon and oil, are highly nutritious, but on account of this oil abounding, they are not readily digested by some persons. In Southern Europe, the Chestnut is a staple article of food. The title "nut" signifies a hard round lump, from *nodus*, a knot.

Leigh Hunt wrote meaningly of the "inexorably hard cocoa nut—*milky at heart.*" In Devonshire a plentiful crop of hazel nuts is believed to portend an unhealthy year:—

"Many nits (nuts)
Many pits (graves)."

When eating almonds and raisins at dessert we get the nitrogenous food of the nuts with the saccharine nourishment of the grapes.

WART-WORT, OR WART-WEED.

THIS name has been commonly applied to the Petty Spurge, or to the Sun Spurge, a familiar little weed growing abundantly in English gardens, with umbels of a golden green colour which "turn towards the sun." Its stem and leaves yield, when wounded, an acrid milky juice which is popularly applied for destroying warts, and corns. But our Greater Celandine (see page 92) or Swallow-wort is better known abroad as the Wart-wort: and its sap is widely given in Russia for the cure, not only of warts, but likewise of cancerous outgrowths, whether occurring on the skin surface, or assailing membranes inside the body. Conclusive evidence has been adduced of cancerous disease within the gullet and the stomach —as well as on the external skin—being healed by this herb. Its sap, or juice, contains chemically, "chelidonine," and "sanguinarine," which latter principle (obtained heretofore from the Canadian "blood root"), is of long established repute for repressing fungoid granulations of indolent ulcers, when powdered over them, and of quickly advancing their cure. Each principle exercises a narcotic influence on the nervous system, and will, thereby, relieve spasmodic coughs. Healthy provers have taken the fresh juice of the Greater Celandine in doses of from twenty to two hundred drops, at repeated intervals; the results of the larger portions being drastic purgation, with persistent nervous torpor, and with an outbreak on the skin of irritating, sore, itching eruptions. In some of the provers active inflammatory congestion of the right lung ensued, with turgidity of the liver. The root beaten into a conserve with sugar will operate by stool, and by urine. For cancerous excrescences from five to ten drops of the fresh juice, or of the mother tincture (H.) should be given steadily three times a day, this quantity being reduced if it should move the bowels too freely. Some of the sap, or tincture, should be also used outwardly as a lotion, either by itself, or diluted with an equal quantity of cold water.

WATER PLANTS (Other).

(Water Dropwort, Water Lily, Water Pepper.)

THE Water Dropwort—Hemlock (*Œnanthe crocata*) is an umbelliferous plant, frequent in our marshes and ditches.

It is named from *oinos*, wine, and *anthos*, a flower, because its blossoms have a vinous smell. A medicinal tincture is made (H.) from the ripe fruit.

The leaves look like Celery, and the roots like parsnips. A country name of this plant is Dead-tongue, from its paralyzing effects on the organs of the voice. Of eight lads who were poisoned by eating the root, says Mr. Vaughan, five died before morning, not one of them having spoken a word. Other names are Horsebane, from its being thought in Sweden to cause in horses a kind of palsy; (due, as Linnæus thought, to an insect, *curculio paraplecticus*, which breeds in the stem); and Five-fingered-root, from its five leaflets. The roots contain a poisonous, milky juice, which becomes yellow on exposure to the air, and which exudes from all parts of the plant when wounded. It will be readily seen that because of so virulent a nature the plant is too dangerous for use as a Herbal Simple, though the juice has been known to cure obstinate and severe skin disease. It yields an acrid emetic principle. The root is sometimes applied by country folk to whitlows, but this has proved an unsafe proceeding. The plant has a pleasant odour. Its leaves have been mistaken for Parsley, and its root for the Skirret.

The *Œnanthe Phellandrium* (Water Fennel) is a variety of the same species, but with finer leaves. Pliny gave the seeds, twenty grains for a dose, against stone, and disorders of the bladder. Also they have been commended for cancer.

In this country Water Lilies, or Pond Lilies, comprise the White Water Lily—a large native flower inhabiting clear pools and slow rivers—and the Yellow Water Lily, frequent in rivers and ditches, with a yellow, globose flower smelling like brandy, so that it is called "Brandy bottle" in Norfolk and other parts. Its root and stalks contain much tannin.

This latter Yellow Lily (*Nuphar lutea*) possesses medicinal virtues against diarrhœa, such as is aggravated in the morning, and against sexual weakness. A tincture is made (H.) from the whole plant with spirit of wine. The second title, *lutea*, signifies growing in the mud; whilst the large white Water Lily is called *Nymphœa*, from occurring in the supposed haunts of the nymphs: and Flatter-dock.

The root stocks of the Yellow Water Lily, when bruised, and infused in milk, will destroy beetles and cockroaches. The smoke of the same when burnt will get rid of crickets.

The small Yellow Pond Lily bears the name of Can-dock, from the shape of its seed vessel, like that of a silver can or flagon, and this perhaps has likewise to do with the appellations, "Brandy bottle" and "Water can:" which latter may be given because of the half unfolded leaves floating on the water like cans.

The root of the larger white Water Lily is acrid, and will redden the skin if the juice is applied thereto.

An Ointment may be made with this juice to stimulate the scalp so as to prevent falling out of the hair. The root contains tannin and mucilage, it is therefore astringent and demulcent. Also the expressed juice from the fresh leaves of this white Water Lily, the "one sinless flower," if used as a head wash, will preserve the hair.

> "Oh, destinée des choses d'ici bas! descendre des austerités du cloitre dans l'officine Cancanière du perruquier!"

Dutch boys are said to be extremely careful about plucking or handling the Water Lily, for, if a boy fall with the flowers in his possession, he is thought to immediately become subject to fits.

The Water Pepper (*Polygonum Hydropiper*) or Arsmart, grows abundantly by the sides of lakes and ditches in Great Britain. It bears a vulgar English name signifying the irritation which it causes when applied to the fundament; and its French sobriquet, *Culrage*, conveys the same meaning:—

> "An erbe is the cause of all this rage,
> In our tongue called *Culrage*."

The plant is further known to rustics as Cyderach, or Ciderage, and as Red-knees, from its red angular points. It possesses an acrid, biting taste, somewhat like that of the Peppermint, which resides in the glandular dots sprinkled about its surface, and which is lost in drying. Fleas will not come into rooms where this herb is kept. It is called also "lake weed." A tradition says that the plant when placed under the saddle will enable a horse to travel for some long time without becoming hungry or thirsty. The Scythians knew this herb (*Hippice*) to be useful for such a purpose.

The Water Pepper had its virtues first taught by a beggar of Savoy. It is admirable against syphilis, and to arrest sexual losses: being long adored because "healing the original sin."

Farriers use it for curing proud flesh in the sores of animals, and when applied to the human skin, the leaves will serve the purpose of a mustard poultice. Also, a piece of the plant may be chewed to relieve toothache, as well as to cure small ulcers of thrush in the mouth, and pimples on the tongue.

The expressed juice of the freshly-gathered plant has been found very useful in jaundice. From one to three

in her portraits. Therefore, the plant is known as Woodrowel.

When freshly gathered, it has but little odour, but when dried it exhales a delightful and lasting aroma, like the scent of meadow grass, or of peach blossoms.

A fragrant and exhilarating tea may be made from the leaves and blossoms of the sweet Woodruffe, and this is found to be of service in correcting sluggishness of the liver. "When it is desired," says Mr. Johns, "to preserve the leaves merely for their scent, the stem should be cut through just below and above a joint, and the leaves pressed in such a way as not to destroy their star-like arrangement."

Gerard tells us: "The flowers are of a very sweet smell, as is the rest of the herb, which, being made up into garlands or bundles, and hanged up in houses, in the heat of summer, doth very well attemper the air, cool and make fresh the place, to the delight and comfort of such as are therein."

The agreeable odour of this sweet Woodruffe is due to a chemical principle named "coumarin," which powerfully affects the brain; and the plant further contains citric, malic, and rubichloric acids, together with some tannic acid.

Another species of the same genus is the Squinancy Woodruff (*Asperula cynanchica*), so called from the Greek *cynanche*, which means quinsy, because an excellent gargle may be made from this herb for the troublesome throat affection here specified, and ~~for~~ any severe sore throat. Quinsy is called cynanche, from the Greek words, *kuon*, a dog, and *ancho*, to strangle, because the distressed patient is compelled by the swollen state of his highly inflamed throat, to gasp with his mouth open like a choking dog.

This plant is found growing in dry pastures, especially on a chalky or limestone soil, but it is not common; it has very narrow leaves, and tufts of lilac flowers.

Reverting to the Sweet Woodruff, the dried herb may be kept amongst linen, like lavender, to preserve it from insects.

> She—"Fresh Woodruff soaks
> To brew cool drink, and keep away the moth."
> —*A. Austin, Poet Laureate.*

It was formerly employed for strewing churches, littering chambers, and stuffing beds. Withering declares that its strongly aromatic flowers make an infusion which far exceeds even the choice teas of China. The powdered leaves are mixed with fancy snuffs, because of their enduring fragrance.

WOODSORRELL (*See also* "*Docks.*")

THIS elegant little herb, called also French Sorrel, Rabbits' food, Shamrock, and Wood Sour (*Oxalis acetosella*), is abundant throughout our woods, and in other moist, shady places. It belongs to the natural order of Geraniums, and bears the provincial names of Sour trefoil, Cuckoo's bread, or Gowk's-meat, and Stubwort (from growing about the stubs of hewn trees). Its botanical title is got from the Greek word *oxus*, sharp, or acid, because of its penetrating sour taste. This is due to the acid oxalate of potash which it contains abundantly, in common with the Dock Sorrel, and the Garden Rhubarb.

By reason of this chemical salt being present in combination with less leafy matter than in the other plants which are akin to it, the Wood Sorrel makes a lighter and more palatable salad.

In olden days the Monks named this pretty little

woodland plant *Alleluia*, because it blossoms between Easter and Whitsuntide, when the Psalms—from the 113th to the 117th, inclusive—which end with the aspiration, "Hallelujah!" were sung.

St. Patrick is said to have shown on the ternate leaf of the Wood Sorrel to his rude audience the possibility of a Trinity in Unity.

The herb has been long popular as a Simple for making a fever drink, which is thought to be somewhat sedative to the heart, and for helping to cure scurvy. Also, it has proved useful against intermittent fever.

Towards assisting to digest, by their free acid, the immature fibre of young flesh meats, the Wood Sorrel leaves are commonly eaten as a dressing with veal, and lamb. But too habitual use of such a salad or sauce has led to the formation of gouty crystals (oxalate of lime) in the urine, with considerable irritation of the kidneys. Externally, the bruised leaves are of excellent service for cleansing and stimulating foul sores and ulcers, being first macerated in a Cabbage leaf with warmth.

This familiar harbinger of Spring, with its three delicate leaflets on a long stalk, and its tiny white flowers, having purple veins like those of the Wood Anemone, bears the fanciful name of Fairy-bells in Welsh districts.

Fra Angelico placed the claret-stained flowers in the foreground of his pictures representing the Crucifixion. After the doctrine of signatures, because of its shape like a heart, the leaf of the Wood Sorrel was formerly esteemed as a cordial medicine. It was called in Latin *Panis Cuculi*, meaning the "Cuckoo's bread and cheese." The leaves, when bruised, make with sugar a capital conserve which is refreshing to a fevered stomach, or, if boiled in milk, they form an agreeable sub-acid whey.

Twenty pounds of the fresh plant will yield four ounces of the oxalate of potash, commonly known as salt of lemons or salt of sorrel, which is often used for taking ink stains out of linen. Francus, an old classical author, concluded by experiment that the herb is of value (*cordis vires reparare*) to recruit the energies of the heart, and (*anginum abigere*) to dispel the quinsy. Its infusion makes an excellent anti-putrescent gargle. There is also a yellow variety of the Wood Sorrel.

WORMWOOD.

THE common Wormwood (*Artemisia absinthium*) has been partly considered here together with Mugwort, to which it is closely allied. It is a Composite herb of frequent growth on waste ground, being a bushy plant with silky stems, and collections of numerous small heads of dull yellow flowers. The name Wormwood is from *wehren*, to keep off—*mought*, a maggot or moth; and *absinthium*, from-*a*-negative—*psinthos*, delight, in allusion to the very bitter taste.

The whole plant is of an aromatic smell and bitter flavour. The flowers, when dried and powdered, destroy worms more effectually than worm seed, whilst the leaves resist putrefaction and help to make capital antiseptic fomentations.

Wormwood tea, or the powdered herb in small doses, mixed in a little soup, will serve to relieve bilious melancholia, and will help to disperse the yellow hue of jaundice from the skin.

This herb was formerly thought to possess the power of dispelling demons, and was thus associated with the ceremonials of St. John's Eve, owning the name, on the Continent, of St. John's Herb, or St. John's Girdle. Both it, and the Mugwort were dedicated to Diana:

put into the nose, assuredly it will stay the bleeding of it," which must be the effect of action according to similars. Or if using Yarrow in the same way as a love charm, the following lines were repeated :—

"Green 'arrow! green 'arrow!
You bear a white blow;
If my love love me
My nose will bleed now."

The leaves have a somewhat fragrant smell, and a bitterish taste. The odour of the flowers, when rubbed between the fingers, is aromatic. In consequence of this pungent, volatile principle, the herb has proved useful in hysteria, flatulence, heartburn, colic, and epilepsy; also, it is employed in Norway for the cure of rheumatism, and sometimes chewed for toothache.

Yarrow is one of the few aboriginal English plants, having held the primitive title, *Gearwe*. Greek botanists seem to have known the identical species which we now possess, and to have used it against hæmorrhagic losses. It yields, chemically, a dark-green volatile oil, and achilleic acid, which is said to be identical with aconitic acid; also resin, tannin, gum; and earthy ash consisting of nitrates, phosphates, and chlorides of potash and lime.

For preparing an infusion of the plant, half an ounce should be boiled down in half a pint of water to six ounces; one tablespoonful for a dose.

Sir John Hill says the best way of giving Yarrow is in a strong decoction of the whole plant. A hot infusion of the herb taken freely on going to bed at night seldom fails to make short work of a cold.

A medicinal tincture (H.) is prepared from the whole plant with spirit of wine. This, when employed in a diluted form of the first or third decimal strength, and in small doses of from five to ten drops in a table-spoonful of cold water, will act admirably in arresting nocturnal losses in the male; likewise bleeding from the lungs, the kidneys, or the nose, especially in florid, hectic subjects. It has been found by healthy provers that stronger, and larger doses of any preparation of the herb will induce or aggravate one or another of these bleedings.

The fresh juice of the plant may be had, a dessert-spoonful three times in the day; or of the volatile essential oil, from three to five drops for a dose. These medicines greatly stimulate and promote the appetite. "For ague," says Parkinson, "drink a decoction of the herb warm before the fit, and so for two or three fits together."

Externally, a strong decoction of the leaves has been used as an injection into the nostrils to stay bleeding from the nose. It is similarly of service for piles, and for female floodings, because exerting a special local action on the organs within the middle trunk. The bruised herb, or an ointment made from it, is applied by rustics to heal fresh cuts and contusions.

Even in ancient times it was famous as a topical remedy for piles. It is further of benefit for sore nipples as a lotion, and for a relaxed sore throat as a gargle: also as a hair wash.

The leaves were applied in former days as a poultice to wounds; and because of its healing and astringent virtues when so used, the plant gained the names Sanguinary, Thousand leaf, Old Man's pepper, Soldiers' Woundwort. Other local names for it are Staunch grass, Carpenters' weed, and Bloodwort: also, "Old Man's Mustard," "Bad Man's Plaything," and "Devil's Plaything." In Gloucestershire and some other parts, the double-flowered Yarrow is brought to a wedding by the dead bodies lying beneath its sombre shade. So Tennyson writes (*In Memoriam*) :—

> "Old Yew! which graspest at the stones
> That name the underlying dead,
> Thy fibres net the dreamless head,
> Thy roots are wrapped about the bones."

The juice of the tree and of its leaves is a rapidly fatal poison, the symptoms corresponding in a very remarkable way with those which follow the bites of venomous snakes.

No known poison but the Yew produces the lazar-like ulcerations upon the body, on which Marlowe lays such stress—(Jew of Malta) :—

> "In few, the blood of Hydra—Herne's bane,
> The juice of *Hebron*, and Cocytus' breath,
> And all the poisons of the Stygian pool."

The witches in *Macbeth* include it in their accursed brew :—

> "Liver of blaspheming Jew,
> Gall of goat, and *Slips of Yew.*"

The Yew tree is called "Hebon" by Spencer, and "Jew of Malta" by other writers of Shakespeare's time. The leaves are bitter, nauseous, and acrid. The succulent covering of the fruit is soft and slimy, mawkishly sweet, and mucilaginous. The leaves have a dangerous effect on the circulation of the heart, and when taken with any freedom are as fatal as the Foxglove.

Before the new Shakespeare Society, 1882, it was contended and proved to the satisfaction of the Society, that "the cursed Hebena," the "leperous distilment poured into the chambers of mine ears," told of, so pathetically, by the sad ghost of Hamlet's father, was the poison of the Yew, and identical with Marlow's juice of Hebron.

Ray mentions that a gardener employed in clipping a Yew tree at Pisa, could not proceed with his work for more than half-an-hour at a time without being seized with a violent pain in the head. Nevertheless, deer, sheep, and goats can eat the foliage with impunity.

The fresh leaves were administered to three children near Manchester for worms. Yawning and listlessness came on, and the eldest vomited a little, but neither of them complained of any pain. They all died within a few hours of each other.

Because being then green, on the Sunday next before Easter, the branches of the Yew tree have been used as a substitute for the Palms which symbolise the entry of Jesus into Jerusalem.

The symptoms induced by provings of the leaves and juice in toxic quantities, have been sick headache, with giddiness, feeble, faltering pulse, coldness of the extremities, diarrhœa, and general prostration. So that for this combination of symptoms, as in severe biliousness, or as in the auditory vertigo of Menière's disease, small doses of the diluted tincture are found to give prompt and effectual relief. The leaves contain a volatile oil, tannin, and a bitter principle "taxina," which is also furnished by the seeds. An extract of Yew has been pronounced a useful narcotic by more than one physician of repute: and in some parts of Germany a decoction of the wood is a well-known remedy against hydrophobia.

A jelly prepared from the berries has been given for chronic bronchitis, and the leaves have been used for epilepsy; likewise they have been taken by ignorant persons to induce abortion, but with serious injury to the experimenter. In some rural districts the berries are known as "Snots"; whilst the wood and roots are "Wire thorn."

By an old statute of Edward the First, trees were required to be placed in churchyards to defend the church from high winds, the clergy being allowed to cut them down for repairing the chancel when necessary. Perhaps, partly for this reason, the Yew was commonly planted by the side of a newly-built church. That its wood was certainly employed for making bows, we learn from Shakespeare:—

> "Thy very beadsmen learn to bend their bows
> Of double-fatal Yew against thy state."

It was "double-fatal," because the leaves and fruit seeds are poisonous, and the bows made from its branches, as well as arrows armed with its deadly juice, were instruments of death.

Against the maladies which have been specified as indicating the tincture of Yew for their cure, from five to ten drops of the third decimal tincture should be given, with a spoonful of water, every two, three, or four hours, whilst required.

In Switzerland the Yew is known as William's tree, in memory of Tell. Formerly the name was spelt "Eugh," "Yeugh," and "Ewgh."

Spenser says:—

> "The Eugh—obedient to the bender's will."

In olden times the Olitory, or Herb-garden, formed an important annex to all demesnes having any pretensions to completeness, and was under "My Lady's" special charge. In fact, the culture and preparing of Simples formed a part of every lady's education.

"My Lord's" retainers and tenants, when out of sorts, were treated with these wholesome remedies, and were directed to find in Simples the cure for all ordinary ailments.

Good George Herbert, of *Country Parson* celebrity, taught, 1620:—"In the knowledge of *Simples*, wherein the manifold wisdom of God is wonderfully to be seen, one thing should be carefully observed, which is, to know what herbs may be used instead of drugs of the same nature, and to make the garden the shop; for, home-bred medicines are both more easy for the Parson's purse, and more familiar for all men's bodies. So where the Apothecary useth either for loosing, Rhubarb, or for binding, Bole Armena; the Parson useth Damask, or White Roses for the one, and Plantain, Shepherd's Purse, or Knotgrass for the other: and that with better success. As for Spices, he doth not only prefer home-bred things before them, but condemns them for vanities, and so shuts them out of his family, esteeming that there is no spice comparable of herbs to Rosemary, Thyme, Savory, Mints: and of seeds to Fennel and Carraway. Accordingly for salves his wife seeks not the city, but prefers her garden and fields, before all outlandish gums. And, surely, Hyssop, Valerian, Mercury, Adder's tongue, Yarrow, Melilot, and St. John's Wort, made into a salve, and Elder, Camomile, Mallows, Comphrey, and Smallage, made into a poultice, have done great, and rare cures!"

INDEX.

'Farewell, sweet flowers!—whose time is fitly spent
For all delights of colour, and of scent:
And after death for cures!
May I my days with equal uses fill,
Living to work some benefits: and still
Having an end like yours!"

Robert Herrick, 1650.